Refreshed

LIGHTER, SIMPLER COMFORT FOOD

THE YANKEE CHEF
JIM BAILEY

Schiffer Publishing Ltd®

4880 Lower Valley Road • Atglen, PA 19310

Other Schiffer books by Jim Bailey:
The Yankee Chef: Feel Good Food for Every Kitchen,
ISBN 978-0-7643-4191-5

Other Schiffer books on related subjects:
Meet Me in My Cape Cod Kitchen:
Recipes for Seaside Living, Linda Maria Steele,
ISBN 978-0-7643-4984-3

Designed by Justin Watkinson
Cover design by Brenda McCallum
Type set in Tandelle/Century Gothic/Minion Pro

ISBN: 978-0-7643-5057-3
Printed in China

Published by Schiffer Publishing, Ltd.
4880 Lower Valley Road
Atglen, PA 19310
Phone: (610) 593-1777; Fax: (610) 593-2002
E-mail: Info@schifferbooks.com
Web: www.schifferbooks.com

For our complete selection of fine books on this
and related subjects, please visit our website at
www.schifferbooks.com. You may also write for
a free catalog.

Schiffer Publishing's titles are available at special
discounts for bulk purchases for sales promotions
or premiums. Special editions, including
personalized covers, corporate imprints,
and excerpts, can be created in large quantities
for special needs. For more information, contact
the publisher.

We are always looking for people to
write books on new and related subjects.
If you have an idea for a book, please contact
us at proposals@schifferbooks.com.

The information contained in this book is intended for educational purposes only and
is not a substitute for advice, diagnosis, or treatment by a licensed physician. It is not
meant to cover all possible precautions, drug interactions, circumstances, or adverse
effects. You should seek prompt medical care for any health issues and consult your
doctor before using alternative medicine or unsubstantiated treatments or making a
change to your regimen.

Contents

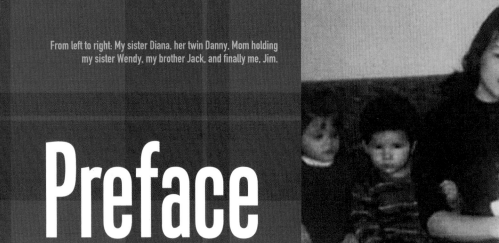

From left to right: My sister Diana, her twin Danny, Mom holding my sister Wendy, my brother Jack, and finally me, Jim.

Preface

I have been blessed with two mothers. My biological and step. Both are equally as important in my life because of two completely different struggles each endured. My biological mother, Marilyn Pearl Moody, was born August 17, 1942, and married my father at the young age of nineteen. My twin brother and I were born within two years and within two more years, another set of twins were born.

Mom and Dad's relationship was beginning to falter by the time I was two years old. After the birth of the second set of twins, Danny and Diana, Mom and Dad parted ways. Dad remarried soon after as did my mother. It was mutually agreed that Jack and I would go live with my Dad (the recipient of the dedication from my first cookbook) and his new wife, my stepmother Anne. Danny and Diana would stay with Mom.

Even though Dad and Mom divorced when I was two, my brother and I spent every summer with her, her new husband, and all my half-brothers and half-sisters whom she had with my stepfather, all of whom I still love and adore.

Then came the springtime of 1979. Mom had been back in Maine from Connecticut and I often went to her house and just plain had fun with my half-siblings. But Mom was sick and I knew it. I will never forget the time when Mom brought me in her bedroom, sat me down beside her, and started talking to me about cancer—breast cancer to be exact.

After a few minutes, she lifted up her blouse and I immediately noticed a very long and bulbous scar. I was unaware of what she had gone through at that time. She had hidden this affliction from me all that time, so when I saw that, I was floored. I don't remember much, but what I do remember was the stun and awe I felt upon seeing her chest where once her breast had been. She had had a mastectomy while living in Connecticut without saying a word to me.

She started telling me about her breast cancer, not in a somber mood but with a rosy outlook. I believe she may have thought the worst was over. Now this was back in 1979 and the medicine, understanding, treatments, and causes were not nearly as understood as they are now.

. . . and it is with this wonder and awe that I dedicate my cooking and life to the remembrance of all those who have suffered and are currently suffering from this awful disease.

I remember not dwelling on it too much after she showed me her battle scar. Mom never mentioned anything negative at all, but had a "glass half full" mentality.

That was the end of the cancer thoughts and worries until the time came when she was admitted to the hospital a few months later. By June of '79, her cancer had reintroduced itself with a vengence. I only went to see her one time while she was in the hospital. She didn't want her children to see her sick and, most likely, she may not have been able to handle seeing her children, knowing whatever she knew about her mortality at the time.

Think about it! You are a young woman of thirty-nine with seven children, all minors. Can you even fathom for one moment what must be going through your mind knowing that you would not be around to see them grow up? You won't be there to protect them, feed them, nourish them, or teach them? It is way beyond my comprehension, and it is with this wonder and awe that I dedicate my cooking and life to the remembrance of all those who have suffered and are currently suffering from this awful disease.

I was at her home on the night of August 16, a day before her birthday. Just me, my half-siblings, along with Danny and Diana, when my stepfather walked in the door. We were all playing air guitars to the song "Honeycomb." He walked over, stopped the music, sat us down, and told us Mom was gone . . . .

We love you, Mom, and with heads bowed down, your children remember you, your grandchildren honor, you and your family misses you . . . every single day!

I am proud to be able to carry memories of Mom and all of you who have struggled with breast cancer in any manner. Consider my pink chefs coat as a personal, silent sigh to you and all those who are no longer with us.

Acknowledgments

I wish to acknowledge Jamie Stern, MS, nutrition consultant and instructor at Husson University in Bangor, Maine. She had an important role in finalizing all aspects of this cookbook from a nutritional standpoint. She has been so patient, friendly, and cooperative as I was writing this book. At the last minute (frequently), I would consult with her and email her question after question, and not once did she bat an eye when it came to offering her expertise in all fields relating to nutritional advice. Although she is not quoted frequently in the book, Jamie was consulted for most of the recipes to suggest ingredient substitution. She was, and continues to be, an invaluable reference for me with regard to healthier versions of all my recipes. Thank you, Jamie.

Also instrumental in putting together this work in a very beautiful way was John Edwards. John Edwards Photography of Glenburn, Maine, was at the ready in less than three days' notice when I approached him about offering the beautiful images seen on pages 108, 184, and 218. Kudos to John.

Jamie Stern, nutrition consultant

Introduction

Welcome to my second cookbook. I think you will find some common denominators between this and my first cookbook, *The Yankee Chef*: Simple food, easily attainable ingredients, and an emphasis in cost conservation and simplicity in preparation.

There are, though, some striking differences as well: Since the publication of *The Yankee Chef*, I have been open and vocal with regard to my "link of pink" and breast cancer awareness. The first Yankee Chef, my grandfather Samuel Bailey, and the second Yankee Chef, my father Jack Bailey, each adored the color pink. My father in particular understood the profound meaning of pink because of my mother's battle. So this book was written with my mother and all breast cancer sufferers and survivors in mind, and to those who love them.

This is not a cookbook to control how you eat, or even a recipe collection developed for breast cancer patients. Instead, the recipes are healthier versions of beloved, popular, and comfort dishes from all over the world.

I limit fat content because of fat's connection to obesity, ill health, and preventable diseases. I use a wide assortment of healthful fruits and vegetables. I've also included some surprising facts about healthy eating and living.

But, above all, these recipes were written with the idea of helping you make good choices so you can enjoy eating— and living. Knowing what we eat is essential to a healthy lifestyle.

The recipes in this book will satisfy you in a way that will have you up and taking a walk after a refreshing meal, rather than slumping down on the couch.

Staying healthy means staying active, getting the right nutrition, and watching out for potential dangers in what we eat. I truly believe that cures for cancer and other maladies are in the near future. While scientists search for that cure, we all need to discover our own path to open-mindedness when it comes to improving the quality of our health.

Improving our children's diets is another priority. Many, like adults, are simply not getting the full benefits of fruits and vegetables consistently. I hope to continue British chef Jamie Oliver's food revolution, getting the next generations to embrace Mother Earth's first line of defense. Fruits and vegetables don't have to be fresh (although that's preferable), but they do have to be present!

Adding fruits and vegetables to as many dishes as possible makes it easy to give nutrition a boost. Even adding fruit purees into the inevitable sweets like cookies and cakes will help in this quest and cut down on fat intake, as well as add more fiber in a diet.

If I were to think of a motto for this new revolution, it would be "Eat for pleasure, not duty." And there is only one way of really doing this for our children: Have good food taste great.

One final word: You will notice throughout the book two of my mottoes: ***It's Just That Simple*** and ***Yanked***. Cooking like a television chef/star doesn't need to be complicated. As The Yankee Chef, by ***Yanking*** a well-known, expensive, complicated, and/or unhealthy recipe, I am transforming it into something everyone can prepare, and enjoy, and it gives me more pleasure than I can describe.

It's Just That Simple!

CHAPTER 1 Quick Breads and Yeast Breads

Let's get one thing straight, finally, about breads in your diet. Controlled and minimal intake of white bread is no more of a health threat than many other foods as long as enjoyed in moderation. Whole grain bread contains good sources of complex carbohydrates while white bread has iron and B vitamins but no fiber. When looking at both on a glycemic level, some whole grain breads have a lower glycemic index but both have relatively higher amounts than many other non grain-based foods.

The solution? Moderation!

And remember that if you just balance your calorie intake with activity that is fun to do or enjoyable, staying healthy is easier.

Nutritionists recommend that children and adolescents should engage in at least one hour a day of moderate-intensity activity with sessions of vigorous activity at least three days a week. This includes going out to play, helping with chores, biking, or anything that simply gets them up off the couch.

These same guidelines note that adults should engage in at least 150 minutes of moderate-intensity or seventy-five minutes of vigorous-intensity activity each week, or an equivalent combination, preferably spread throughout the week. Again, this can be as easy as taking a walk with your children or friends.

When you do something enjoyable, not only does it seem less like exercise and clear the head, but it also takes your mind off eating.

New England Jonnycake

Forget about French crêpes! These New England originals can be enjoyed on their own, spread with creamy butter, or as a substitute for any dessert that crêpes are used for. But why stop with the sweet tooth? I enjoy them as a vegetarian wrap or treat yourself to a Yankee version of chicken and waffles. Simply fry (or bake!) some chicken strips and wrap them up inside, along with sauce and veggies of your choosing.

1 cup yellow cornmeal
1 teaspoon salt
1 teaspoon sugar
2 cups boiling water
About 1 cup milk
2 tablespoons melted butter
    or margarine

In a bowl, combine cornmeal, salt, and sugar. Pour boiling water into the cornmeal mixture and stir to dissolve until lump-free; set aside.

In a separate bowl, whisk together milk and melted butter. Pour the mixture into the cornmeal bowl, and whisk until it is the consistency of crêpe batter, adding more milk if necessary.

Heat a large skillet over medium-high heat with a liberal dose of nonstick cooking spray. When hot, ladle ¼ cup of the batter into the pan. and cook 1–2 minutes or until well browned on the underside. Flip and continue cooking an additional minute. Remove to a plate, and continue until all the batter is used.

Here's an easy, fat-free cornbread recipe for you. Preheat over to 375° F. Grease a 13- by 9-inch baking pan with nonstick cooking spray. In a large bowl, combine 2 cups yellow cornmeal, 1 cup flour, 2 tablespoons sugar, 2 teaspoons baking powder, and 1 teaspoon each baking soda and salt. Blend well. In another bowl, whisk together ¾ cup egg substitute, 1½ cups evaporated fat-free milk, and ¼ cup maple syrup. Mix the wet with the dry and our into prepared pan. It does not need to be lump free. Bake 20–25 minutes or until toothpick inserted in the middle comes out clean. Serve hot.

Sun-Dried Tomato-Basil Biga Bread

Ripping a piece off this often-misshapen low-fat Italian bread will transport you to the Italian table. Whether you call it ciabatta, pane Francese, or pane Pugliese, it is baked to be chewy on the inside and old-world crusty on the outside. The word *biga* refers to the age-old method of pre-fermentation using a wet dough that takes hours and hours to rise. While this recipe does take time, it's authentic and delicious.

1 cup warm water
1 tablespoon dried basil leaves
1 teaspoon sugar
1 (0.25-ounce) envelope
      active yeast
2 cups flour
1 teaspoon garlic salt
½ cup small dice sun-dried
      tomatoes, diced small
Nonstick cooking spray
Water in a spray bottle

MAKES 2 LOAVES

Most white breads only need to be kneaded gently and consistently in order for that perfectly soft and tender texture to shine through. But with *biga* bread, if you have any frustrations or stress to get rid of, now is the time to do it. The more forceful your kneading, the chewier your bread will be, as *biga* should be.

In a large bowl, combine the warm water, basil, sugar, and yeast. Stir for a few seconds to completely wet the yeast. Let sit for 10 minutes, or until it starts to foam.

In a separate bowl, blend the flour and garlic salt and then add to the yeast mixture along with the tomatoes. Using a stout wooden spoon, vigorously stir until the dough forms around the spoon and leaves the side of the bowl. Spray the top with nonstick cooking spray and loosely lay a towel over the top. Leave in a warm, draft-free place to double in bulk (about an hour).

When risen, transfer dough to a well-floured work surface and knead for about 2 minutes, or until it holds together and is elastic. Divide into 2 balls and shape each into oblong logs, about 10-inches in length and only 2–3 inches high.

Place on an ungreased baking pan, spray once again with nonstick cooking spray, loosely cover and let rise for another hour, or until almost doubled in bulk.

Preheat oven to 450° F. Remove towel from bread and poke the top down with your fingers. Spray the top with water and bake 20–22 minutes or until well browned on top and the loaf sounds hollow when tapped. Spray the top of the loaf every 5 minutes for that extra color and crunch. Remove from oven to cool slightly before cutting.

Rascally Radicals

Free radicals are little terrorists that can compromise our health. But what exactly are they?

Briefly, they are atoms that are unbalanced, as they are missing an electron. They roam the body looking for any chemical structure from which to steal the needed electron so they can become stable again.

Some free radicals occur simply as part of our metabolism, through breathing. But stress can mass produce free radicals, as can environmental factors, including pollution and cigarette smoke. Over time, these thieving free radicals can cause irreversible cell damage, which can lead to diseases such as cancer.

Let me also say that our bodies have a way of naturally creating balance, and they can even harness the power of some free radicals to fight off infections and inflammation and keep our immune systems in check. It is the mass production of excess free radicals that we need to be concerned about.

One of the best ways to keep those little free-radical terrorists in check is the intake of antioxidants, which are so friendly to us that they voluntarily give up electrons to the terrorists without hurting themselves. Two of the best antioxidants are Vitamins C and E. The best way to get your daily dose? Eat foods rich in these vitamins, such as fruits and vegetables.

Crispy Savory Sweet Pita Coca

Coca refers to a Mediterranean pizza topped with sweet bell peppers that have been almost caramelized—a perfect alternative to cheesy fat-laden traditional pizza.

4 pita bread rounds
2 large bell peppers, seeded
    and halved
2 tablespoons pure olive oil
1 large onion, peeled, halved
    and sliced
1 cup fresh basil
    leaves, chopped
2 tablespoons powdered sugar
2 tablespoons balsamic
    vinegar
1 cup low-fat ricotta cheese,
    drained well
2 tablespoons milk
1 teaspoon each garlic
    powder, oregano, and
    cracked black pepper

MAKES 4

Place pita rounds on a large baking pan; set aside. Slice peppers into strips; set aside. Preheat oven to 450° F.

Heat oil in large skillet over medium-high heat. When hot, add peppers and onions, stir-frying 4–5 minutes until crisp tender, but not too soft. Reduce heat to low, add basil, sugar, and vinegar and simmer, stirring frequently, for about 4–5 minutes or until all liquid has evaporated.

Evenly divide the pepper mixture over the top of each pita round. Bake 12–14 minutes, or until each pita is crusty and the toppings have started to brown. Remove to cool slightly.

While the cocas are baking, make the topping by whisking together the ricotta, milk, and spices in a small bowl. Drizzling topping on pitas.

Here is another great method for cooking this recipe, resulting in a crispier coca. Preheat broiler and make sure rack is at least 3 inches from heat source. Place the pitas on a baking pan. Evenly divide the cooked pepper mixture on top of each. Place under the broiler and cook until the top is starting to crisp and becomes charred looking, about 3–4 minutes. Remove from broiler and cool slightly before cutting and drizzling ricotta sauce over the top.

Simple Whole Grain Artisan Bread

Why, with the downplay of bread lately, do people keep flocking to artisan bread outlets? Make it yourself, and see why. With so many types of whole grain flours available, I find the best to use is whole grain bread flour. Although slightly denser than all purpse, it is the finest grind available for keeping the entire grain. The crisp crust, hollow sound, and great old "home" flavor is second to none.

1½ cups warm water
1 (0.25-ounce) active yeast
1 teaspoon maple or corn
    syrup, or honey
½ teaspoon each dried
    rosemary and basil
2½ cups whole grain
    bread flour
1 cup white rye or
    all-purpose flour
¼ cup guar gum, optional*
1 teaspoon salt
Cornmeal

In a large bowl, blend the warm water with yeast, maple syrup, rosemary, and basil. Let sit for 10 minutes.

In another large bowl, combine both flours, guar gum, and salt. Add the dry to the wet and mix well with a stout wooden spoon or a mixer with a dough hook or paddle until the dough comes together in the center of the bowl.

Cover bowl with a towel and place dough in a warm spot to rise until it doubles in bulk (about an hour).

When dough is ready, sprinkle some cornmeal on a baking pan and keep a bowl of water handy to wet hands. Remove the dough from bowl with wet hands and shape it into a sphere or ball. Place it on the cornmeal (use parchment paper if you don't have cornmeal) and smooth it all over with wet hands, shaping it into a uniform ball. Loosely place a towel over the top and let sit for another hour.

Preheat oven to 400° F. With your hands, wet the dough again on top quite liberally. With a sharp, serrated knife, make a couple slits on top and sprinkle evenly with some cornmeal. Bake about 30–35 minutes in the upper half of your oven, or until the bread is quite browned and hollow when tapped. The bread may be softer than you like when first removed, but will crisp up as it cools.

*Guar gum strengthens baked breads without adding elasticity, which makes it perfect for artisan breads. It also provides protein from its complex carbs. Can't find it in your health food store, but still want the protein? Simply add 2 eggs to this recipe, lowering the flour content by ¾ cup.

MAKES 1 LOAF

Whole Wheat vs. Whole Grain

Make sure you know the difference between "whole wheat" and "whole grain." Whole grain means the entire kernel of the grain is intact, from the bran to endosperm to the germ. Whole wheat has the bran and germ removed; this results in at least a 25% reduction in protein and a reduction in most of the antioxidants, which are found mostly in the outer layer, or bran.

Also keep an eye out for the word "enriched." It means that the processor of that food product has added back some of the nutrients and vitamins lost in processing.

Gluten-Free Whole Grain Artisan Bread

To be perfectly honest, this is about the best artisan bread you can make without gluten, although the texture may be slightly dry. If you find it truly too dry for your taste, add another teaspoon xanthan gum or reduce water by 3 tablespoons and substitute 3 tablespoons melted butter or margarine.

1⅓ cups warm water
1 teaspoon sugar
1 (0.25-ounce) package active
    dry yeast
1½ cups tapioca starch
1 cup sorghum flour
¾ cup white or brown rice flour
1 tablespoon xanthan gum
1 teaspoon salt
Cornmeal
2 tablespoons whole seeds, for
    example poppy, anise,
    sunflower, sesame or flax

In a large bowl, blend the warm water with sugar and yeast. Let sit for 10 minutes.

In another large bowl, combine starch, flours, guar gum, and salt. Add the dry to the wet and mix well with a stout wooden spoon or a mixer with a dough hook or paddle.

Cover bowl with a towel and place dough in a warm spot to rise until it doubles in bulk (about an hour). When ready, sprinkle some cornmeal on a baking pan and keep a bowl of water handy to wet hands. Remove the dough from bowl with wet hands and shape it into a sphere or ball. Place it on the cornmeal (use parchment paper if you don't have cornmeal) and smooth it all over with wet hands, shaping it into a more uniform ball. Loosely place a piece of film wrap over the top and let sit for another hour.

Preheat oven to 400° F. With your hands, wet the dough again on top quite liberally. With a sharp, serrated knife, make an "x" on top and sprinkle seeds evenly. Bake about 30 minutes, or until the bread is quite browned and hollow when tapped. Every 5 minutes, open the door of the oven to spritz the top of the dough with additional water if desired. This helps to brown and crisp the crust. The bread may be softer than you like when first removing, but will crisp up as it cools.

MAKES 1 LOAF

Going Gluten-Free

It is an odd thing when a disease sparks a diet fad. Celiac sufferers have an all-too-real problem with their small intestines inflaming when gluten is ingested. But today a huge "congregation" follows gluten-free diets, even if they don't have celiac disease. Studies have been head-buttingly contradictory: Some gluten-free dieters report feeling more energetic and losing weight, while others report no difference at all. In fact many have gained weight, often making them more sedentary. What everyone needs to know is that just because something is gluten-free, it isn't automatically healthy. Many food items that are without gluten are high in calories, fat, and carbs.

It is true that going gluten-free allows you to avoid many processed foods, and that definitely helps with maintaining a healthier lifestyle. And I would say that anything that keeps processed foods out of your system is okay in my book.

Sweet Semolina Batard

Simply put, a *batard* is a small French baguette. Usually sweeter than a baguette, this bread uses semolina, which is a coarse grind, high-protein durum wheat. It contains several B-complex vitamins, which greatly aid in converting food into usable energy, thereby supporting your metabolism. And with your metabolism boosted, there is no reason *not* to take that walk after dinner.

1 cup warm skim milk
½ cup brown sugar
1 (0.25-ounce) package
    dry yeast
1¼ cups semolina flour
1¼ cups all-purpose flour
2 eggs, beaten
1 teaspoon salt
Nonstick cooking spray
1 tablespoon cornmeal
1 teaspoon maple syrup
1 tablespoon sesame seeds

In a large bowl, mix milk, brown sugar, and yeast. Let sit for 10 minutes, or until it starts to foam. Stir in both flours, eggs, and salt until the dough comes together and leaves the side of the bowl. This is best accomplished with a dough hook on a tabletop mixer but is easily accomplished with a sturdy, wooden spoon as well. Spray the top of the dough with nonstick cooking spray, loosely cover with a towel, and set in a warm spot to rise until the dough doubles in bulk.

MAKES 1 LOAF

When dough has doubled, remove and place on a floured work surface. Knead for a minute until it is elastic and smooth before forming into an oblong shape. Place the loaf on an ungreased baking sheet that has been sprinkled with corn meal. Brush maple syrup over the top, followed by sesame seeds. Cover with a light towel and let rise for about an hour, or until dough has almost doubled in size again.

Preheat oven to 350° F. Make a couple slashes on top with a sharp, serrated knife and bake until golden brown on top, about 25–30 minutes. Remove from oven to cool.

Fill up on Fiber

I have heard story after story of cancer patients having issues with constipation or diarrhea. To combat this, you want to get more soluble fiber in your diet, such as oats, bran, and barley. Adding soluble fiber by increasing fruits and vegetables is recommended for constipation sufferers only.

An easy example of the difference between insoluble and soluble fiber can be described by taking a carrot and dropping it into your bathtub. When you retrieve it, the carrot didn't absorb any water or become altered in any way. This is insoluble fiber. If you pour rolled oats in this same water and retrieve them, they are sticky and begin to degrade. This is soluble fiber.

The Perfect English Muffin Bread

Not only is the fat and calorie content in this recipe low, it is the one and only English Muffin Bread recipe you will ever need. When you slice this bread and toast it, you will notice those little peaks that brown up just as if you had fork-split a muffin. As for flavor? Again, it is the best!

1¼ cups warm skim milk
1½ teaspoons sugar
1 (0.25-ounce) package
    dry yeast
2½ cups flour
1 teaspoon salt
1 teaspoon baking soda
1 egg, beaten
1 tablespoon butter or
    margarine, melted
Nonstick cooking spray

In a large bowl, whisk together milk, sugar, and yeast until well blended. Let sit for 15 minutes, or until the yeast starts to foam.

Stir in flour, salt, baking soda, egg, and butter until the dough comes together and leaves the side of the bowl. This is best accomplished with a dough hook on a tabletop mixer but is easily accomplished with a sturdy, wooden spoon as well. Spray the top with nonstick cooking spray, loosely cover the dough with a towel and set in a warm spot to rise until the dough doubles in bulk.

MAKES 1 LOAF

Spray a loaf pan with nonstick cooking spray and dust with cornmeal, making sure you coat the bottom and sides of the pan. Sprinkle a work surface with a mixture of half flour and half cornmeal. Turn dough out and knead for a minute or so, or until smooth and no longer sticky. The dough will be heavier than normal yeast breads, but that is expected with this type of dough. Form into a loaf, pinch to seal if needed and place, pinched side down, into prepared pan. Spray the top again with nonstick cooking spray, loosely cover with a towel and let rise again until the dough doubles in bulk (about an hour).

Preheat oven to 350° F and remove towel. Bake 23–25 minutes, or until lightly browned on top. Remove from oven to cool a few minutes before removing from pan onto a plate to cool completely.

Whole Grain Irish Maslin Bread

Maslin literally means brass, but it also refers to a variety of grains used in the baking of bread. So keeping with tradition, in a way, I am including different grains as well as a surprise ingredient that I think you will find a perfect fit.

If you don't have buttermilk, the perfect substitute is mixing 1 tablespoon vinegar or lemon juice in the same amount of whole milk and letting it sit for 30 minutes or even longer. It will curdle, which is exactly what you want. The interaction of this with baking soda gives this perfectly salty/sweet bread that distinctive hollow sound and the flavor will remind you of an old-world bake shop in Ireland.

Nonstick cooking spray
2 cups all purpose flour
1 cup whole grain bread flour
½ cup any whole grain cereal
    mix, crushed
½ cup rye flour
1 tablespoon baking soda
1 ½ teaspoons salt
3 tablespoons butter or
    margarine, cold
1¼ cups buttermilk
¼ cup molasses
1 egg, lightly beaten
Honey or maple syrup for
    brushing the top

MAKES 1 LOAF

Preheat oven to 375° F and position rack to the upper portion of the oven.

Grease a baking pan with nonstick cooking spray. In a large bowl, combine both flours, crushed cereal, rye flour, baking soda, and salt. Add butter and cut in using either 2 knives, scissor fashion, or a fork. Stir in buttermilk, molasses, and egg, mixing well.

Turn out onto well-floured work surface and knead for a minute, or until smooth and elastic. Brush off excess flour and place in the middle of the prepared pan. Brush the top with honey and sprinkle extra rolled oats over the top, slightly pressing into the dough. Mark the top with a serrated knife with two 1-inch deep gashes.

Bake 40-45 minutes, or until very well browned all over. Remove to cool slightly before serving.

Original and Versatile Naan Bread

Although I adore naan as it is classically prepared with white, all-purpose flour, I have always sought to add as much flavor as possible without adding more ingredients. This is the best tasting naan recipe you will ever make. Of course you can use all-purpose flour if desired, but this recipe gave me exactly the taste I was hoping for. And topping this Asian, leavened flat bread with crushed garlic, cooked onion, minced lamb, nuts and dates, or mashed potatoes makes for classic presentations.

1 (0.25-ounce) package
    active yeast
1 teaspoon sugar
⅔ cup warm water
2 tablespoons butter or
    margarine, melted
2 tablespoons pure olive oil
6 tablespoons plain yogurt
1 egg, slightly beaten
2 ⅔ cups white rye flour
½ teaspoon salt
½ teaspoon garlic
    powder, optional

In a large bowl, blend the yeast, sugar, and water and let sit for 10 minutes, or until the yeast starts to foam. Stir in the butter, oil, yogurt, and egg. With a sturdy wooden spoon, add the flour, salt, and garlic powder, vigorously mixing until the dough leaves the side of the bowl. You can use a mixer with a dough hook if desired.

Using naan as pizza is a favorite of my children. Simply spread pizza sauce and low-fat cheese on a piece of naan, top with whatever meat and cooked veggies you desire, and put the naan under the broiler for a couple minutes. For a breakfast treat, take leftover naan and spread it with some cooked thinly sliced ham, followed by chopped eggs and a drizzle of low-fat Hollandaise sauce; broil for a couple of minutes.

Transfer to a floured work surface and knead for a couple minutes, or until it is no longer sticky and is smooth, adding more flour if needed.

Place dough back in the bowl, loosely cover with a towel, and let rise in a warm spot until the dough doubles in bulk (about an hour). Remove to a well-floured work surface and divide into 8 small balls. Roll each ball out in a tear-drop shape about ¼-inch thick and about 6 inches in diameter. Stack on a plate with film wrap between naans.

Spray a large skillet with cooking spray and place over medium heat. As it is heating, grab one naan and stretch it back into the teardrop shape (it will have shrunk while sitting). Place naan in hot skillet and cook about 1–2 minutes on one side. When you notice large bubbles or blisters appear*, it is time to flip it and cook the other side until browned. While it is cooking, get the next naan ready to grill. Remove cooked naan to a dish, add more oil to skillet, and repeat until all naans are cooked. Be careful *not* to spray the pan directly over a gas flame.

MAKES 24 (6-INCH) PIECES OF NAAN.

*Don't worry if you have black blisters on your bread; that is quite typical of naan and actually makes it taste perfect.

Welsh Rarebit Bread

Welsh Rarebit, for those unfamiliar, is generally made with a strong, dark beer and cheese. I have made this bread using hard apple cider. No beer can even come close to the flavor profile.

Nonstick cooking spray
3 cups flour
¼ cup sugar
1 tablespoon baking powder
2 teaspoons dried mustard
16 ounces hard or regular
　　apple cider, divided
3 tablespoons Worcestershire
　　sauce
2 tablespoons butter or
　　margarine, melted
6 ounces shredded, reduced
　　fat cheddar cheese

Preheat oven to 350° F. Spray loaf pan with nonstick cooking spray; set aside.

In a large bowl, combine flour, sugar, baking powder, and mustard. Stir in 12 ounces apple cider, Worcestershire sauce, melted butter, and cheese until a thick batter is formed. Pour into prepared pan, leveling the top but not smoothing it out. This is what will give it a great "spiked" crust.

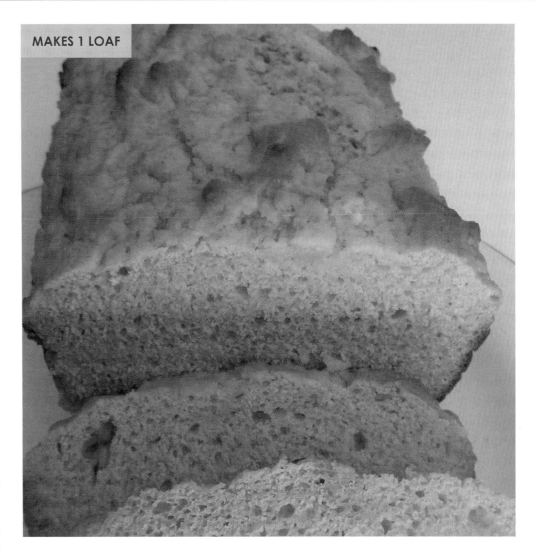

MAKES 1 LOAF

Pour remainder of hard cider evenly over the top and bake 32–34 minutes, or until the bread is firm and bounces back when touched in the middle. Remove from oven to cool for a few minutes before transferring to a plate to cool completely, uncovered.

New England Sausage and Cornbread Stuffing

I don't generally use boxed breads but with all the baking and cooking that needs to be done during the holidays, why not? You may have a tendency to skip toasting the corn muffin cubes, but I highly urge you *not* to do so! It lends an incredible texture and taste.

Nonstick cooking spray
2 boxes (8.5 ounce each) corn
    muffin or corn bread mix
1 link chicken sausage, sliced
1 teaspoon butter or margarine
1 small onion, peeled
    and minced
1 rib celery, thinly sliced
½ cup roughly chopped,
    roasted bell pepper
1 cup fresh sage leaves,
    chopped*
½ cup egg substitute
½–1 teaspoon garlic powder
1–2 cups fat-free chicken or
    turkey broth
½ teaspoon salt
¼ teaspoon black pepper

Preheat oven to 400° F. Spray two 8 × 8 × 2–inch baking pans with nonstick cooking spray. Make cornbread according to package directions. Pour into prepared pans and bake 18–20 minutes, or until lightly browned on top and cornbread springs back in the center when touched. Remove from oven to cool completely.

Cut cornbread into 1-inch cubes and place on baking pan, evenly spacing in a single layer. Bake an additional 10 minutes at 400° F, or until well toasted but not browned, stirring halfway through the baking. Remove from oven to cool, and reduce oven temperature to 375. Toss corn bread cubes with egg substitute; set aside.

Spray a 13 × 9–inch square baking pan with nonstick cooking spray; set aside. Add sausage to a large skillet over medium heat. Cook 5–6 minutes or until no longer pink, making sure to turn slices over. Use a slotted spoon to remove meat to a bowl and discard drippings. Return skillet to burner, and add butter until melted. Add onion and celery, cooking until the celery is soft, 3-4 minutes, stirring frequently. Add bell pepper and sage leaves. Mix well and cook an additional 1–2 minutes, or until sage is wilted and everything is combined well. Remove from heat to cool 15 minutes.

Put bread cubes in a large bowl. Pour vegetable mixture, egg substitute, and garlic powder into bread cubes, as well as cooked sausage. Toss to combine. Add 1 cup broth. Toss well and add more broth if needed to moisten. Season to taste with salt and pepper. Pour into prepared pan.

Bake, uncovered, at 375° F for 40-45 minutes, or until top is crisp and the middle, when touched, is firm.

*You can use 2 teaspoons rubbed, dried sage if desired.

SERVES 8–10

The Holy Trinity is the combination of onion, celery, and carrots, in a 2:1:1 ratio and is the basis for hundreds of dishes, stocks, and broths. In France, it is called *mirepoix*. while the Italians refer to it as *soffritto*, *odori* or *battuto*. In Louisiana, Cajun chefs use celery, onions, and bell peppers. The Chinese Holy Trinity is garlic, ginger, and chiles, and in Poland, it is less well defined. A mixture of carrots, parsnips, and parsley root may be the sworn stock base from one chef while celery root, carrots, and leeks is used by another.

High-Rise Apple Crisp Scones

This unusual and delicious scone would be perfect as a Sunday brunch dish or enjoyed by itself with a hot cup of coffee.

Nonstick cooking spray
2 apples of your choice,
    peeled and cored
¾ cup rolled oats
¾ cup sugar, divided
4 tablespoons melted butter or
    margarine, divided
1 tablespoon cinnamon,
    divided
2 ½ cups flour
1 tablespoon baking powder
1 teaspoon baking soda
1 teaspoon nutmeg
½ cup raisins
½ cup sour cream or yogurt
¾ cup apple jelly, melted and
    stirred until smooth
1 egg, beaten

Preheat oven to 350° F. Grease well a 9-inch round cake pan with nonstick cooking spray.

Mince 1 apple and add to a bowl with rolled oats, 3 tablespoons sugar, 2 tablespoons melted butter, and 1 teaspoon cinnamon. (You should have no more than ¾ cup minced apple. If you have more, simply add the rest into the flour mixture below). Mix well and set aside.

Dice remaining apple and add to a large bowl with flour, remaining sugar, baking powder, baking soda, nutmeg, and remaining cinnamon. Blend well and add raisins, sour cream, apple jelly, and egg. On a well-floured work surface, knead just until the dough holds together (about 10 seconds of folding it over onto itself). Place in prepared cake pan and evenly top with rolled oats mixture. Bake 45–50 minutes, or until firm when pressed in the center with no other part of the scone moving. Remove from oven to cool slightly before digging in.

SERVES 8–10

Is Coffee the New Super Antioxidant?

Well, yes and no. Joe A. Vinson, PhD, a chemistry professor at the University of Scranton in Pennsylvania, has found in his research that coffee just may be that golden ticket. The average adult consumes about 1,300 milligrams of antioxidants a day from coffee, which makes it the number one source of antioxidants in Americans' diet. The closest competitor was tea (294 mg), then bananas, dry beans, and corn. This doesn't mean that coffee as a food is the highest in antioxidant levels: It simply means that with the combination of the amount of coffee we drink and the number of antioxidants per serving, coffee tends to be our main source of antioxidants.

Tropical Coconut Bread

Although tropical in name, this sweet bread is simply a must at any Sunday brunch. The second Yankee Chef, my father, Jack Bailey, made this for me for the first time at a luncheon many, many years ago and I have never forgotten how refreshing the taste was. And I don't think you will soon forget either.

Nonstick cooking spray
1½ cups shredded, sweetened coconut, divided
3 tablespoons maple syrup
2 bananas, sliced
1 cup evaporated skim milk
2½ tablespoons butter or margarine, melted
2 teaspoons rum extract
2 cups flour
1 cup sugar
2 teaspoons baking powder
3 egg whites, beaten

MAKES 1 LOAF

Preheat oven to 350° F.

Spray an 8 × 8-inch square baking pan with nonstick cooking spray.

In a small bowl, blend ½ cup coconut with maple syrup; set aside. In the bowl of a food processor or blender, combine sliced bananas, milk, melted butter, and rum extract. Puree on high until smooth, about 15 seconds; set aside.

In a large bowl, combine well the flour, remainder of coconut, sugar, and baking powder. Add the wet into the dry, along with egg whites, stirring until well combined. Transfer to the prepared pan and evenly sprinkle the prepared coconut mixture on top. Bake 30–32 minutes, or until firm on top when touched. Remove from oven to cool before slicing.

Go Bananas!

Vitamin B6, of which bananas have an abundance, is the workhorse of all vitamins, as it is involved in more body functions that most other nutrients and it aids in more than 100 metabolic processes. Keeping your metabolism up, in turn, helps you get off that couch and take a walk.

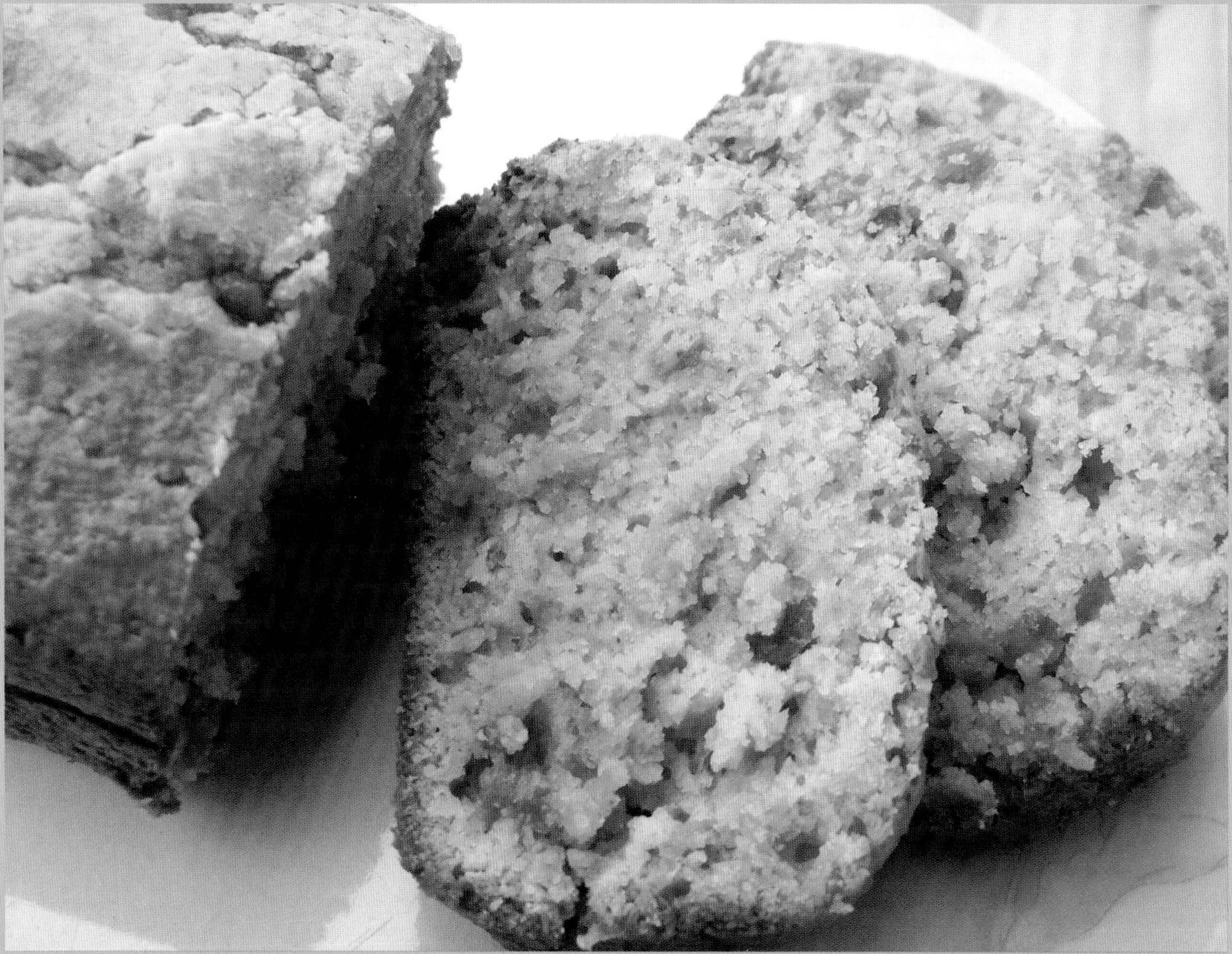

Old-Fashioned Orange-Spice Graham Bread

This is a simple, spot-on coffee cake-like dessert bread that is sweet and delicious. If you have any left over the next day, I highly suggest either spraying each side with butter-flavored spray and grilling for a crispy, warm indulgence or using the bread to make a great french toast breakfast.

Nonstick cooking spray
¾ cup buttermilk
¼ stick butter or
    margarine, melted
¼ cup orange juice
    concentrate, thawed
2 eggs, beaten
1 egg white, beaten
½ cup brown sugar
¼ cup granulated sugar
1 cup flour
1 cup crushed graham
    crackers
2 teaspoons baking powder
1 teaspoon each of cinnamon
    and allspice
½ teaspoon nutmeg

Preheat oven to 350° F. Spray a loaf pan with nonstick cooking spray, on bottom and sides; set aside.

In a large bowl, combine buttermilk, butter, orange juice, and eggs and whisk well.

In another bowl, combine remainder of ingredients, stirring well. Add the wet to the dry and blend well. It doesn't matter if there are lumps or not—in fact a few lumps help prevent gluten from forming, creating a soft, slightly crumbly texture.

Pour into the prepared loaf pan and bake 35–37 minutes, or until the sides are pulling away and the top springs back when touched. Remove to cool for a few minutes in pan before transferring to a rack or plate.

MAKES 1 LOAF

Butter's Bonus

Butter is a very rich source of selenium, a vital antioxidant. It contains more selenium per gram than either herring and wheat germ, both known for their robust levels of this antioxidant.

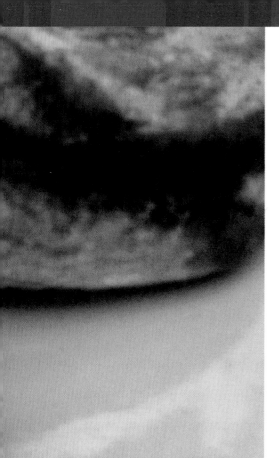

New England Pumpkin Cobbler Swirls

With four flavors that are quintessential Yankee, these swirls are supereasy to make, yet in a class all their own.

1 cup flour, plus more
    for kneading
1/2 cup cornmeal
1/2 teaspoon salt
2 teaspoons baking powder
2 teaspoons cinnamon
1/2 teaspoon nutmeg
2 tablespoons butter or
    margarine
1/2 cup pure pumpkin,
    not spiced
1/4 cup maple syrup
1/2 cup blueberry preserves
1/4 cup apple jelly
1 teaspoon lemon juice

Preheat oven to 350° F.

In a large bowl, combine flour, cornmeal, salt, baking powder, cinnamon, and nutmeg. Cut in butter with a fork until very small beads are formed. Add pumpkin and maple syrup, mix well, and turn out onto a well-floured work surface. Knead for a least 2 minutes, adding more flour as needed to prevent sticking and until it is smooth; divide in half.

Roll out one half onto a 10- by 5-inch rectangle. Spread half of the preserves evenly to within one inch of all sides. Working from the long side, roll up tightly, pinching to seal. With the seal side facing up, use a knife to cut halfway through the top of the "rope," from one end to the other, lengthwise.

Grabbing one end, start coiling it tightly, forming a spiral, pinching the end onto itself. Repeat with other dough half.

Place on ungreased baking pan and bake 22–24 minutes or until firm to the touch.

Meanwhile, empty apply jelly into a bowl, add lemon juice, and microwave on high for 30 seconds. Remove to whisk smooth. Drizzle equal amounts of apple jelly mixture over each and serve hot.

MAKES 4

Sources such as Breastcancer.org note that diet is thought to be partly responsible for about 30% to 40% of all cancers. That truly is a staggering assumption, and one that this author truly believes. The nonprofit group recommends getting nutrients "from a variety of foods, especially fruits, vegetables, legumes, and whole grains." They also recommend limiting fat intake and mixing up protein options to reduce the consumption of red meat.

"New" Fashioned Hot Cross Buns

For this twist on a classic, I have cut the usual powdered sugar glaze in half and added that New England flavor that is cranberries. I think you will save this recipe to hand down to the next generation.

¾ cup dried cranberries
2¾ cups water, divided
1 tablespoon plus
    1 teaspoon sugar
1 (0.25-ounce) package
    active yeast
2 ½ cups flour
2 tablespoons butter or
    margarine, melted
2 teaspoons cinnamon
1 teaspoon nutmeg
1 teaspoon salt
Grated zest from 1 lemon
Nonstick cooking spray
1 cup powdered sugar
Juice from 1 lemon
    (about 1 tablespoon)

MAKES ABOUT 15 ROLLS

In a small saucepan, bring cranberries and 1¾ cups water to a boil over medium-high heat. Cook 10 minutes and remove from heat. Remove ½ cup cranberries and place in a bowl; set aside. Remove 2 tablespoons of the cranberry juice and place in a small bowl; set aside for glaze. Transfer the remainder of the berries and liquid to a blender or food processor and puree until smooth. Transfer to a bowl; set aside.

In a large bowl, combine 1 cup warm water, sugar, and yeast, whisking well. Let sit for 10 minutes, or until yeast starts to foam. With a sturdy wooden spoon (or using a dough hook on a standing mixer) stir in flour, melted butter, cinnamon, nutmeg, salt, and lemon zest until well mixed. Add cooked cranberries, continuing to stir until dough leaves the side of the bowl. Cover loosely with a kitchen towel and let rise in a warm place until almost double in bulk (about an hour).

Turn dough out onto lightly floured work surface and knead for 2–3 minutes, or until smooth and elastic. Pinch off balls of dough about the size of ping-pong balls, creating 15 rolls. Place each on a baking pan greased with nonstick cooking spray, spacing 2 inches apart. Spray the top with nonstick cooking spray and let rise until almost double in bulk (another hour).

Preheat oven to 350° F. With a pair of scissors, snip a cross on top of each roll and bake 12–14 minutes, or until lightly browned on top. Remove to cool completely on a rack or plate.

In a bowl, whisk together powdered sugar, lemon juice, and the 2 tablespoons of reserved cranberry liquid.

When rolls are cooled, whisk and drizzle reserved cranberry puree in cross on top of each roll. Place in refrigerator for 5 minutes, then drizzle powdered sugar glaze over each roll and serve.

A Cup of Cranberries

The antioxidant values of foods are expressed in Oxygen Radical Absorbance Capacity (ORAC) units. Each food is assigned a point value based on its ability to neutralize free radicals. It is universally suggested that we include at least 3,000 ORAC units in our daily diet, with anything above 8,000 being optimal. What does the average American consume? How does 800 a day sound? Pretty sad, isn't it? Cranberries are one of the top antioxidant-rich foods. With a total antioxidant value of about 9000 ORAC units, just one cup of berries provides all the antioxidants you need in a single day.

Here are the USDA's TOP 20 Antioxidant-Rich Foods (in ORAC units). (Learn the ORAC values of other common foods at superfoodly.com.)

1 Small red bean (dried): 13,727 per ½ cup
2 Wild blueberry: 13,427 per 1 cup
3 Red kidney bean (dried): 13,259 per ½ cup
4 Pinto bean: 11,864 per ½-cup
5 Blueberry (cultivated): 9,019 per 1 cup
6 Cranberry (whole): 8,983 per 1 cup
7 Artichoke (cooked) (hearts): 7,904 per 1 cup
8 Blackberry: 7,701 per 1 cup
9 Dried Prune: 7,291 per ½ cup
10 Raspberry: 6,058 per 1 cup
11 Strawberry: 5,938 per 1 cup
12 Red Delicious apple: 5,900 per apple
13 Granny Smith apple: 5,381 per apple
14 Pecan: 5,095 per 1 ounce
15 Sweet cherry 4,873 per 1 cup
16 Black plum: 4,844 per plum
17 Russet potato (cooked): 4,649 per potato
18 Black bean (dried): 4,181 per ½ cup
19 Plum: 4,118 per plum
20 Gala apple: 3,903 per apple

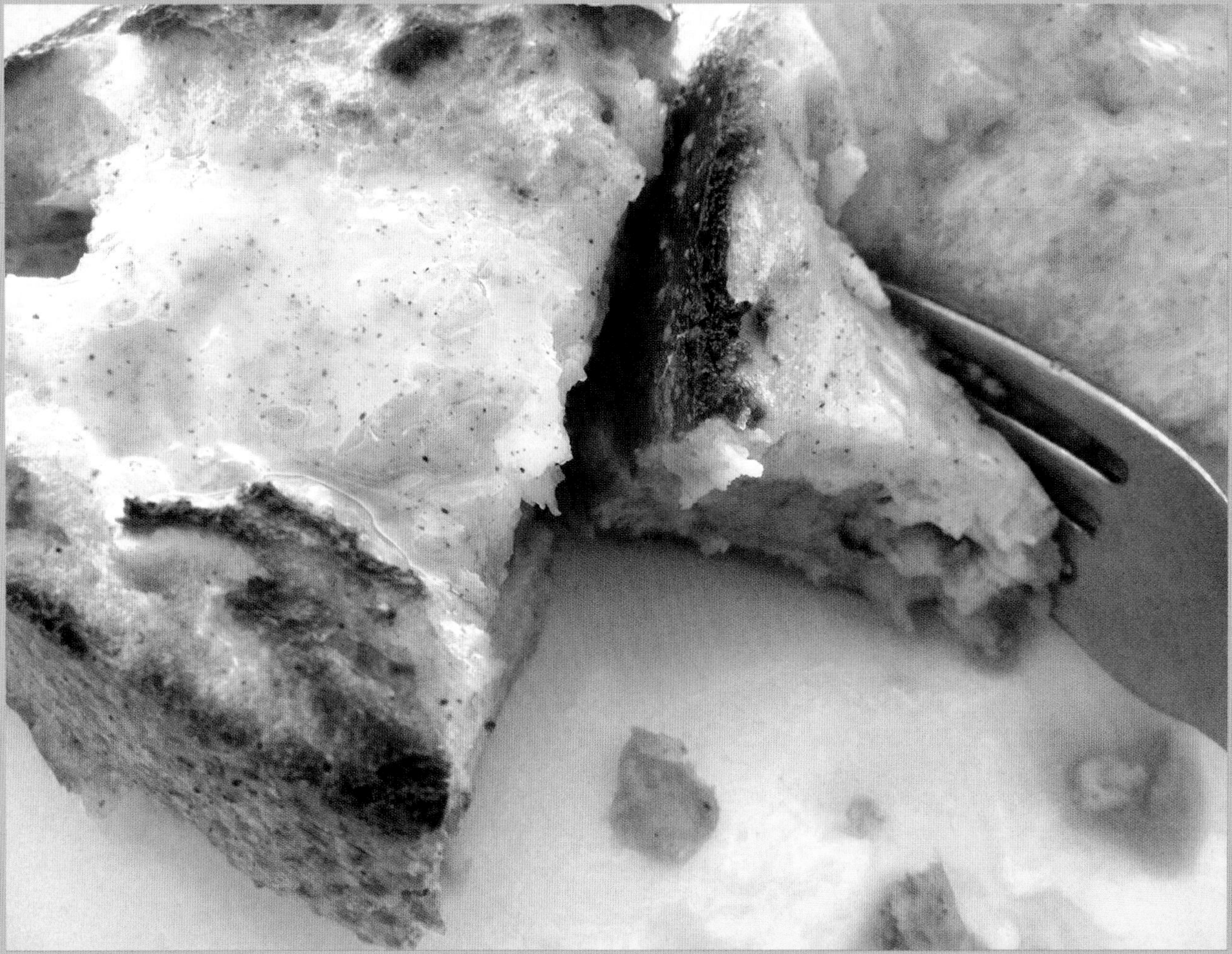

Banana "Crème" French Toast

This recipe is out of this world. Making your own crème fraîche is simple and transforms this ordinary breakfast dish into a recipe to serve anytime. Believe it or not, it will take longer to cook this perfect french toast than it will to prepare it.

½ cup sugar
½ cup egg substitute
1¼ cups plus 1 tablespoon cup
    skim milk, divided
½ teaspoon cinnamon
1 teaspoon vanilla extract or 2
    teaspoons imitation vanilla
Nonstick cooking spray
3 bananas, mashed
1 tablespoon maple syrup
3 (4-inch) thick slices
    french bread

In a small saucepan, make crème fraîche by combining sugar, egg substitute, 1¼ cups milk, and cinnamon. Whisk well and bring to scalding over medium heat, whisking frequently. Reduce heat to low and whisk constantly for 4–5 minutes, or until thickened. Remove from heat, stir in the vanilla, and transfer to a shallow bowl and refrigerate for 15 minutes, uncovered.

Meanwhile, preheat oven to 375° F. Spray a pie tin with nonstick cooking spray; set aside.

In a bowl, stir the mashed bananas and maple syrup very well. With a pointed steak knife, make a deep slit in each bread slice, forming a pocket, but don't cut all the way to the other side. Spoon equal amounts of banana mixture into each bread pocket. Remove crème fraîche from refrigerator and whisk in remainder of milk until smooth. Dip filled bread slices into crème fraîche, turning over a few times to thickly coat each side. Place in prepared pie tin and bake in the hottest part of the oven for 25–30 minutes, or until starting to brown on top. This step can be quickened by baking for 15 minutes then transferring to the broiler for about 3 minutes to brown on top.

Remove and serve as is or with maple syrup drizzled on top.

MAKES 3 SERVINGS

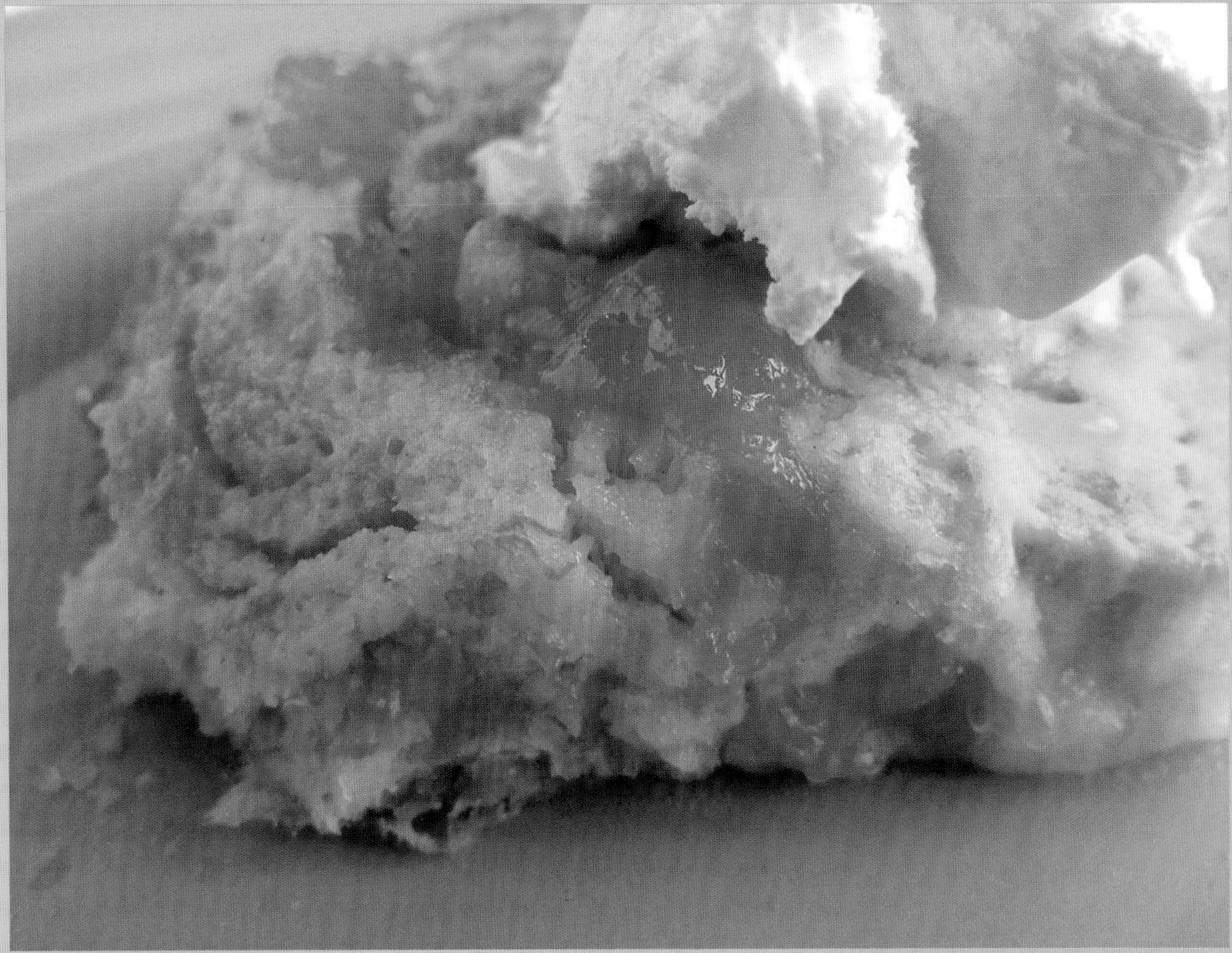

Sticky Orange Bolts

You can opt for navel oranges if desired, but know that both clementines and mandarin oranges are far more flavorful and give the perfect power punch to this super sticky treat. The juice is absorbed into these rolls, almost caramelizing on top, giving you lusciousness in the middle and crunch on top. And why the "bolts"? I have no idea where the name originated and have yet to find a comparable recipe so named. The first Yankee Chef, my grandfather, made these albeit a little differently, and called them as such, so I am "paying it forward."

1 pound clementine or
    mandarin oranges
1 cup frozen orange juice
    concentrate, thawed
    and divided
Butter-flavored nonstick
    cooking spray
2 cups flour
¾ cup sugar, divided
4 teaspoons baking powder
1 teaspoon salt
3 tablespoons cold butter
    or margarine
½ cup plain yogurt, plus more if
    needed
Whipped topping,
    frozen yogurt or ice
    cream, optional

Grate 1 tablespoon orange rind from clementines; set aside. Peel all oranges, seed, and roughly chop; set aside. Whisk 1 cup water to ½ cup orange juice concentrate; set aside. Spray a 2-inch-deep oven-safe pan or casserole dish with nonstick cooking spray.

In a large bowl, combine flour, ½ cup sugar, baking powder, orange rind, and salt until blended well. Cut in butter until it resembles crumbs. Stir in half the chopped oranges, remainder of concentrate, and yogurt until it just holds together. If you need to add another tablespoon of yogurt, or two, go ahead now.

Transfer dough to a lightly floured work surface and knead for a minute or two until it comes together well and is no longer sticky. Roll out into a rectangle about 10 × 14 inches. The dough should be about ½–¾-inch thick. With a glass rim or cookie cutter, cut out circles of dough and place on prepared pan, slightly apart. You can also cut squares or triangles if desired. Spray the top of each with nonstick cooking spray, sprinkle with remainder of sugar, and pour the reserved orange juice mixture over the top.

Turn on oven to 425° F. After a couple minutes, or when it reaches 300 degrees, pop the rolls in oven. Let cook for 20 minutes and then shut off oven, leaving rolls inside. After 10 minutes, remove rolls and enjoy while warm.

Did you know . . .
- Wild oranges are nonexistent.
- There was no name for the color orange until 1542. Very few things in nature were orange, so historians and authors before that time simply described things using the words copper, gold, or amber.
- The larger the navel on an orange, the sweeter it will be.
- Look closely. If you see an orange in any painting depicting the Last Supper, it is wrong. Oranges were not cultivated in the Middle East for another 800 years.

Cranberry Sweetheart Scones

These scones truly come from my heart. My mother would have adored these lightly sweetened but truly tart and tasty scones. These are much better when made one day and eaten the next.

Nonstick cooking spray

3 cups fresh cranberries

1 cup sugar, divided

Grated rind from 2 large
    oranges, divided

3 cups flour

1 tablespoon baking powder

3 tablespoons cold butter
    or margarine

¾ cup evaporated skim milk

Juice from 2 large
    oranges, divided

½ cup egg substitute

¾ cup dried or candied
    cherries, chopped

2 cups powdered sugar, or
    more as needed

MAKES 4 FULL-SIZE SCONES

Grease a large baking pan with nonstick cooking spray; set aside.

In a small saucepan, combine the fresh cranberries, ⅔ cup sugar, half the orange rind, and enough water to cover. Place on high heat and boil until you hear the cranberries pop, about 3 minutes. Remove from heat. Transfer to a bowl, liquid and all, and mash lightly. Place in refrigerator to cool at least one hour before making the rest of the recipe.

Preheat oven to 375° F. In a large bowl, mix well flour, remainder of sugar, and baking powder. Cut in the butter until it resembles small peas.

In a separate bowl, mix together milk, half the orange juice, half the orange rind, and all of the egg substitute. Blend the wet with the dry and fold in all but ¼-cup cherries. Mix only until combined.

Turn out the dough onto floured work surface and knead just a couple times to hold together. Divide the dough in half and roll each into a 12 × 6-inch rectangle. Cut each rectangle into 6-inch squares, then cut each square into equal triangles.

Top half the triangles with a tablespoon cooked cranberries (they will have thickened upon standing) and place a plain triangle of dough over the top. Press to seal around the edges and place on prepared baking sheet. Repeat with remaining dough, leaving an inch between each scone. Brush excess flour from the top of each and bake 14–16 minutes, or until browned on top. Remove to completely cool while making glaze.

Whisk the remainder of the orange juice with powdered sugar until smooth. Stir in the remainder of the chopped cherries. If the glaze isn't thick enough to still be white, add more powdered sugar. Pour glaze over each scone. Let the glaze set for 15 minutes in the refrigerator before serving.

Apple Glazed Cinnamon Roll Cups

Prepare this recipe entirely the night before so all you have to do is pop them in the microwave in the morning. All you have to do with the apple glaze is heat it, according to directions, on the stove top while your coffee is brewing.

½ cup evaporated skim milk
2 tablespoons butter
     or margarine
¼ cups sugar
1 (0.25-ounce) package
     active yeast
¼ cup warm water
2 eggs
1 egg white
3 cups flour
2 tablespoons cinnamon
¾ cup brown sugar
½ cup raisins
Nonstick cooking spray
½ cup frozen apple juice
     concentrate, thawed

In a small saucepan, heat the milk until just scalding. Don't boil! Stir in the butter and sugar. Remove the milk mixture from heat and cool until tepid, stirring to help the butter melt.

In a small bowl, combine yeast and water. Stir and set aside for 10 minutes to foam.

In a large bowl, beat the eggs and egg white using an electric mixer. Add in the yeast and milk mixture, beating well. Using a wooden spoon, mix in the flour, 1 cup at a time, until a soft dough forms.

Turn the dough out onto a generously floured work surface and, with floured hands, knead gently until the dough is smooth and elastic, about 5 minutes. Return the dough to the bowl and cover with film wrap. Let rise in a warm place until the dough doubles in size (about 1 hour). Divide the dough in half and form into 2 balls. Cover with plastic and let sit for 10 more minutes.

In a small bowl, combine the cinnamon, brown sugar, and raisins; set aside. Spray a 12-cup muffin tin with cooking spray. Using a rolling pin, roll each ball of dough into a 16 × 8–inch rectangle. Spray the dough with cooking spray and sprinkle each rectangle with half of the cinnamon mixture.

Starting at the long side, roll up each rectangle and slice each roll into 6 pieces. Place cut side

MAKES 12 ROLLS

up in prepared muffin tin. Cover and let rise until doubled (about 30 minutes).

Preheat the oven to 350° F. Brush each roll with the apple juice concentrate and bake until golden brown, about 15 minutes.

Serve warm with even more of this sticky glaze brushed over each.

Raisin Reason

Although raisins are a great snack and many references tout their health benefits, the truth is that they are simply delicious to eat. They aren't nutritionally outstanding in any sense. With 500 calories per cup, they provide half the recommended daily allowance (RDA) of carbs and a quarter the RDA of fiber. On the other hand, raisins have zero fat or cholesterol and only a hint of sodium.

Something to consider: Some raisins, such as golden raisins, are treated with sulfur dioxide, which can aggravate asthma and other allergies in some people. When buying raisins, read the label: Be sure they are sun-dried because these are not treated with sulfur.

Apple Cranberry Sticky Buns

These are so incredibly sticky and tasty I want to sit down with my paper, cup of coffee, and enjoy. You can substitute prepared cinnamon rolls in a tube for this recipe if desired.

Nonstick cooking spray
2 cups brown sugar
1½ cups chopped apple
1½ cups dried cranberries
1½ cups chopped nuts of
    your choice
1 batch Cinnamon Roll Cups*
    (see recipe on page 37)

Preheat oven to 350° F. Heavily spray a 12-cup muffin tin (or two 5-cup tins) with nonstick cooking spray.

Evenly divide the brown sugar into cups and then evenly spread the chopped apples, cranberries, and chopped nuts on top of the brown sugar. Push one cinnamon roll into each muffin cup, slightly pushing down into the cups so that the dough meets the sugar/fruit mixture.

Bake 25–30 minutes, or until browned on top. Immediately remove from oven and let cool 5 minutes. Carefully, and quickly, invert onto a large serving plate or platter and enjoy while hot and sticky.

*Follow recipe for Cinnamon Roll Cups, stopping directly after cutting them.

MAKES 12 STICKY BUNS

Want a great sweet sauce for these buns? In a saucepan, mix together 2 cups pureed pumpkin, 1 cup apple cider, and 1 teaspoon lemon or lime juice. Whisk well and heat over medium until hot. Remove and enjoy.

CHAPTER 2 Soups, Sides, and Sauces

Aaaah, that familiar call from the kitchen that "Soup's on!" can mean almost anything: Soups can include a wide variety of meats, vegetables, fish, seafood, and poultry, all combined in a fragrant, delicious broth.

These recipes offer the comfort of traditional, long-simmering soups but also offer an ease and quickness of preparation that is so often needed in today's busy world.

The sides and sauces in this chapter are equally delicious, nutritious, and easy— *It's Just That Simple!*

Spicy Asian-Style Soba Noodle Soup

Why just an eighth of a pound of noodles for this recipe? The abundance of other ingredients and the thickness of the soba noodle create a perfect combination for a tasty and not overly spiced soup. If you want more heat, add some red pepper flakes, but I think you will agree it is perfect just the way it is.

2 ounces dry soba noodles,
    cooked and drained
1 tablespoon chili sauce
1 cup bottled clam juice*
1 cup fat free beef broth
¼ teaspoon garlic powder
1 teaspoon molasses
1¼ teaspoons soy sauce
¼ cup sliced, cooked carrots
¼ cup cooked spinach,
    well drained
1 (6-ounce) can chopped
    clams, drained
Pinch of dry ginger
Pinch of black pepper

Add all ingredients to a large saucepan, stir very well, and bring to scalding over medium-high heat. That is it!

For a richer, deeper flavor, boil the noodles in juice/broth mixture until done. Add remaining ingredients, stir well, and serve very hot.

SERVES 2

*Don't have any? Simply add the juice from the can of chopped clams and add more beef broth to equal 1 cup.

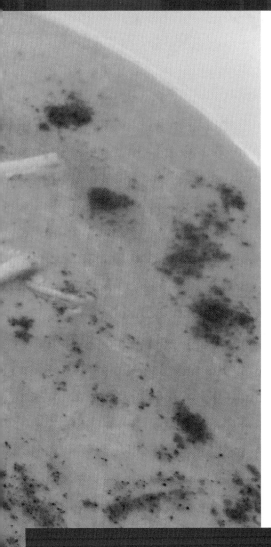

New England Curried Pumpkin Soup

For those who don't wish to go through the hassle (well worth it, I might add) of preparing the pumpkin, simply use four (15-ounce) cans of pureed, pure pumpkin.

2 small pumpkins
 (2–3 pounds each)
2 cups fat-free chicken broth
1 cup apple juice
¼ cup maple syrup
1 teaspoon seeded, minced
 jalapeño pepper
2 teaspoons curry powder
1 teaspoon cinnamon
½ teaspoon each salt, dried
 ginger, and nutmeg
1 cup plain yogurt
½ cup milk

For matchstick topping:
2 10-inch flour tortillas

For the Maple Cream:
¼ cup maple syrup
1 tablespoon plain yogurt

Preheat the oven to 350° F. Cut pumpkins in half. Scoop out seeds and place pumpkins skin-side down on baking sheet. Bake 35–45 minutes, or until soft. Remove and set aside until they are cool enough to handle.

Make matchstick toppings: Cut flour tortillas into thin slices, or any desired shape. Place on an ungreased baking pan and pop in 350-degree oven just for a few minutes, until starting to crisp and firm. Immediately remove from oven and pan to prevent burning; set aside.

Make Maple Cream: Heat a quarter cup maple syrup until hot to the touch, then stir in 1 tablespoon plain yogurt until color is even; set aside.

Scoop pumpkin flesh into food processor and puree until smooth. Pour pureed pumpkin into saucepan and add chicken broth, apple juice, maple syrup, jalapeño, and spices. Bring to a boil, then reduce to low and simmer 15 minutes.

Remove from heat and stir in yogurt and milk until smooth. Evenly divide soup among serving bowls, swirling some Maple Cream into each bowl and adding a large pinch of crisp tortilla matchsticks.

Depending on how rich you want it, or how cold it is outside, you can use mascarpone or any thickness of cream in place of yogurt. Just remember, the thicker the dairy product you use, the thicker the soup will be.

MAKES ABOUT 3 (1½ CUP) SERVINGS

The Power of Pumpkin

1 cup pure cooked, mashed pumpkin has only 50 calories, no fat or trans fats, no cholesterol, a trace amount of sodium, 11% of daily dietary fiber, 20% of RDA of Vitamin C and . . . almost 250% Vitamin A, according to the National Institutes of Health. Vitamin A (retinol) is keenly associated with eyesight and helps you adjust from coming inside, from out. And as with most foods, it is what we add to pumpkin that alters its nutritional values. No wonder our ancestors could read by candlelight!

According to the American Association for Cancer Research, tomatoes and lemon juice may have anti-tumor properties associated with breast cancer. Naringenin is a flavanone found in both and these researchers have found that naringenin may inhibit the growth of mammary tumor cells.

Red Jasmine Gazpacho

There are few soups that I truly enjoy during the warmer months, but gazpacho would rank as number one. Not only is this often-altered Spanish soup tasty and refreshing but when you add a wide variety of vegetables, along with fruit as a natural sweetener, the nutritional value soars.

2 pounds ripe tomatoes,
    chopped
3 cups diced watermelon,
    without seeds
1 pound cucumbers,
    peeled, seeded and
    roughly chopped
1 each red and yellow bell
    pepper, seeded and
    roughly chopped
1 jalapeno pepper, seeded
1 tablespoon lime or
    lemon juice
3 tablespoons red wine vinegar
2 tablespoons pure olive oil
1 cup jasmine tea
Salt and black pepper to taste

Those who can't tolerate tomato seeds should start by discarding seeds (otherwise proceed to the food processor step): Place a fine meshed sieve over a large bowl. Cut tomatoes in half and squeeze each to release as much juice and seeds as possible into the sieve With the back of a spoon, press against the sides of the sieve to release even more juice from the pulp. Discard seeds and chop the tomato.

Put all ingredients in the bowl of a food processor or blender and puree until desired consistency is reached. You may need to do this in batches. Season to taste with salt and pepper. Serve immediately at room temperature or refrigerate until ready to serve.

MAKES 6 SERVINGS

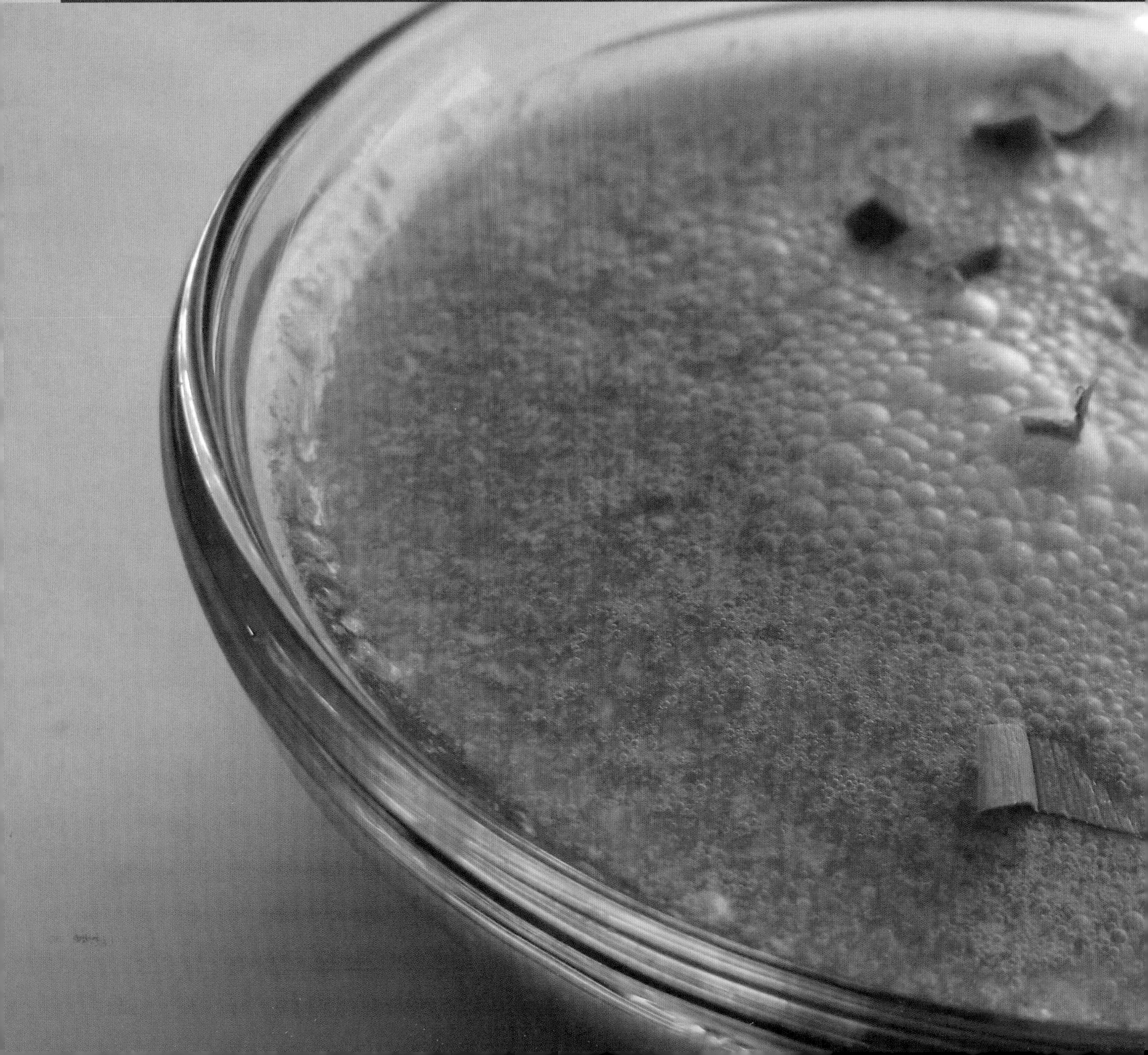

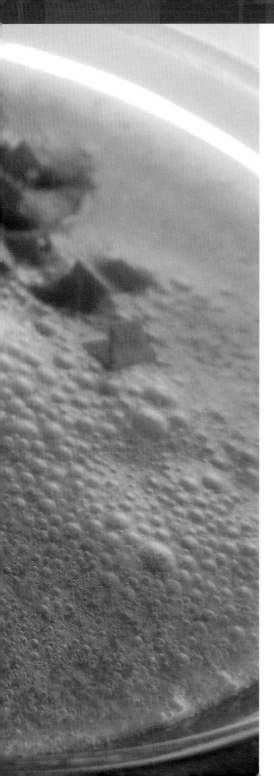

Beautiful Spring Gazpacho

There has been much debate over the difference, if any, between cilantro and coriander. But I must confess, humbly, that it is only here in America that we have it right. Everywhere else in the world, the terms cilantro and coriander and are used interchangeably, also going by other names such as Chinese parsley and dhania, to name just two. The truth is that *Coriandrum sativum* is the seed while the plant itself, the leaves, is cilantro.

1 pound green tomatoes,
    room temperature*
1 pound cucumbers,
    peeled, seeded and
    roughly chopped
1 each yellow and green bell
    pepper, seeded and
    roughly chopped
¾ cup light coconut milk
3 tablespoons freshly
    chopped cilantro
2 tablespoons apple
    cider vinegar
2 tablespoons pure olive oil
2 peaches, peeled, pitted and
    roughly chopped
Salt and black pepper to taste

First, remove seeds from the tomatoes, if desired (otherwise simply chop the tomatoes): Place a fine meshed sieve over a large bowl. Roll tomatoes with the palms of your hands against the counter to loosen the pulp inside. Cut tomatoes in half and squeeze each to release as much juice and seeds as possible into the sieve. With the back of a spoon, press against the sides of the sieve to release even more juice from the pulp. Discard seeds and chop the tomato.

Combine tomatoes and remaining ingredients in the bowl of a food processor or blender and puree until desired consistency is reached. You may need to do this in batches. Season to taste with salt and pepper. Serve immediately at room temperature or refrigerate until ready to serve. Garnish with diced cucumbers, peaches, or tomatoes if desired.

MAKES ABOUT 6 SERVINGS

Shoreline Christmas "Stew"

Oysters have been part of our American holiday custom for centuries. Oysters were plentiful here on our New England shores and have been used in stuffing since the Puritan era. Did you know that oyster stuffing, as well as other types of stuffing, was originally stuffed between the skin and meat of the turkey? For the first hundred or so years of New England colonization, there was rampant debate about which method tasted better: loosening the skin around a fowl to stuff or simply packing stuffing into the cavity of a dressed bird.

Regardless, oyster stew is a New England classic. I have taken this meal in itself and added even more New England ingredients, and I think you will find it satisfying and delicious.

1 pound chestnuts in shells
   (or pre-peeled and
   cooked in a jar)
1 slice turkey bacon, diced
½ small onion, peeled
   and minced
1 rib celery, sliced thinly
1 cup diced white potatoes
1 cup diced sweet potatoes
3 cups fat-free vegetable broth
1 teaspoon dried chives

1 pint (16 ounces) raw
   oysters, drained
3 ounces fresh Louisiana or
   salad shrimp, drained
1 cup almond milk
½ teaspoon salt
½ teaspoon dried thyme
¼ teaspoon black pepper

Place chestnuts in a large bowl and cover with boiling water for 30 minutes. Remove from water and carefully use a knife to slit an "X" on the rounded bottom of each chestnut. Place on a large, microwave-safe dish and cover with a wet paper towel. Heat, on high, for 2 minutes. Remove to let cool to room temperature before peeling and chopping.

Meanwhile, in a large saucepan, cook the bacon over medium heat until almost crispy. Drain and add the chopped chestnuts, onion, and celery and continue cooking, with the bacon, until celery is crisp tender, about another 3–4 minutes. Add the potatoes, vegetable broth, and chives. Bring to a boil, reduce heat to medium-low, and simmer until the potatoes are fork tender without falling apart, about 6–7 minutes. Add oysters and shrimp, cooking another 4–5 minutes or until the edges of the oysters start to curl. Add the milk, salt, thyme, and pepper. Serve immediately.

MAKES 6 SERVINGS

Salmon and Couscous Chowder

MAKES 4 SERVINGS

If you have never cooked with couscous, you are missing out on a great additive to many recipes. North African in origination, and super popular in French stews, it was only logical to add it to cream-style chowder.

FYI, we here in New England have our rice pudding while in Egypt, they have couscous pudding; both are sweet, creamy, and delicious.

1 (15-ounce) can salmon
2 tablespoons pure olive oil
½ onion, sliced and chopped
2 cloves garlic, crushed
1½ cups fat-free
    vegetable broth
1 pound sweet
    potatoes, diced
1 small carrot, chopped finely
½ cup whole wheat couscous
3 cups evaporated skim milk
1 teaspoon black pepper
Pinch of salt
½ teaspoon dried thyme or 1
    tablespoon chopped, fresh

Place salmon, with juice, into a bowl and remove any bones and black skin; set aside.

Crushing garlic is easily accomplished by laying a peeled garlic clove on a cutting board and placing the flat side of a large knife over the top. Gently press down until you hear the clove "break." You can then either keep rubbing the side of the knife against the garlic to form a paste or simply start chopping until desired consistency is reached.

In a large saucepan, mix olive oil, onion, and garlic. Cook over medium heat for 3–4 minutes, or until onion is soft. Add vegetable broth, potatoes, carrot, and couscous, stirring to combine. Cook 10–12 minutes, covered, or until potatoes are softened. Reduce heat to low and add milk, black pepper, salt, and thyme. Stirring occasionally, bring to scalding uncovered. Add salmon, stir to combine, and serve hot.

Cider Press Lamb Stew

I simply cannot say enough good about apple cider, especially when added to any dish that contains lamb. It is something about the subtle sweetness of sweet apples that just pairs naturally with lamb and this recipe is a perfect example.

2 pounds stew lamb, trimmed
    (or trimmed, deboned,
    and cubed lamb chops,
    or cubed, boneless
    leg of lamb)
½ teaspoon grated lemon rind
2 cups apple cider or
    juice, divided
¼ cup cornstarch plus 2
    tablespoons, divided
2 tablespoons pure olive oil
½ cup minced red onion
2 garlic cloves, crushed
Juice from 1 lemon
1 cup fat-free vegetable broth
    plus 3 tablespoons, divided
½ teaspoon salt
¼ teaspoon black pepper
½ teaspoons cinnamon
1 pound potatoes, peeled and
    cubed (about 2 cups)
¾ cup sliced carrots

Combine lamb with lemon rind and 1½ cups cider. Toss to coat, cover, and refrigerate at least 12 hours, stirring every couple of hours.

Remove lamb from cider mixture and discard marinade. Drain lamb chunks well and toss with ¼ cup cornstarch.

Heat oil in large saucepan over medium-high until hot. Add lamb, onions, and garlic. Cook, stirring frequently, until well browned, about 6–8 minutes. Add remaining cider, lemon juice, 1 cup broth, salt, pepper, cinnamon, potatoes, and carrots. Bring to a boil, reduce heat to low, cover and simmer 40–45 minutes, or until lamb and vegetables are tender. Meanwhile, whisk together 2 tablespoons cornstarch with 3 tablespoons vegetable broth until smooth. Stir into stew until well incorporated and simmer an additional 2 minutes, or until thickened. Serve hot.

MAKES 4 (1¼ CUP) SERVINGS

Apple Cider vs. Juice
The difference between apple cider and juice? The filtering process. I adore apple cider not only because it retains more of the bulk (ending in a much healthier intake of fiber) but because of the flavor is associated with less filtering. Apple juice lasts much longer because it isn't as fresh. *It's Just That Simple!*

Super Spuds

Some researchers believe a diet of potatoes, oatmeal, and milk can sustain a human indefinitely. I will add that potatoes have:

• twice as much potassium as bananas;
• more than twice as much Vitamin C as an orange; and
• 75% more fiber when baked than an apple.

Remember too that about 20% of the potato's nutrition is in the skin.

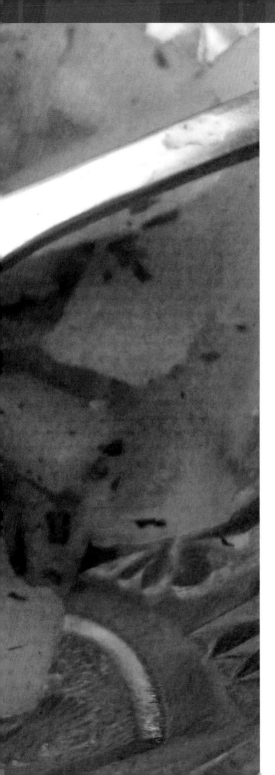

Watermelon Rind "Pickles"

By doing your own pickling, you are able to adjust the spices to suit your taste. This side dish is naturally fat free, great tasting, and a surprise topping for everything from burgers to fish to your favorite grilled protein during the summer months.

4 cups small diced watermelon
    rind, green skin removed
½ cup powdered sugar
½ cup apple cider vinegar
3 tablespoons chopped,
    fresh cilantro (or 1
    tablespoon dried)
1 tablespoon dry mustard
1 teaspoon turmeric, optional
½ teaspoon dried,
    ground cloves
½ teaspoon celery salt

Add all ingredients to a large saucepan. Add enough water to cover rind by 2 inches. Bring to a boil over medium-high heat. Once boiling, reduce heat to low and simmer until most of the liquid has been absorbed and the rind is fork tender, but not mushy. Transfer entire contents to a bowl; cover and refrigerate until cold before serving.

MAKES ABOUT 2½ CUPS

Spicy-Tart Cranberry Chutney

I think you will find this chutney to be a better side than ordinary cranberry sauce. If you don't want to bother with crystallized ginger, simply add 1 tablespoon dried (but, please, just once a year, try the candied ginger!).

¼ cup dried apricots,
   finely chopped
½ cup brown sugar
½ cup raisins
1 cup pomegranate juice
3 cups fresh cranberries
1 Granny Smith apple, peeled,
   cored, and chopped
1 teaspoon grated lemon zest
¼ cup lemon juice
¼ cup crystallized
   ginger, chopped
½ teaspoon red pepper flakes

In a saucepan, combine apricots, brown sugar, raisins, and pomegranate juice; bring to a boil. Reduce heat to simmer and stir, while simmering, for 5 minutes. Stir in cranberries, apple, and lemon zest; simmer for 10 minutes more. The cranberries will start popping, warning you that they are done. Simply place a lid askew over the top to prevent splattering, or if you have a screen, that would work great.

Remove from heat and stir in lemon juice, ginger, and pepper flakes. Mash slightly, cover, and refrigerate at least 3 hours.

Tart to Sweet Apple Relish

Many people associate relish with burgers and dogs. This condiment also has chopped fruits and vegetables with a little sauce thrown in. What usually sets relish apart from other, similar condiments is that the ingredients are pickled and a pickling spice or liquid binds everything together. Many people will argue that chutney and relish are different because one has fruit while the other has vegetables. While this is basically correct, in a very broad sense, nowadays, everyone is putting everything into each, so this difference is now almost extinct.

1 Granny Smith apple, cored, peeled, and diced
1 Asian pear, cored, peeled, and diced
1 Fuji apple, cored, peeled, and diced
½ cup dried raisins
½ cup dried blueberries
1-inch slice of fresh ginger, grated*
½ cup apple cider vinegar
½ cup sugar
1 tablespoon lime juice
1 teaspoon cayenne pepper
½ teaspoon minced garlic in oil
½ teaspoon salt
Fresh dill, for garnish

MAKES ABOUT 3 CUPS

Combine all the ingredients, except dill, in a large pot and bring to a boil over high heat. Reduce heat to low and simmer 20–22 minutes, or until the mixture reaches the consistency of jelly or preserves. Make sure you stir quite often to prevent scorching on bottom.

Remove from heat to cool to room temperature before transferring to a bowl. Cover and refrigerate until needed. It will thicken upon standing.

*The best way to do this is to peel down one inch of a fresh ginger-root and grate on the largest holes of a grater.

Asian-Style Hot Mustard

For a no-frills Chinese hot mustard, simply mix ¼ cup hot water with ¼ cup dry mustard and whisk well. Add a pinch of salt and let sit, covered, in your refrigerator for at least an hour. You can also purchase mustard seed and grind it yourself for a much more, shall I say, robust flavor. The recipe here is great on grilled sausages, burgers, and hot dogs, and especially brushed on salmon to be cooked. Where does the "hot" come in? The chemical reaction between the liquid and the powdered mustard will give you the heat you desire—trust me! To make a thinner mustard, add more apple juice; for thicker, less juice.

¼ cup dry mustard
3 tablespoons apple juice
    or water
2 tablespoons apple
    cider vinegar
½ teaspoon salt
½ teaspoon brown sugar
Pinch each of allspice, onion
    powder, and garlic powder

Whisk all ingredients together well, cover, and refrigerate at least one hour before using.

MAKES ABOUT ½ CUP

Originally, Chinese mustard was served with just brown mustard seeds that were hand-ground and mixed with water directly before serving. You can still do this at home but just remember that this liquid/powder reaction makes for a very hot mustard, so taste it first before serving. After a day, the heat will begin to subside.

Yanked Hoisin Sauce

This recipe for a thin version of hoisin sauce is great for basting steaks, burgers, or chicken while cooking on your grill (directions for a thicker version are also given). This is also a great glaze for grilled chicken and apples; use it as a dip for egg rolls or add some to your stir-fry or noodle dishes. Although this is as close to authentic hoisin sauce as you can get, many chefs use peanut butter instead of black beans. Either way is perfectly acceptable, although beans are much lower in fat. By adding molasses *and* maple syrup, this is truly a great *Yanked* recipe.

1 cup cooked black
   beans, drained
2 teaspoons garlic powder
¼ cup soy sauce
3 tablespoons hot
   sauce, optional
2 tablespoons maple syrup
2 tablespoons molasses
1 teaspoon Chinese
   5-spice powder

Add all ingredients to the bowl of a food processor or blender and puree until as smooth as possible, about 15 seconds on high. Remove and pour through a wire sieve, pressing the bean "bulk" against the sieve; discard pulp.

To make a thicker sauce, add 1 tablespoon cornstarch before pulsing in blender and transfer to a small saucepan. Bring to a slight boil over medium heat for 1 minute, or until thickened. Remove from stove and cool.

MAKES ABOUT 1¼ CUPS

The Magic of Beans

For concentrated levels of complete protein, seek out beans! Beans are a favorite because they lack the fat, calories, and cholesterol found in the other sources of proteins such as eggs, yogurt, cheese, and meats. Plus, beans will nourish your body with other vitamins and minerals.

Creamy Blueberry Curd

When you look into the health benefits of blueberries (among them: they're filled with antioxidants and support heart health), you will find yourself not only making this blueberry curd recipe often but coming up with recipe ideas of your own.

Enjoy this "spread" simply on your favorite cracker (don't forget some sliced cheddar cheese as well), as a dip for fruit, heated and poured over fresh biscuits, or with pancakes, waffles, english muffins, or toast.

1 cup fresh blueberries
2 tablespoons lime juice
½ cup (1 stick) butter
    or margarine
3 tablespoons maple syrup
    or honey
2 eggs, lightly beaten
3 egg whites, lightly beaten

In a food processor or blender, puree blueberries and lime juice for 15 seconds or until pureed well. Pour into a fine wire strainer over a bowl, pressing on the sides of strainer with a spoon to get every bit of liquid out. Discard the pulp. (Note: If you like your curd with lumps, skip this step with the strainer.)

Combine all ingredients in a medium saucepan, and place over medium heat until boiling. Reduce heat to low and continue simmering 8–10 minutes, or until thickened and smooth. Remove from heat, cover, and refrigerate until cooled and thickened completely, about an hour.

MAKES ABOUT 1½ CUPS

Maple Syrup's Secrets

I truly believe that cures for many of today's diseases will be found in our flora or fauna. Navindra Seeram, PhD, a researcher for the University of Rhode Island, seems to agree. He has extensively experimented with and written about the health benefits of maple syrup. In a 2013 article in the *Journal of Functional Foods*, he wrote, "I continue to say that nature is the best chemist, and that maple syrup is becoming a champion food when it comes to the number and variety of beneficial compounds found in it. It's important to note that in our laboratory research we found that several of these compounds possess anti-oxidant and anti-inflammatory properties, which have been shown to fight cancer, diabetes, and bacterial illnesses."

Banana Monkey Jam

This "jam" is the end-all, beat-all of fruit spreads. While the banana will not brown as you keep this in the refrigerator, if desired, add a couple drops of yellow food coloring for an even more vibrant yellow tone.

1 cup granulated sugar
½ cup brown sugar
2 pounds (1 bunch) ripe
    bananas, sliced thin
1 cup apple juice
2 tablespoons butter
    or margarine

MAKES ABOUT 4–5 CUPS

Add all ingredients together in a large saucepan. Over high heat, bring to a boil. Reduce heat to low and continue cooking until banana jam is thickened and much of the moisture has dissipated, stirring often to prevent burning, about 12–15 minutes. Mash bananas periodically with a potato masher. When moisture has evaporated, remove from heat and transfer to a bowl. Cover and cool completely before serving.

Cheesy Succotash Grill

Want a great and filling grilled cheese sandwich that is truly satisfying? Using succotash ingredients gives you the satisfaction of protein without the fat. As you know, succotash has been around for centuries in New England and for many moons before Europeans came ashore here.

2 rounds of pita bread
Nonstick cooking spray
1 cup pepper jack
    cheese, shredded
1 cup whole kernel corn
½ small tomato, diced
¼ cup onion, diced
½ cup great northern beans,
    cooked (or other cooked
    and drained beans or
    cooked grain)*
½ cup cooked chicken, diced

For the Pumpkin Mayonnaise:
¼ cup Greek yogurt
2 tablespoons pumpkin
½ teaspoon chili powder
¼ teaspoon cumin
¼ teaspoon both salt and
    black pepper

Make Pumpkin Mayonaise by combing all ingredients in a small bowl and mixing well. Set aside.

Use a sharp knife to separate each pita bread into two thin halves. Spray the outer halves of the pitas with cooking spray and heat them in a large skillet over medium-low heat.

Spread Pumpkin Mayonnaise over warm pita slices and top with equal amounts of half the cheese, corn, tomato, onion, beans, and chicken. Top the filling with remainder of the cheese and then top the sandwich with another pita slice with additional Pumpkin Mayonnaise.

Cook in skillet over medium-low heat, flattening down with a spatula, until sandwich starts to crisp. Carefully flip over to finish crisping on the other side. Remove and enjoy.

Cool Beans

Beans are a superb source of B vitamins, a folic acid (a.k.a. folate or folacin). Folic acid has many health benefits: it helps create healthy fetuses and reduces osteoporosis, and some studies have shown a positive effect on cervical cancer. It has also been found to help in the prevention of heart disease.

Light and Airy Garden Apps

"Oh, man!!!" That's what my eldest son said when he dove into these eggy, veggie laden, and gooey appetizers. He enjoyed them *while* he was downloading another kind of app he is more familiar with—honest to goodness.

Nonstick cooking spray
1 cup egg substitute
2 egg whites
½ cup grated zucchini,
    skin and all
½ cup grated summer squash,
    skin intact
1 (8-ounce) jar sun-dried
    tomatoes, chopped
¼ cup fat-free sour cream
¾ cup reduced fat Colby
    cheese, shredded
½ teaspoon salt
¼ teaspoon black pepper

MAKES 12 MINI MUFFINS

Preheat oven to 350° F. Spray a 12-cup mini muffin tin with nonstick cooking spray.

In a large bowl, beat egg substitute and egg whites until well combined, and add the remainder of ingredients, mixing well. Evenly divide among the muffin cups and bake 12–14 minutes, or until set in the middle. The sides of the apps will become dark and caramel in color, lending a great crunch.

Remove from oven and let cool 5 minutes. Run a dull butter knife around the edges to remove apps from the pan, and serve while warm.

Super Crispy Acorn Bites

MAKES 12 SERVINGS

These bites are the perfect appetizer for any gathering. Perfectly spiced and simple in flavors, this recipe can only be enhanced by your imagination. Substitute a wide variety of breads, trying even rye or pumpernickel. For your maple syrup, try Grade A Light Amber right on up to Grade A Dark Amber.

½ of a 1 pound acorn squash,
   peeled and seeded
1 cup low-fat cheddar
   cheese, shredded
½ cup brown sugar
1 teaspoon garlic powder
1 teaspoon chili powder or
   cayenne pepper
Salt and black pepper to taste
Nonstick cooking spray
12 slices your favorite bread
1 cup maple syrup

Cut squash into ½-inch-thick wedges and then cut into very thin pieces. The pieces should be no larger in circumference than a dime. Place in a bowl and toss with cheese, brown sugar, garlic and chili powders, salt, and black pepper to taste; set aside.

Spray a 12-cup mini muffin tin with nonstick cooking spray. Using a glass with a lip that has the same diameter as the top of the muffin tin cups, cut out circles of bread. Lay each into the muffin tin firmly, pressing on the bottom and sides.

Take remainder of each slice of bread used and cut into very small cubes. Toss with maple syrup in a bowl; set aside.

Evenly divide the seasoned squash pieces into each bread bowl and top with maple bread cubes. Bake at 350° F 16–18 minutes, or until a toothpick inserted in the middle goes in easily, showing that the squash is cooked. The tops should be browned nicely. Remove, and let rest for a minute before lifting each out to serve while hot.

Spiced Cranberry Ketchup

MAKES ABOUT 2 CUPS

Whether you use this sweet and spicy ketchup on your hamburgers or as a dip for french fries or onion rings, it is such a refreshing change of pace from tomato-based condiments. This Yankee-style ketchup is great to dip chicken nuggets into as well, or maybe follow President Nixon's approach to ketchup and dollop some on top of your cottage cheese . . . on the other hand, maybe not.

2 cups fresh or frozen
    cranberries
½ cup apple juice
¼ cup onions, minced
¾ cup sugar
¼ cup apple cider vinegar
¼ cup balsamic vinegar
¼ cup tomato paste
2 teaspoons Dijon-style mustard
½ teaspoon cinnamon
¼ teaspoon both salt and
    black pepper
Pinch of ground cumin

In a small saucepan, combine cranberries with the apple juice and onions. Cover and cook over medium heat until you hear the cranberries start popping, about 10 minutes. remove from heat and let sit until cool to the touch. Then pour the cranberry mixture through a fine mesh sieve, pressing against the sides. Discard the cranberry bulk and return to the saucepan.

Add the remainder of the ingredients and bring to a boil over medium heat. Once boiling, reduce heat to low and simmer 10–12 minutes, uncovered, or until thickened. Remove from heat, transfer to a bowl, and cover. Refrigerate at least 3 hours or until completely cooled.

Sweet Potato Brulee

Broiled brown sugar glaze sitting atop fragrant sweet potatoes. Need I say more?

6 cups hot mashed sweet
    potatoes (about 4 pounds)
¾ cup plain yogurt
3 tablespoons butter or
    margarine, softened
2 tablespoons dried chives
½ teaspoon salt
½ teaspoon saffron threads (or
    substitute turmeric)
¼ teaspoon cinnamon
Pinch of dried nutmeg
Nonstick cooking spray
½ cup brown sugar
3 tablespoons crushed nuts of
    your choice (optional)

MAKES ABOUT 7 CUPS

Preheat broiler.

Combine first 8 ingredients in a bowl. Spoon potato mixture into an 11 × 7–inch baking pan coated with nonstick cooking spray. Mix the brown sugar with nuts and sprinkle over the top of sweet potato mixture. Broil 2 minutes or until sugar melts. Let stand until melted sugar hardens, about 3 minutes.

Oh-So-Sweet Sweet Potatoes

Sweet potatoes are known for their high carotenoid and phenolic content. Beta-carotene, lycopene, and lutein—different varieties of carotenoids—act as antioxidants and have strong cancer-fighting properties. According to *Current Pharmaceutical Biotechnology*, phenolic compounds also fight certain cancers. Other good sources of cancer-fighting carotenoids are squash, kale, broccoli, cabbage, and cauliflower.

"Old-Fashioned" Homemade Cran-Apple Sauce

This has got to be one of the easiest and uniquely delicious apple sauce recipes out there. Although the soda has sugar, there is no other added sugar—just nature's sweetener. My son sat down to this for dessert and ate the whole bowl. Don't worry if any of the apple tidbits are slightly firm, by the way; that adds character, bite, and its own uniqueness. The taste of golden ginger ale is the perfect complement to apple sauce, but experiment with other flavors such as cherry, root beer, orange, or lemon lime.

6 large sweet apples, peeled, cored, and diced fine
3 tablespoons maple syrup
3 tablespoons whole berry cranberry sauce
1 teaspoon cinnamon
1 (12-ounce) can golden ginger ale*

Add everything to a large saucepan with a lid. Over medium heat, bring to a boil, lay the lid on askew, and continue cooking and intermittently stirring for about 20 minutes, or until apples have dissolved into even smaller pieces. You can mash the apples at any point once softened to help the cooking along. Once soft, you will notice the liquid has evaporated and the apple sauce has thickened substantially. If need be, add more soda, but a very little at a time.

MAKES ABOUT 2 ½ CUPS.

Want to make your own ginger ale or other flavored sodas? By using something called "ginger bug," you can take advantage of beneficial bacteria and yeast to flavor drinks and make them bubbly. Here's how: Cut a 2-inch piece of peeled ginger and grate it, making about 3 tablespoons. Place this in a mason jar and add 3 tablespoons granulated sugar and 1 teaspoon molasses. Stir in 2 cups filtered water, stir with a wooden or plastic spoon, and lightly cover with a coffee filter held on by an elastic. Let sit for 5 days, shaking it once a day and adding a teaspoon more of both grated ginger and sugar. At the end of 5 days, simply strain off a ¼ cup and mix it with up to 32 ounces of water. (Or try it with iced tea or fruit juice.) Pour this mixture into an airtight container for 3 days and that's it. Open it up, and enjoy your carbonated, delicious beverage.

When done, remove from heat and transfer to a bowl. (Before you cover the bowl with film wrap, have a taste!) Refrigerate overnight.

In the morning you will notice the applesauce has thickened even more. (Taste it again—quite a difference from yesterday, huh?)

*Or use ginger beer, but either way, you want the spiciest true "heated" flavor of ginger ale without being overly sweet. I find that Polar brand is one of the best and lets the flavor of ginger come to the tongue. Bear in mind that ginger beer will contain up to about 10% alcohol.

Raisin "Figgy" Pudding Preserves

For a great, warm, and homey taste during the holidays, spread some of this comfort preserve on absolutely anything you desire.*

2 cups apple juice
1½ cups raisins
2 ounces candied (or crystallized) ginger
½ teaspoon cinnamon
½ teaspoon nutmeg
2 (3-ounce) pouches liquid pectin

In a food processor or blender, pulse first 5 ingredients until ginger and raisins are pulp-like in size (about 1 minute). Remove to a large saucepan and bring to a boil over high heat. Stir in the pectin and cook for 1 minute longer, stirring constantly. Remove from heat and carefully ladle the jelly into four half-pint jars, leaving a half-inch space on top. Seal with lid and refrigerate until set, about 6 hours or longer.

Once this is set, take a fork and mix it up a little; the raisins that may have settled on the bottom while hot.

MAKES ABOUT 2 CUPS

*Although this recipe contains no figs, many recipes call for this substitution in figgy pudding. If you want to stay true to the classic, use ½ pound fresh figs, trimming off both ends first before adding to food processor. Add, also, 1 tablespoon lemon juice. If using dried figs, boil 6 ounces of them in apple juice for 10 minutes, over medium heat, until they start to soften and plump. Remove from heat and let sit in hot juice for 1 hour. Add this to the food processor with candied ginger, cinnamon, and nutmeg, and then continue with the recipe.

Homemade GMO-Free Pectin

Many people are increasingly concerned about Genetically Modified Organisms (GMOs) and avoid any processed foods that may contain them. Dextrose is one of these foodstuffs that often contain GMOs and is a commonly found ingredient in commercial pectin. To avoid GMOs, make your own pectin at home for jams and jellies. Simply quarter 8 large, tart apples into a large saucepan with a quart of water and a couple tablespoons of lemon juice. Boil for 30 minutes, strain, and boil for 30 more minutes, or until reduced by half. Pour into sterilized jars. That's it.

When ready to use for jelly, for every cup of fruit juice, add a ¼ cup homemade pectin and the same amount of sugar; proceed as directed in your recipe. For preserves or jams, add a ¼ cup homemade pectin per cup of mashed fruit or berries with no added sugar.

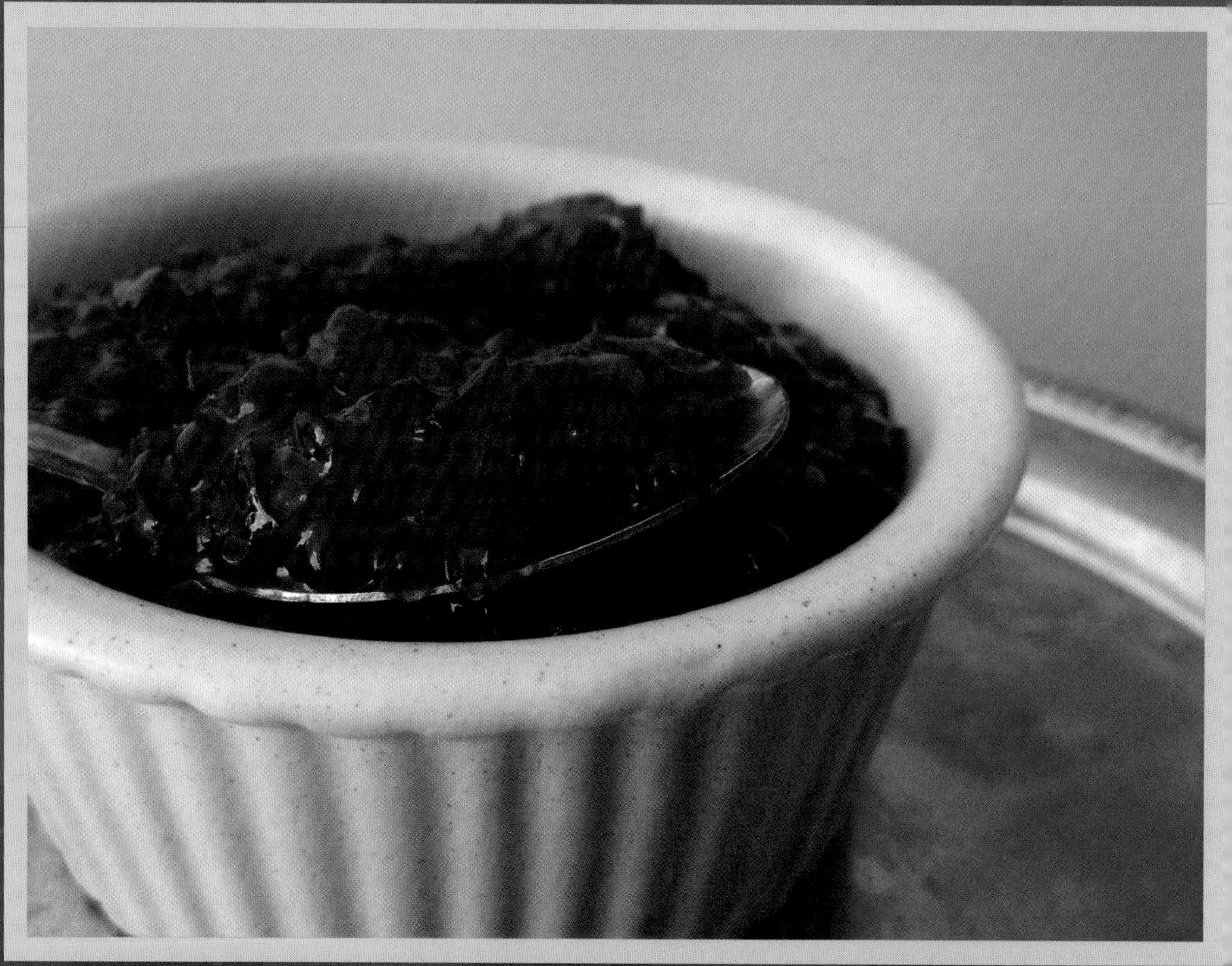

Sugar Plum Jelly

I do so wish that sugar plums were real plums but I am out of luck. Sugar plums were originally sugar-covered nuts (to explain loosely) and now they are the exact opposite, nut- and seed-covered sugar confections. So why the word plum in the title? Because a few centuries ago, the word plum meant something that was great, desirable, or very tasty. This is fantastic on any fruited quick bread or coffee cake, toast, English muffins, or just plain ol' crackers.

2 cups plum juice (Sunsweet
    brand makes a great one)
¾ cup sugar
Juice of one large
    orange, strained
1 teaspoon grated orange zest
2 (3-ounce) pouches
    liquid pectin*

In a large saucepan, bring plum juice, sugar, orange juice, and grated orange zest to a boil over high heat, stirring almost constantly. Stir in the pectin and boil for 1 minute, stirring constantly. Remove from the heat and pour into 3 half-pint jars. Seal with lids and refrigerate 6 hours, or longer, until set. I always mix it up before using.

MAKES ABOUT 2 CUPS

*Yes, you can substitute powdered pectin for liquid pectin. Liquid pectin is used in jelly recipes that require cooking first, while powdered pectin can be used in the same recipes, even if you aren't cooking them. One tablespoon liquid equals 2 teaspoons powdered. In the recipe for Sugar Plum Jelly, each pouch is 3-ounces (6 tablespoons total), equivalent to ¼ cup powdered pectin. While Certo brand liquid pectin comes in 6-ounce pouches, Sure Jell also comes in 3-ounce pouches. I also use the pink box at times, which is called Sure Jell Liquid Pectin for Less. This means that the pectin will set up with less sugar.

Sun-Dried Tomato Tapenade

Did you know that olives contain monosaturated fats? And concentrated amounts of it to boot? This particular fat significantly helps to lower cholesterol *and* is tough as nails. Unlike polysaturated fats, monosaturated fats help cells fight off free radicals, the cancer-causing agents that literally destroy cells and damage tissue. So now have a big ol' bite of this deliciously unique tapenade. *It's Just That Simple!*

1 cup sun-dried tomatoes
   in olive oil
1 (15-ounce) can pitted black
   olives, or olives of your
   choice, drained
2 tablespoons minced onion
2 garlic cloves, peeled and
   roughly chopped
1 tablespoon fresh basil
   leaves or 1 teaspoon
   dried, chopped
¾ cup pure olive oil
½ cup balsamic vinegar
½ teaspoon cracked
   black pepper
3 pita rounds, quartered
Nonstick butter-flavored
   cooking spray

MAKES ABOUT 2½ CUPS

You can go ahead and buy sun-dried tomatoes at the store and spend over $5, or make your own for less than $2. Simply get a 10-ounce container of cherry tomatoes and slice them in half. Place parchment paper on a baking sheet and spray with nonstick cooking spray. Put the tomatoes, cut-side up, onto the paper and sprinkle with whatever spices you want. I use a pinch of sugar, black pepper, oregano, basil, and garlic powder. Then I plop those bad boys in a 225-degree oven for about 3 hours, or until they look all dried up and shriveled. Remove to a bowl after they have cooled and drizzle with extra-virgin olive oil to evenly coat. Transfer them to an air-tight container and you have some great additions to salads, burgers, entrees, or whatever you can think of.

Add all ingredients, except pita and cooking spray, to the bowl of a food processor of blender and pulse on medium until chopped, but not mushy. Remove, transfer to a bowl, cover and refrigerate at least 2 hours for the flavors to meld.

When ready to serve, preheat oven to 400° F. Spray both sides of cut pita and place on a baking pan, Bake 5–7 minutes, or until very crispy. Serve pita chips on the side.

New England Shore Corn Pudding

The combination of lobster and corn pairs two naturally sweet items so well together, I think you will find yourself making this on Thanksgiving. Just remember, serve this as a side along with either soup, bread, or the main course. You can even heighten the flavor by roasting cleaned ears of corn in the oven first for 20 minutes at 400° F. Remove, let cool enough to handle, and then remove the corn kernels.

Nonstick cooking spray
4 cups cooked lobster
    meat, chopped
4 ears of corn, silk and
    husk removed*
2 cups buttermilk
4 strips turkey bacon, chopped
½ red bell pepper, minced
4 scallions or green onions,
    sliced thinly
3 eggs
5 egg whites
¼ cup flour
1 teaspoon salt
1 teaspoon sugar
1 cup shredded Monterey
    Jack cheese

SERVES 8

Preheat oven to 350° F. Coat eight 8-ounce ramekins or one shallow 2-quart casserole dish with nonstick cooking spray. Remove corn kernels from each ear using a sharp knife.

Holding ear of corn with the stem up (it is easier if you cut off the tip of the ear so that it stands up more securely), run the knife from top to bottom over a plate.

In the bowl of a food processor or blender, puree half the corn with ½ cup buttermilk.

In a large skillet, cook bacon over medium-high heat until almost crisp: drain fat. Add remaining corn kernels, pepper, and scallion; saute for 5 minutes.

In a bowl, whisk remaining buttermilk, eggs, egg whites, flour, salt, and sugar. Stir in lobster, pureed corn, sauteed vegetables, and cheese.

Divide among ramekins or pour into a large casserole. Set individual casseroles or large casserole in a baking pan that has at least two inch-high sides. Place in oven; pour hot water into baking pan to 1 inch. Bake for 35–40 minutes, or 5–10 minutes longer for large casserole dish, or until knife inserted in center comes out clean. Let stand for 15 minutes before serving.

*Take the easy route if you wish. Use one (15-ounce) can of whole kernel corn, drained, or the equivalent in frozen corn. Just look for labels that show the corn is non-GMO.

CHAPTER 3 Salads and Vegetables

I believe there will be a day when scientists, researchers and natural food advocates will come together at a table and all agree on one point: that fruit and vegetable consumption will ward off breast cancer, if not combat and kill it. I truly believe that the cure for breast cancer lies somewhere in nature, and I believe specifically in the plant kingdom.

In all major studies to date, there is no direct link between an abundance of fruits and vegetables and their effects on breast cancer, but it is known that they play an integral part indirectly. The consumption of vegetables has been determined to be associated with a lower risk of ER-negative breast cancer, according to a study published January 24, 2013, in the *Journal of the National Cancer Institute.*

It would be nice to stick with one guideline when it comes to what should be consumed on a daily basis for fruits and vegetables, but the USDA continually changes its RDAs and Harvard's Healthy Eating Plate program "one-upped" them with its own rendition. So let's do this logically: If you can involve fruits and vegetables in at least every other meal, and snack at least once a day on a fruit and once a day on a vegetable, I strongly urge you to do so. Even a 100% fruit or vegetable juice drink counts as a serving. One thing to keep in mind, when you involve raw leafy greens: It takes 2 cups to equal 1 cup from the vegetable group. Include 2–2½ cups veggies on a 2,000 calorie a day diet.

Think about this. When the health craze was all about Vitamin C, greens were on the list. When the Vitamin A fad was in full swing, greens were part of that. When many people were fanatically watching their calcium, again, greens were part of that diet. And when iron entered the ring for a round or two, greens stepped up and took the challenge. From the roots to the greens themselves, these mineral and vitamin-rich natural foods always come out on top.

And don't just picture yourself having to eat a head of broccoli: The recipes in this book show great, creative ways of introducing fruits and vegetables in your diet that will be enticing and have you looking forward to dining and snacking in a healthful way.

Primavera Vegetable Salad

You simply cannot get more colorful than this dish. And when you combine the flavors and textures with eye-appeal, you have the perfect dish. This "laundry list" of ingredients may look intimidating, but this dish is easy to put together and inexpensive as well. *It's Just That Simple!*

2 tablespoons pure olive oil
1 yellow bell pepper, seeded
    and diced
½ onion, minced
2 cups frozen, fresh, or canned
    (drained) non-GMO corn
2 tomatoes, seeded (if desired)
    and diced
1 cup frozen peas
1 cup tomato juice
1 (15½-ounce) can kidney
    beans, rinsed and drained
1 tablespoon chopped,
    fresh cilantro
1 lime, juiced and zest grated
1 tablespoon chili sauce
1 tablespoon apple
    cider vinegar
1 teaspoon ground cumin
2 teaspoons chili powder
Pinch of red pepper flakes
Salt and pepper to taste

In a medium saucepan, heat olive oil over medium-high until shimmering. When oil is hot, add pepper and onion. Cook until onions are soft, about 7–9 minutes, stirring frequently. Add the corn, tomatoes, and peas, continuing to cook until the tomatoes have softened just a little, about 3–4 minutes. Add remainder of ingredients, stir to combine, and continue cooking an additional 3 minutes. Remove from heat, transfer to a large bowl and cover.

Refrigerate at least 3 hours, if not overnight, and serve cold.

Bell peppers, tomatoes, artichokes, spinach, red wine, and celery have very high amounts of apigenin, a flavonoid. Strong antioxidant and anti-inflammatory properties are known benefits of apigenin, thus preventing free radical damage.

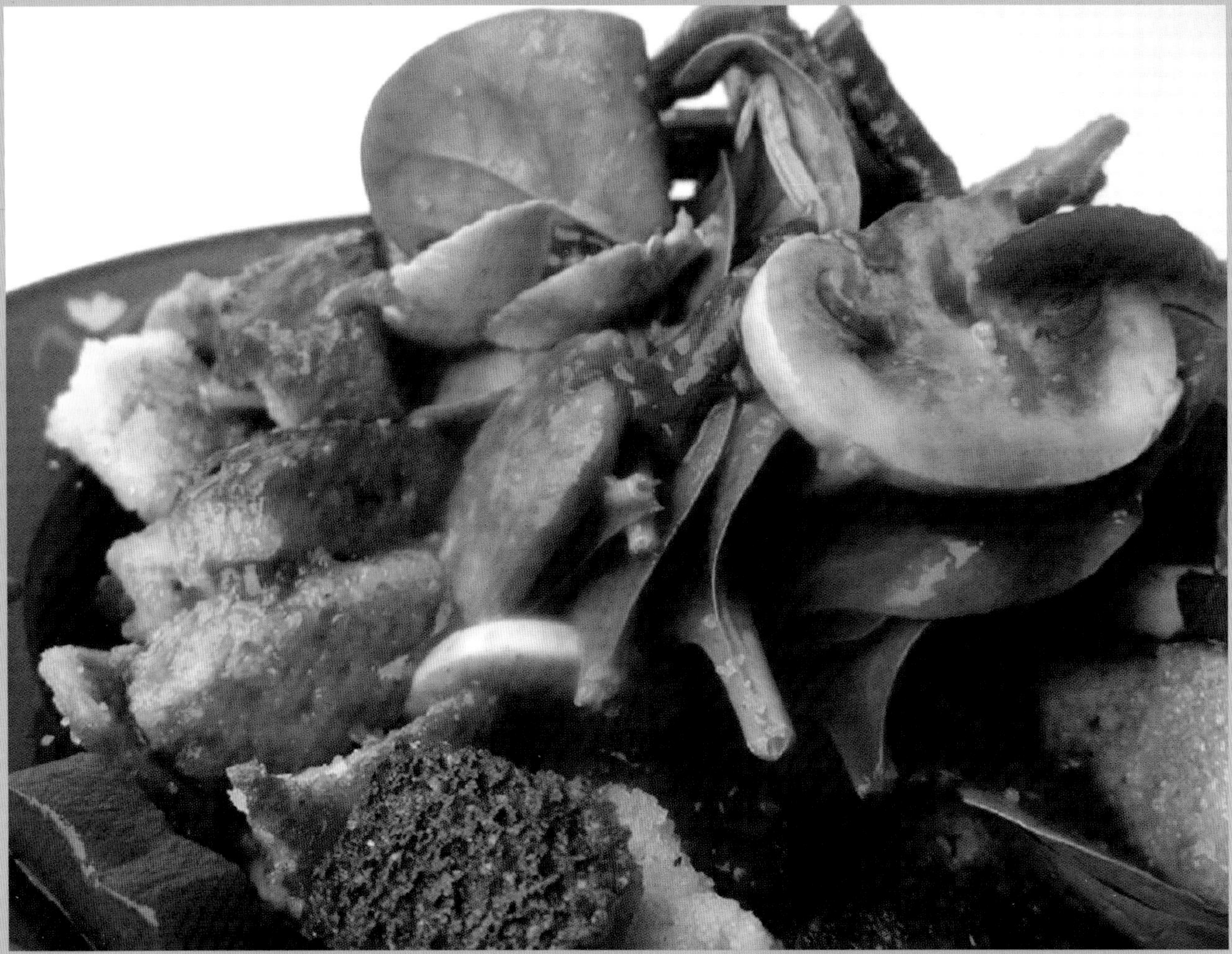

New England Johnnybread Salad

Want an easy and flavorful salad this grilling season or any time of year? This Yankee-inspired salad is a great entrée as well, but especially suited to prevent you from returning over and over again to the "grill-master" for another burger.

Nonstick cooking spray
1 box (8.5 ounce) corn muffin
   or corn bread mix
1 egg
½ cup skim milk
2 tablespoons butter
   or margarine
1 green onion, sliced thinly
1 green, red, or yellow
   bell pepper, seeded
   and chopped
2 plum tomatoes, seeded
   and julienned*
4 ounces fresh baby spinach
3 ounces mushrooms, sliced

For Tangy Sausage Dressing:

½ pound low-fat chicken
   sausage links, sliced
   ¼-inch pieces
¼ cup apple cider vinegar
¼ cup Worcestershire sauce or
   soy sauce
¼ cup ketchup
3 tablespoons sugar
1 tablespoon brown sugar

Preheat oven to 400° F. Spray an 8-inch square baking pan with nonstick cooking spray.

Stir muffin mix, egg, and milk until combined. Pour into prepared pan and bake 18–20 minutes or until lightly browned on top and it springs back in the center when touched. Remove from oven to cool completely. Cut cooled cornbread into cubes; set aside.

In a large skillet, melt 2 tablespoons butter or margarine over medium-high heat. Add green onion, green pepper, and julienned tomatoes. Grill, stirring frequently, until softened, about 2–3 minutes. Add the cornbread cubes and continue cooking until cornbread is starting to crisp, another 3–4 minutes. Remove from heat and set aside.

Make Tangy Sausage Dressing: Cook sausage slices in a large skillet, over medium heat, until no longer pink in the middle, about 2–3 minutes, turning each slice over. With a slotted spoon, remove cooked sausage to a dish; set aside. Discard fat and wipe skillet clean. Return skillet to heat and add vinegar, Worcestershire, ketchup, sugar, and brown sugar. Bring to a boil, stirring to lift up sausage browned bits from the bottom of the pan, and let reduce slightly, about 4–5 minutes. Add the sausages back into the skillet, and mix well.

Toss spinach, mushrooms, and cornbread mixture in a large salad bowl. Pour Tangy Sausage Dressing into bowl of greens and toss. Evenly divide among bowls and serve immediately.

SERVES 4–6

*You can also simply add chopped, fresh tomatoes on top of salad when serving.

Want to make your own inexpensive, tasty, crispy, and healthy croutons? Slice whole grain bread of your choice into 1-inch thick slices. In a bowl, whisk together olive oil with garlic powder, onion powder, dried basil, dried oregano, and black pepper. There is no need for salt here. Lightly brush this flavored oil over both sides of bread slices and lay out on a sheet pan for a couple of hours (or overnight, if desired). When ready to bake, cut each slice into squares of desired size and place back onto sheet pan, in a single layer. Bake at 250° F for at least 30 minutes, turning over a couple times, or until crispy and well dried out.

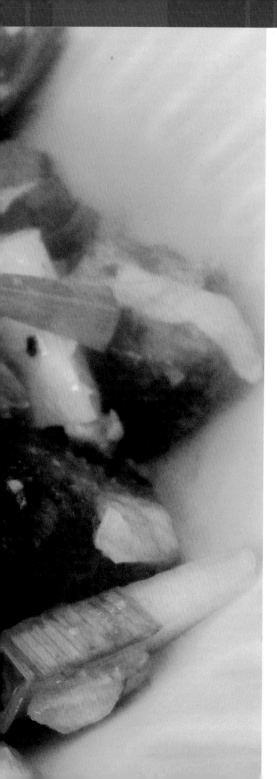

Yanked Fattoosh

Ordinarily prepared with stale flat bread that has been crisped, I opted for croutons because it gives a better crunch and texture to this Middle Eastern bread salad. And don't be fooled by the moniker "bread salad." With the addition of lamb and chilies in adobo sauce, this is one fare that you can proudly serve at any function.

1 (6-ounce) boneless lamb
    chop, trimmed and diced
    into bit-sized pieces
2 tablespoons pure olive oil
1 cup croutons
Grated rind from 1 lemon
Juice from 2 lemons
3 cups salad greens of
    your choice
3 cups fresh spinach leaves
2 tablespoons fresh cilantro,
    chopped
¼ cup fresh mint, chopped
½ cup onion, minced
½ can chilies in adobo sauce,
    drained and chopped
1 small cucumber, peeled
    and chopped

In a large skillet, heat olive oil over medium heat. When hot, add lamb and cook until desired doneness. Remove and set aside.

In a large bowl, combine remaining ingredients and toss well. Add cooked lamb and toss to combine.

SERVES 3–4

Yanked Carrot Slaw

I do love this side dish but I always thought of it as too much on the sweet side. Many people add pineapple tidbits and use either mayonnaise or salad dressing. It's time to **Yank** this recipe for a bolder, up-to-date style. The result is a carrot "slaw" that embodies a little more saltiness without adding salt and some spice without being too overpowering.

6 ounces extra-sharp,
   low-fat cheddar cheese,
   cubed small
½ pound shredded carrots *
½ cup raisins
2 cups plain yogurt
1 apple or pear, peeled, cored
   and chopped
½ cup spiced peanuts,
   optional
½ teaspoon Chinese
   5-spice powder

Put everything in a large bowl, and combine well. Cover and refrigerate for at least 30 minutes before serving.

SERVES 4

*You can either buy carrots already shredded or simply buy 2 or 3 large carrots, peel, and shred using the large holes on a box grater.

Carrots Are Tops

Bone growth and vision are given a huge boost when it comes to Vitamin A, or retinol, a remarkable, fat-soluble vitamin. Carrots are a tremendous source, with 1 cup of carrots offering over 500% of your daily needs. One cup of cooked carrots contains over 26,000 international units of Vitamin A. To put this into perspective, the average adult woman only needs about 2,300 units a day while men should have 3,000 per day. 'Nuff said!

Summer Seashore Salad

This is one of my absolute favorites when it comes to a salad preparation using either octopus or squid. The taste of octopus is so mild that, at times, the flavor is lost with more assertive co-ingredients. Not the case here, folks! If I were to choose a dish to try my first taste of octopus, this would be it. As for the cost of fresh octopus or squid? I called a supermarket in the middle of June and the price was $7/pound. That, my friends, is cheaper than that steak you're probably ready to throw on the grill.

2 tablespoons pure olive oil
2 garlic cloves, peeled
    and crushed
½ pound fresh octopus or squid
    meat, sliced
½ red bell pepper, julienned
1 Asian pear, peeled, cored
    and chopped
1 cup frozen peas
1 cup frozen cauliflower florets
½ teaspoon cayenne pepper
1¼ cups apple juice
Salt and black pepper to taste

In a large skillet, heat oil over medium-high heat. When oil is hot, add garlic and continue to cook and constantly stir for 1 minute. Add the octopus, bell pepper, and Asian pear. Cook, stirring frequently, for 6–7 minutes, or until octopus is cooked through. (If using frozen, precooked octopus, cook the same way but the time may be reduced, as you will only be cooking until heated through.)

Add peas, cauliflower, cayenne pepper, and apple juice. Stir to combine and cook an additional 4–6 minutes, or until apple juice has reduced and everything is hot throughout. Remove, season to taste, and serve while hot.

SERVES 4

A Boost of Taurine

Need a little energy boost and recuperative management from exercise? Many will turn to an energy drink. I say stop and get some octopus or squid on the way home instead. Octopus contains taurine, an organic acid that acts as an antioxidant. Studies suggest that also helps protect against stress effects from exercising. Energy drink makers have known about this acid for a number of years, which is why many of the drinks contain taurine.

Summertime Chopped Salad

I have been on an *eating light* kick for quite some time now, and you know, I *do* feel good. Even though every fiber of my body is crying out for more meat, I feel so great after eating and filling up on food that is low in fat. Sure, that carnivorous craving is always lingering, but with a little help with flavor and will power, I feel good after every meal.

A delightfully tasty and a true feel-good dish, try eating more robust salads such as the one below for that perfect frame of mind.

(Note: The directions call for using a mezzaluna, a double-bladed cutting tool; it is a glorified pastry cutter, actually, with double the cutting blades, which aren't sharp by the way. Keep a mezzaluna handy for chopping and mincing in the summer.)

4-6 ounces gnocchi

4 ounces sugar snap peas, trimmed and cut in half

1 cup whole kernel corn

1 head romaine, Boston bibb, or iceberg lettuce, roughly chopped

1 cucumber, peeled, seeded, and chopped

1 carrot, peeled and shredded

3 ounces pancetta ham, sliced thin

½ red bell pepper, cored and coarsely chopped

½ small onion, roughly chopped

SERVES 4

Your favorite vinaigrette dressing to taste

Salt and pepper to taste

Cook gnocchi according to package directions, drain. Refrigerate until ready to use.

Meanwhile, over medium-high heat, boil snap peas in enough water to cover them by an inch. After 3 minutes, while still crisp tender, carefully strain and immediately plunge in very cold water to stop the cooking. Remove from heat and drain.

Mix everything except cooked gnocchi in very large bowl. With your mezzaluna, chop all the ingredients until a small dice, or desired size, is achieved. As you are cutting the salad, the ingredients will automatically blend together.

Toss in the gnocchi and blend well. Divide among serving dishes, sprinkle with parmesan cheese, and serve.

Asian Veggie Omelets

Every once in a while, I make breakfast for lunch or supper. Asian-style omelets like these are eaten throughout the day in that part of the world, and after a few bites, you will see why.

Nonstick cooking spray
1 rib celery, minced
3 green onions, sliced thin
2 ounces (about a cup)
    mushrooms, minced
1 cup fat-free vegetable or
    chicken broth
1 tablespoon cornstarch
1 teaspoon brown sugar
2 tablespoons soy sauce
2 cups egg substitute
½ teaspoon each salt, black
    pepper, and chili powder
8 ounces beans sprouts,
    chopped
8 ounces fresh bok
    choy, chopped
Pure olive oil, as needed

SERVES 4

Grease a small skillet with nonstick cooking spray. Add celery and onions, cooking until the celery is softened over medium heat, about 3 minutes, stirring occasionally. Add the mushrooms and cook until soft, about another 3 minutes. Remove from heat, drain any juice accumulated, and set aside.

In a small saucepan, whisk together broth, cornstarch, sugar, and soy sauce and cook over medium heat until the mixture boils and thickens, about 4–6 minutes. Set aside, covered to keep warm.

In a large bowl, stir together egg substitute, spices, bean sprouts, bok choy, and celery mixture.

Add a half tablespoon oil to a skillet over medium heat until hot. Pour in ¼–½ cup measures of omelet batter to skillet and cook until browned on both sides, about 2–3 minutes per side. Transfer to plate and continue until all omelets have been made. Pour soy sauce mixture over the top and serve immediately.

Golden Delicious Grilled Broccoli and Cheese

This is the epitome of broccoli and cheese. I adore the flavor the cheese takes on when charred just a tad and mixed with the earthy taste of the broccoli. These are also so easy to make.

3 cups cooked broccoli, roughly chopped,
2 eggs, lightly beaten
½ cup butter-flavored crackers, crushed
½ cup quinoa, cooked*
⅓ cup parmesan cheese, grated
¼ teaspoon cayenne pepper or chili powder
¼ teaspoon black pepper
1 ¾ cups low-fat cheddar cheese, shredded
2 tablespoons pure olive oil

MAKES ABOUT 6 PATTIES

Mix everything, except the oil, in a bowl until well combined.

In a large skillet, add the oil over medium heat. When hot, scoop out ¼ cup mounds of the broccoli mixture and add to the skillet. Flatten to about an inch thick. Cook until browned on the bottom, about 2–4 minutes. The mixture may not look as if it is holding together at first, but it will bind together beautifully as the cheese melts. Turn over and continue cooking an additional 2–4 minutes, or until browned on the bottom. Transfer to a serving plate.

*To cook quinoa, simply place a ¼ cup quinoa in a cup cold water and swish around with your hand. Let it sit in water for 5 minutes, then drain through a sieve and rinse for another minute under cold running water. Place quinoa in a saucepan with ½ cup water and bring to a boil over high heat. Cover, reduce to low and simmer 5 minutes. Remove from heat, keeping the lid on, and let sit for 5 minutes. Fluff with fork and add to recipe.

Rocky Barren Potato Latkes

Such a simple recipe but intense with the flavor of blueberries hidden among the rocky barrens of Maine.

1 pound russet potatoes
½ small onion, minced
3 tablespoons matzo meal or cracker crumbs
2 strips turkey bacon, cooked and crumbled
2 egg whites, beaten
2 tablespoons plain yogurt or sour cream
1 teaspoon lemon juice
½ teaspoon both salt and black pepper
Nonstick cooking spray
1 cup blueberry garlic jelly*

Peel and grate the potatoes on the largest holes of your food grater. Transfer to a large bowl and cover with cold water, swishing it around slightly. Remove to a colander to drain, pressing down to extract as much liquid as possible.

Return potatoes to bowl and add onion, matzo meal, bacon, egg whites, yogurt, lemon juice, and salt and pepper, mixing well.

Spray a large skillet liberally with nonstick cooking spray. Place pan over medium heat and spoon 3 tablespoon measurements of the latke mixture into pan when hot, leaving an inch or so between each as you flatten them with a

SERVES 4 (2 LATKES EACH)

Can't find blueberry garlic jelly or don't want to bother with ordering online? Here is a recipe to make your own. In a food processor or blender, pulse 3 cups frozen (thawed) blueberries, 1 teaspoon garlic powder, and ¼ teaspoon each of cinnamon and dried ginger on high until they are as small as you can get, about a minute. You should have 2 cups blueberry puree. Add ½ cup sugar, 1 tablespoon apple cider vinegar (or red wine vinegar) and bring to a boil over medium heat, stirring often. When it has slightly reduced, about 5 minutes later, remove from heat and stir in 1 packet (1/4 cup plus 2 tablespoons) liquid pectin. Bring to a boil once again for one minute, constantly stirring. Pour into a bowl, cover and refrigerate for at least 4 hours, or until completely set.

spatula. Cook until well browned on the bottom, about 6–8 minutes, then flip over and continue cooking until browned on bottom. Remove to a platter and cover to keep warm as you repeat with remaining latke mixture.

In the meantime, place the blueberry jelly in a microwave-safe bowl, cover loosely with film wrap, and heat for 30 seconds, or until hot and bubbling. Carefully remove wrap, stir until smooth, and serve with latkes.

*I have found that the best blueberry garlic jelly is made by Worcester's in Maine. If you get a chance, take a peek at their website (www.wildblueberryproducts.com), where they feature my recipe!

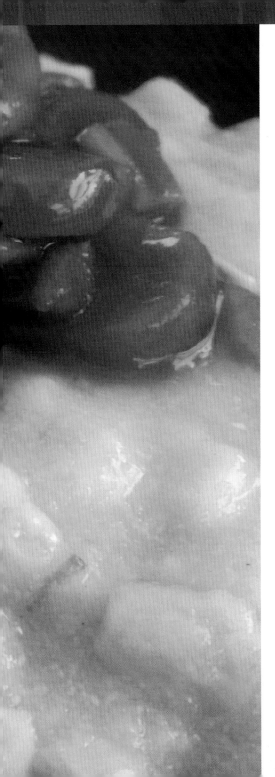

Fresh Corn Polenta with Balsamic Carrots

Talk about a dish that truly doesn't need any meat. The tastes and textures of this veggie-rich dish will keep you from thinking about any protein boost.

2 cups fat-free vegetable
    or chicken broth
¼ cup cornmeal
2 cups fresh corn kernels,
    cooked (about 3 ears)
2 tablespoons fresh
    cilantro, chopped
1 cup carrots, cooked
    and sliced
3 tablespoons balsamic
    vinegar
1 tablespoon pure olive oil
¼ cup canned green
    chilies, chopped
4 ounces low-fat provolone
    cheese, very thinly sliced

In a large saucepan, mix broth and cornmeal well and bring to a boil over high heat, stirring occasionally. Reduce heat to low and continue cooking, stirring often, until creamy and smooth, about 4 minutes. Stir in the corn and cilantro and cook an additional 2 minutes.

Meanwhile, in a large skillet over medium-high heat, add carrots, vinegar, and olive oil. Stir to combine and cook 4 minutes, or until the carrots are hot. Fold in the chilies.

Ladle the polenta into 4 serving bowls, top with equal amounts of cheese slices and dollop a ¼ cup of the carrot mixture over the top of each bowl. Let sit for 1–2 minutes to allow the cheese to melt, then serve.

SERVES 4

Tangy Cuke Bowl

This is a great recipe to enjoy even in the middle of winter, alongside a roast beef, oven roasted turkey, or even during lunch with a cold sandwich. If you have a hard time slicing the cucumbers in thin strips lengthwise, cut them to whatever size you want.

¼ cup rice wine vinegar
¼ cup pure olive oil
2 garlic cloves, peeled
    and crushed
½ teaspon dried dill or 1
    tablespoon freshly chopped
½ teaspoon brown sugar
¼ teaspoon each of salt and
    cracked black pepper
2 tablespoons grated
    parmesan or
    romano cheese
2 large cucumbers, peeled
    and sliced thinly lengthwise
½ (14.5-ounce) jar roasted
    red bell peppers, julienned
    or chopped

In a small bowl, whisk together vinegar, olive oil, garlic, dill, brown sugar, salt and black pepper and parmesan cheese. In another bowl, add the cucumber and bell peppers. Pour vinegar mixture over cucumbers, toss to combine, and refrigerate at least 30 minutes before serving.

SERVES 6–8

Say Cheese!

For those of you who try to shy away from all cheeses because of the calorie content, consider this. parmesan cheese only has 20 calories per tablespoon. And there is an array of lower fat/calorie cheeses available today, including part-skim mozzarella cheese that only has 70 calories per ounce. Just keep in mind that any cheese that says "reduced fat" is required to have at least 25% less fat than regular. So eat up, but in moderation.

Yanked Red Flannel Hash

Classically, and rightfully, made hash is a chopped combination of leftover vegetables from a true New England boiled dinner with beets, onions, turnip, potatoes, carrots, and corned beef. This recipe is a variation on the theme; hence the moniker *Yanked*.

I truly believe I have elevated this dish so that it will not only appeal to the younger generation, but it fits perfectly with any gathering, formal or otherwise.

Red Flannel Hash has an amusing beginning. The story goes that during the mid-nineteenth century in New England, a lumberman's wife made him a plate of hot, grilled, chopped hash before he was to leave for the woods. She began pouring his coffee as he was digging in, when he looked up and asserted that his breakfast looked like the red flannel shirt he had donned for the day.

Another Yankee link to this recipe is the polenta itself. I often laugh when I see polenta served at fine dining restaurants around the world because we Yankees have been stirring yellow cornmeal into boiling water since the early seventeenth century and enjoying it with butter or a drizzle of cream on top. We also let the leftover cornmeal mush firm up overnight so that it could be sliced and fried the next morning. It was a lowly meal but easy to make and very, *very* cheap, as it still is today.

My take on this classic Yankee dish takes out the protein and gives it a whole new twist. By all means add some chopped ham in this recipe, if you wish, but I think you will find it more than satisfying without it.

This dish is not only fragrant but beautiful as well, with a pink hue from the beets soaking into all the vegetables.

For the marinade:
½ cup apple cider vinegar
½ cup apple juice
1 tablespoon brown sugar
1 tablespoon soy sauce
1 teaspoon garlic powder
½ teaspoon cayenne pepper
Salt and black pepper to taste

1 ear of corn
Nonstick cooking spray
½ pound carrots, halved lengthwise and crosswise
1 onion, peeled and sliced into ½-inch rings
½ pound beets, peeled and sliced ½-inch thick
1 bell pepper, halved and seeded
1 pound potatoes, sliced ½ inch thick
Greens from beets
6–8 thick slices polenta*
3 ounces sharp, low-fat cheddar cheese, shredded or shaved

In a bowl, whisk together all marinade ingredients together and set aside.

Pull down husk on the corn, removing the hair. Soak for 30 minutes in water.

Meanwhile, heat grill on medium. Spray the vegetables on all sides with nonstick cooking spray. Lay carrots, onion, beets, bell pepper, and potatoes on the grill and close lid. Watching carefully, char both sides of all veggies just until you can see the marks, remembering that bell peppers take less time. No need to cook vegetables thoroughly; we are after the charred flavor.

Remove the vegetables and reduce grill heat to low. On a cutting surface, chop charred vegetables into roughly 1-inch cubes. Evenly divide into 4–5 large pieces of tin foil. Place the beet greens in a smaller piece of foil. Drizzle a couple tablespoons marinade into each and crimp well. Place back onto the grill, along with polenta slices and corn. Close lid and cook 20–25 minutes, rotating corn frequently, or until the corn husk has darkened and the kernels are done. Take a peek, carefully, to make sure vegetables are done as well. You don't want them mushy, just cooked.

Remove all items from the grill, emptying the vegetable packets into a large bowl along with greens. Stir to combine. Cut the stem end of the corn off and remove husk. With cut side down, slice off the kernels of corn onto a plate.

To serve, place a couple slices of charred polenta slices on each plate, evenly divide vegetables over polenta, followed by some of the grilled corn and shavings of cheddar cheese.

*Simply buy a roll of premade polenta from the supermarket or spend far less by making it yourself. See my recipe, page 104.

SERVES 3–4

Curried California Veggie Au Gratin

The touch of curry in this dish brings everything together rather nicely. I used yellow curry powder, but use any curry your heart desires. Be careful and remember that there are differing levels of heat in each blend.

1 (12-ounce) bag of California-style frozen vegetables
2 tablespoons pure olive oil
¼ small onion, minced
1¼ cups fat-free chicken or vegetable broth
2 tablespoons cornstarch mixed with
   3 tablespoons water
¼ cup evaporated skim milk
½ cup shredded low-fat Swiss cheese
1 teaspoon curry powder
Salt and black pepper to taste

SERVES 4

Preheat oven to 400° F. Place the frozen vegetables on a baking pan and roast until thawed and hot, about 12–14 minutes.

In a medium saucepan, add oil over medium heat. Add onion and saute until soft, about 4–5 minutes, stirring frequently. Add broth, stir to combine, and bring to a boil, raising heat to medium-high if desired. With one hand stirring, pour the cornstarch slurry into the broth, stirring well. Add milk, stir well, and remove from heat. Stir in the cheese until melted. Add curry and season to taste with salt and pepper; set aside. Remove vegetables from oven, portion onto 4 individual serving plates and top with cheese sauce.

Crisp Fried Yellow Tomatoes

Yup! We said yellow tomatoes! There are some of us who adore the less acidic taste of a yellow tomato. Of course you can vary this recipe by using green tomatoes and once in a while you may even see purple tomatoes in your market.

2 yellow tomatoes
Salt and cracked black pepper
    to taste
½ cup evaporated skim milk
1 egg white, beaten
½ cup yellow cornmeal
¾ cup flour
½ cup dried bread crumbs
½ teaspoon cayenne pepper
Pure olive oil, as needed
1 (10.5-ounce) can prepared
    crab bisque
¼ cup skim milk
1 red tomato, diced, to garnish
    on top
parmesan cheese, for
    garnish, optional

SERVES 4

Slice tomatoes into ½ inch slices and sprinkle each side with salt and cracked pepper; set aside.

In a large, shallow bowl, whisk together evaporated milk and egg white; set aside.

In another large shallow bowl, blend cornmeal, flour, bread crumbs, and cayenne pepper; set aside.

In a saucepan, whisk together crab bisque and milk. Heat over low and keep warm while cooking tomatoes.

Dip tomatoes in crumbs, then egg wash and crumbs again, making sure you pat the crumb mixture firmly onto each side of the tomato. Set on a plate and repeat with remaining slices. In a large skillet, heat 2 tablespoons oil over medium heat until shimmering. Add as many tomato slices as will fit and cook 3–5 minutes per side, or until lightly browned. Remove and repeat with any remaining slices, adding more oil as needed.

To serve, ladle equal amounts of warmed crab bisque onto each of four serving plates. Lay two grilled slices of green tomato onto bisque and top with chopped red tomatoes and a sprinkling of parmesan cheese. Serve immediately.

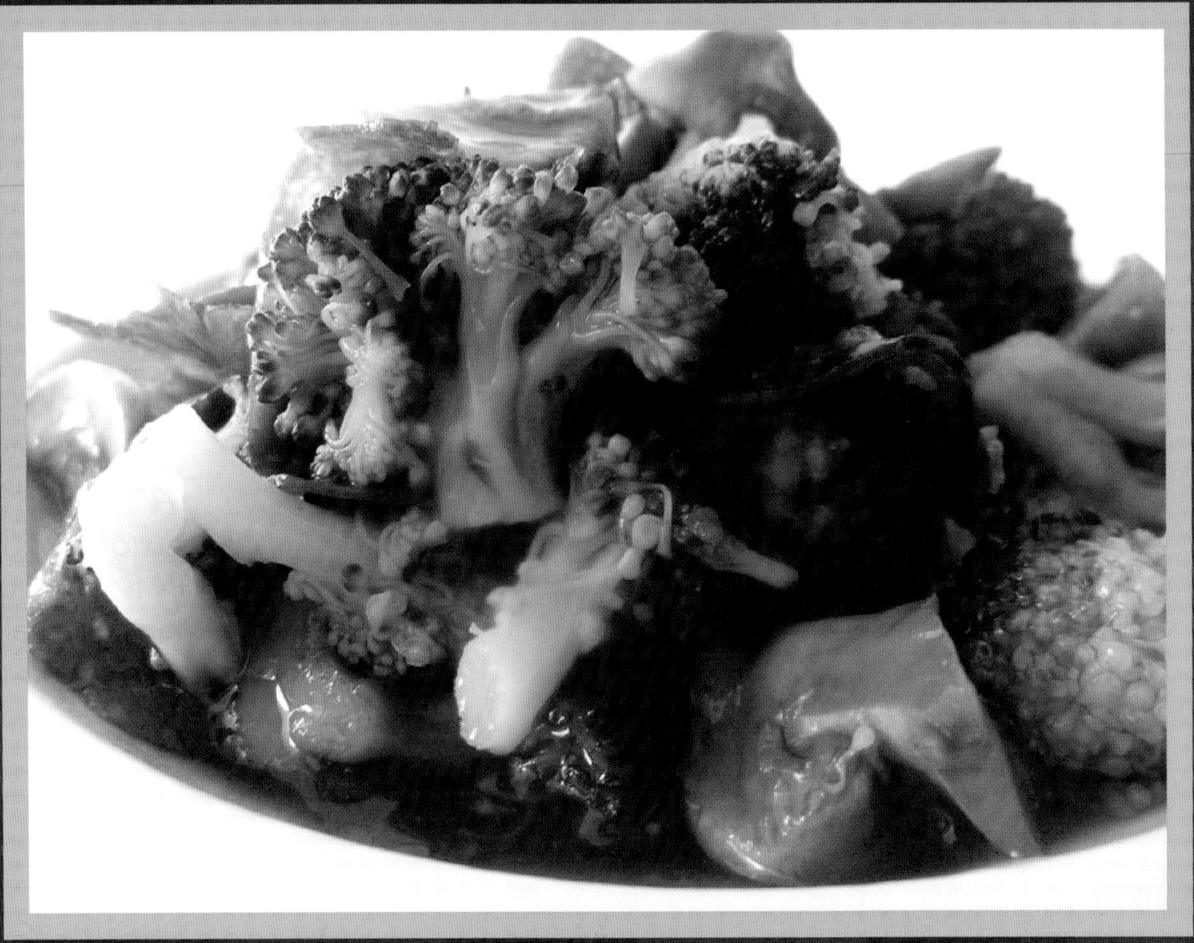

New England Broccoli-Mushroom Skillet

This is a quick, tasty treat to satisfy that hunger without feeling any guilt. I am amazed at how diverse certain New England ingredients are when used in recipes not generally associated with certain food items. Here, the soy sauce offsets the sweetness of the Yankee-land maple syrup. I think you will be pleasantly surprised as well.

¾ cup frozen apple juice
    concentrate, thawed
¼ cup maple syrup
2 teaspoons soy sauce
2 teaspoons butter
    or margarine
½ teaspoon black pepper
Pinch of cayenne pepper
2 tablespoons pure olive oil
½ pound button mushrooms,
    quartered
3 cups broccoli florets, cooked*
2 ounces thinly sliced prosciutto

Combine the first 6 ingredients, mixing very well; set aside.

Heat oil in a large skillet over medium-high heat. Add mushrooms and cook until fork tender, about 3 minutes. Add broccoli and prosciutto and continue cooking until heated through.

Carefully remove broccoli mixture to a bowl with a slotted spoon. While skillet is still on the heat, add the maple mixture and bring to a boil. Immediately add the broccoli and prosciutto back into the pan, toss to coat and remove. Serve immediately with croutons dotting the top if you would like.

SERVES 5

*Cauliflower would be a perfect substitution here.

'Tis the Season Sweet Potato Pancakes with Fruited Maple Syrup

You can substitute canned pumpkin for the sweet potatoes if desired without any noticeable difference in the taste. Also use any leftover potatoes. The subtle flavor of the sweet potato is so spot-on when combined with the textural kick of the syrup, it makes you feel like you should be shoveling a foot of snow . . . *naaaah*.

½ cup brown sugar
2 teaspoons baking powder
2 teaspoons pumpkin pie spice
1 cup buttermilk
2 tablespoons butter or
    margarine, melted
4 egg whites, lightly beaten
1 (16-ounce) can sweet
    potatoes, drained
    and mashed
1½–2 cups flour
Nonstick cooking spray

For the Fruited Maple Syrup:
¾ cup cranberry juice
½ cup chopped, dried fruit
1 cup maple syrup

Combine first 3 ingredients in a small bowl; set aside.

In a large bowl, mix together buttermilk, butter, egg whites, and sweet potatoes, combining well. Whisk in the sugar mixture. Stir in the flour, a little at a time, until it is pancake consistency.

Spray a skillet liberally with nonstick cooking spray and place over medium heat until hot. Pour the pancake batter by the ¼-cup and cook for 2–3 minutes, or until starting to bubble around the edge. Flip and continue cooking an additional 2 minutes, or until nicely browned. Repeat with remainder of pancake batter.

To make the syrup: In a medium saucepan, boil the cranberry juice and chopped, dried fruit together for 6–7 minutes on medium-high, or until fruit is softened and the liquid has reduced by half. Remove from heat and add maple syrup. Serve over pancakes.

SERVES 4, EACH WITH 3 PANCAKES

Simple and Fragrant Roasted Cauliflower

Want something different yet exciting in flavor? Use red wine vinegar for that acidic taste. I enjoy the simplicity of apple cider vinegar but balsamic introduces that special touch as well. For an Asian twist, combine 2 tablespoons rice wine vinegar with 1 teaspoon soy sauce and ½ teaspoon brown sugar.

1 head cauliflower
2 tablespoons your
    favorite vinegar
2 tablespoons pure olive oil
½ teaspoon dried rosemary
½ teaspoon dried
    thyme, crushed
Salt and pepper to taste
½ cup grated parmesan
    cheese

Peel leaves off cauliflower head and cut off protruding stem. Preheat oven to 450° F.

Cut cauliflower in half and remove the inside hard portion of the stem. Cut both halves into small, 1–1½ inch in diameter florets.

In a large bowl, toss florets with next 5 ingredients until well coated. Spread out onto a large baking sheet in a single layer. Roast 20–22 minutes, stirring half-way through, or until starting to brown.

Carefully remove from oven, sprinkle cheese over the top evenly and return to oven to continue cooking an additional 10 minutes, or until cauliflower has softened. Serve immediately.

SERVES ABOUT 6

Call on Cauliflower

Cauliflower contains the organic compounds isoflavones and indoles, as well as the chemical group isothiocyanates. These sound like man-made additives to processed foods, don't they? Actually, they offer serious hope in blocking cancer cell growth and contribute to DNA repair, immune support, and keeping cancer inflammation at bay.

Cape Cod Carrots

SERVES 4

What better way to expound on the classic Carrots Vichy than this delicately flavored side dish that adds a touch of Cape Cod?

1 pound carrots
12 ounces golden ginger ale
1 (8-ounce) can jellied
    cranberry sauce
    (about ¾ cup)
2 teaspoons dried dill
    or rosemary
2 teaspoons butter
    or margarine
1 teaspoon molasses, optional

Peel and slice carrots and place in a medium saucepan.

In a blender or food processor, pulse the ginger ale with cranberry sauce and dill until smooth, then add to the saucepan. Add enough water or more ginger ale to saucepan to cover carrots if needed. Cook over medium-high heat until carrots are tender.

With a slotted spoon, remove carrots to a bowl, then reduce heat to medium, and add the butter. Continue boiling liquid until reduced by half or thickened, about 3–4 minutes longer. Remove glaze from heat, transfer to carrots, and toss with molasses. Remove immediately and serve hot.

Arlene Wright-Correll of Kentucky's Home Farm Herbery is also a cancer survivor and touts the benefits of dill: "As a 21-year cancer survivor I am always interested in healthy information and especially the qualities of culinary herbs such as dill because Vitamin A and beta carotene are natural flavonoid antioxidants. Just 100g of dill weed sprigs provide 7718 IU or 257% of recommended-daily levels of this vitamin. Vitamin A is also required for maintaining healthy mucus membranes and skin and is essential for good eye-sight."

Crab Stuffed Tomatoes

SERVES 4

This recipe, as with all baked stuffed tomato recipes, is very delicate when removed from the oven or broiler. Just be careful and use one hand to steady the tomatoes while lifting with the other.

4 tomatoes
2 tablespoons low-fat
    mayonnaise
2 tablespoons yogurt
2 tablespoons minced onion
2 teaspoons Old Bay seasoning
1 teaspoon roasted green
    peppers in oil, well drained
    and minced
1 teaspoon dried
    chipotle pepper
Salt and pepper to taste
1 pound crabmeat,
    squeezed dry

Preheat oven to 350° F.

Slice off the top of each tomato, saving the tops. Core the tomatoes leaving about ¾-inch of tomato all around the inside wall. Place all the other ingredients except the crabmeat in a large bowl and mix well. Fold the crabmeat in gently so as not to break up the lumps. Spoon mixture into the tomatoes filling them a little over the top. Place the reserved tops off-center a bit.

Bake 10–12 minutes, or until tomatoes are beginning to soften. Crank the broiler up and finish them off at least 3–4 inches from heat source for about 5 minutes, or until crisp and starting to blacken on top. Serve with cole slaw and/or crusty, warm french bread.

Let me guess, you don't have Old Bay seasoning in your cupboard. This seasoning, originally named Delicious Brand Shrimp and Crab Seasoning, is the ultimate seafood seasoning and is a New England original. If you don't have it in your cupboard, here is a perfect substitution:

Combine 1 tablespoon celery seed, 1 teaspoon paprika (preferably smoked Spanish-style), ¾ teaspoon black pepper, 4 bay leaves, ½ teaspoon dried mustard, ¼ teaspoon cardamom, ¼ teaspoon ground cloves and ¼ teaspoon nutmeg. Mix it all together and remember to remove the bay leaves after the recipe is completed.

Yanked Harvard vs. Yale Beets

Even though that great Harvard vs. Yale rivalry is more pronounced in football, they have met on the baseball diamond more often, starting back in 1867. In 1875, these two teams met on the football field for the first time, and since then it has always been referred to as The Game. There seems to have been a rivalry in the kitchen as well. Did you know that Harvard Beets—a creamy, deliciously sweet and sour side dish—was pitted against Yale Beets? Harvard Beets have stood the test of time because of the recipe's tanginess, whereas Yale Beets were just plain sweet.

Here, I will give you both recipes, done over in The Yankee Chef's style, and you tell me which you prefer.

Want to use fresh beets instead of canned? Cut off the tops and rinse about 3 beets that are 3–4 inches in diameter. Place the beets in a large saucepan. Add enough water to cover by 4 inches. Bring to a boil over medium-high heat and cook until the beets are tender, about 45 minutes. Drain, reserving 2 cups of the liquid. Slip the skin off the cooked beets by rubbing them under cold water. Leave very small beets whole; slice larger beets.

For Harvard Beets:

1 (13-ounce) can sliced beets
1 teaspoon cornstarch
⅓ cup sugar
¼ cup balsamic vinegar
1 teaspoon lime juice
½ teaspoon salt
Pinch of ground cloves
2 tablespoons butter or
    margarine
2 strips turkey or pepper
    bacon, cooked and
    crumbled, optional

Drain beets and reserve beet juice. In medium saucepan combine cornstarch and sugar, add reserved beet juice, vinegar, lime juice, and salt. Bring to a boil over medium-high heat until thickened and smooth, stirring almost constantly. Reduce heat to low and add sliced beets, stirring gently until beets are warmed through, adding the butter at the last minute and stirring in completely. Remove from heat and sprinkle with crumbled bacon before serving, if desired.

For Yale Beets:

Follow recipe for Harvard Beets but substitute ¼ cup orange juice for the vinegar. Sprinkle grated orange or tangerine zest on top, instead of bacon.

SERVES 4

SERVES 4

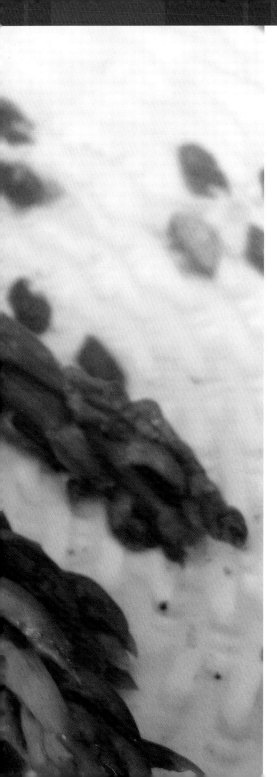

Indian Marketplace Potato Salad

If there was one accompaniment I would serve with this recipe it would be spicy Chinese Red Barbecue found on page 194.

6 large potatoes,
    about 3 pounds
1 tablespoon curry powder
1 teaspoon cumin seed
1 teaspoon dried mint
1 tablespoon pure olive oil
¼ teaspoon ground cloves
½ cup fat-free vegetable broth
⅓ cup rice vinegar
1 pound asparagus spears
    or green beans, cooked
    and cold

Peel (or leave skin on) potatoes and boil, until tender. Drain, cool, and dice to your liking.

In a small saucepan, combine curry, cumin seed, mint, and oil. Mix well and place over medium heat, cooking and occasionally stirring for 3 minutes, or until the cumin is very fragrant.

Remove from heat and whisk in the cloves. Add broth and vinegar, whisking to combine. Pour over the potatoes, toss, and add salt and pepper to taste.

Cover and refrigerate at least one hour. Divide asparagus among 5 plates and top with equal amounts of potato salad.

SERVES 6

Free Radical Frenzy

It has only been the past few decades that free radicals have become an issue, and two reasons stick out to me as the main reasons. First of all, more and more of the foods we eat are being processed instead of being produced at family farms. We have become a hurried and impatient society for a number of reasons and that reflects directly into the kitchen.

Second is the level of pollution in the air and chemicals in every aspect of our lives. I think it is because of this changed lifestyle and nutritional depletion that free radicals are attacking our bodies more ferociously than ever in the history of the human race, resulting in diseases invading every part of our bodies.

Your Own Polenta

salt
2 cups cornmeal
parmesan cheese to taste

Line the bottom of a loaf pan with tin foil and generously grease with cooking spray.

Heat 6 cups water and salt in a large pot to boiling over medium-high heat. Begin whisking the water and add 2 cups cornmeal in a very thin, steady stream. Vigorously whisk to prevent lumps while adding the cornmeal.

Reduce heat to low once all the cornmeal has been added and blend in however much parmesan cheese you desire.Continue cooking until very thick, stirring frequently. This step will take about 3–4 minutes, making sure that a spoon can stand up in it before transferring to prepared pan.

In pan, smooth out the top so it is level and let sit at room temperature 5 hours or overnight. When ready to serve (or cook with it, as in the Saucy Polenta Lasagna recipe), cut into 16 equally thick slices.

MAKES 16 SLICES

Saucy Polenta Lasagna

This is one luscious lasagna. Creamy, cheesy, and completely satisfying without meat. Add other cooked vegetables such as carrots, broccoli, kale . . . the list goes on and on.

2 cups low-fat ricotta cheese
2 egg whites, beaten lightly
1 teaspoon garlic powder
½ teaspoon red pepper flakes
16 polenta slices*
1 (10-ounce) package frozen
    spinach, thawed and
    squeezed dry
1 cup prepared
    marinara sauce
¾ cup parmesan cheese,
    shredded
¼ cup fresh basil, thinly sliced

SERVES 6

Preheat oven to 400° F.

In a large bowl, blend ricotta, egg whites, garlic, and red pepper flakes together well; set aside.

Spread out a ¼ cup marinara sauce in the bottom of a loaf pan. Lay polenta slices on top, not overlapping. Place half of the ricotta mixture and half spinach over the top, smoothing out evenly. Add another layer of polenta slices, then half of remainder marinara sauce and half the parmesan cheese, evening out. Add another layer of polenta slices, followed by remaining ricotta and remaining spinach. Top with one last layer of polenta, remaining marinara, and basil and sprinkle rest of parmesan cheese evenly over the top. Bake for 45 minutes, or until the top is bubbling. Remove and serve hot.

*Simply buy a roll of premade polenta from the supermarket or spend far less by making it yourself. See my recipe, page 104.

According to the World Health Organization, high intake of fruit and vegetables, particularly of the green leafy variety, can decrease overall cancer risk by as much as 15%.

As many of you know, if corn is left on the stalk when the first frost of the season comes, the sugar quickly turns into starch. Parsnips, on the other hand, is completely the opposite. When this vegetable is still in the ground during the first frost, the starch turns to sugar. That is why many centuries ago, the English used parsnips to sweeten cakes and jams and parsnips were even commonly found in bread.

Crisp Parsnip Sticks with Spiced Blueberry Compote

What to do, what to do . . . with parsnips? Admit it! Once a staple around our holiday tables, parsnips have been fading in popularity in the last generation. I believe in carrying on our heritage and support bringing this antioxidant-rich root vegetable back into our lives. This recipe combines the sweet taste of cooked parsnips with the natural sweetness of blueberries and a punch of red pepper

2 parsnips, peeled
2 tablespoons pure olive oil
1 tablespoon parmesan
  cheese
½ teaspoon each garlic, onion,
  and chili powders

For the Spiced Blueberry Compote:

1 cup blueberry preserves
1 tablespoon orange juice
1 teaspoon lemon juice
½ teaspoon red pepper flakes

Prepare the Spiced Blueberry Compote: Blend blueberry preserves, orange juice, lemon juice, and red pepper flakes well in a small bowl. Cover and refrigerate while continuing with recipe.

Cut parsnips into "french fries" and place in a large bowl. Pour olive oil over the parsnips and toss to evenly coat. Add parmesan cheese, garlic powder, onion powder, and chili powder. Toss well to coat all parsnip fries.

Transfer to a nonstick baking pan, or an oven pan with parchment, foil, or waxed paper in a single layer. Place in the oven and then turn it on to 450° F. Let bake 14–16 minutes once the temperature hits 450° F, turning over once, or until crisp and golden. Remove from oven to serve immediately with Spiced Blueberry Compote.

When ready to serve, place jelly in microwavable bowl, cover with film wrap, and heat for 10–15 seconds, or until it is just barely warm. Remove film wrap and whisk well.

SERVES 3

CHAPTER 4 Grains, Beans, and Pasta

Each grain has its own distinctive flavor, from rye's strong taste to the mellowness of barley and oats. Millet and cornmeal offer rich and sweet flavors and if it is earthiness you are seeking, look no further than wheat berries, spelt, or buckwheat.

A number of recipes in this book use grains' inherent health benefits because I truly believe that they, along with fruits and vegetables, are the main course, with meat as the side-kick. To easily understand the parts of grains, allow me to simply explain what their anatomy is and why different parts offer different rewards. Of course, the husk is the outside and covers the bran, which is the grains' incredible dietary fiber source. The germ is directly underneath the bran and offers certain enzymes, proteins, Vitamin A, and minerals. And at the core of each grain is the endosperm, where the carbs are stored.

Glossary of Grains

Amaranth: This gold and granular grain that is speckled with black pepper-like flakes is high in protein and available whole, powdered, or puffed.

Barley: One of the first cultivated plants, it is usually sold pearled but also comes in quick-cooking, hulled whole, grits, flakes, and flour.

Buckwheat: Triangular in shape and related to the rhubarb plant, it is sold as kasha, whole or cracked and unroasted in grits or ground into flour.

Bulgur: These are wheat kernels that have had a hot bath in steam and then dried and cracked. Bulgur is very seldom cooked but is used after being soaked in boiling water. Bulgur is sold either fine, medium, or coarse.

Corn: Of course we all know that you can buy corn yellow, white, or both colors on the ears. But did you know that you can purchase it in a wide assortment of colors including blue, red, and black? This is *not* the sweet corn we eat off the cob.

Cornmeal: Simply dried corn kernels of varying colors that comes in fine, medium, or coarse textures.

Couscous: A coarsely ground pasta of durum wheat, originating in Africa. They are cooked and then dried to be again cooked by . . . well, the cook. (Before I start getting all sorts of feedback from readers telling me that couscous isn't a grain, I shall like to say one thing: *I know that*! It is made of semolina (a ground wheat grain) and prepared much like other grains. So with the majority of its makeup as a grain and the preparation almost identical, I am adding it to this section, much as many other cookbook authors do.)

Grits: Usually referred to as hominy, this is often found as a dried corn product. But did you know that you can also find grits as oats or barley?

Groats: A coarser grind of grits

Kamut: A very old form of wheat that is explosive in protein. It is generally available whole or processed into cereals and pasta.

Kasha: Buckwheat that has been roasted and sold either whole or cracked in either fine, medium, or coarse textures.

Millet: A very nutritious, sweet-flavored grain of a yellow color. The hulls have been removed and it is ground coarsely when you buy it.

Oats: These protein-rich grains have been a mainstay on our breakfast tables for generations.

Quinoa: Incan in origin, and pronounced *keen-wah*, these tiny seeds are truly not a grain but a fruit. This is one of the best "grains" to eat, as it relates to protein, calcium and iron and is sold whole, ground, or processed into pasta. Quinoa should be well rinsed to remove the bitter-tasting coating called saponin.

Rye: Very low in gluten, it is mainly ground into flour but can be found as rye berries and meal.

Spelt: Large, brown, and with a great nutty flavor, this grain is sold whole, rolled, and ground and can often be tolerated by people with wheat allergies.

Wheat: Although it is our most important grain and is one of the most exported of all grains, it is not only found as flour but as cracked, bulgur, grits, shredded wheat, germ, flakes, puffed, and cream of wheat.

A Handy Bean Guide

It isn't very tempting to consider cooking beans from scratch for a recipe anymore, is it? I concur, even though our much busier ancestors always found the time. Beans were at the top of our food chain in the early colonization of America and the natives always grew them along with corn. The corn stalks provided a type of trellis for the beans to climb, and the beans provided a ground cover for the corn.

Here is a handy tip sheet for the times when you are able to devote time to cooking dry beans.

Great Northern Beans:	1 cup	presoaked	beans cooked in	3 cups liquid	equals	2 cups	cooked
Kidney Beans:	1 cup	presoaked	beans cooked in	3½ cups liquid	equals	2 cups	cooked
Lentils:	1 cup	unsoaked	beans cooked in	4 cups liquid	equals	3 cups	cooked
Lima:	1 cup	presoaked	beans cooked in	4 cups liquid	equals	2 cups	cooked
Navy:	1 cup	presoaked	beans cooked in	3½ cups liquid	equals	2½ cups	cooked
Whole dried peas:	1 cup	presoaked	beans cooked in	3½ cups liquid	equals	2 cups	cooked
Pinto:	1 cup	presoaked	beans cooked in	4 cups liquid	equals	2½ cups	cooked
Red Beans:	1 cup	presoaked	beans cooked in	3½ cups liquid	equals	2½ cups	cooked
Split Peas:	1 cup	unsoaked	beans cooked in	3½ cups liquid	equals	2½ cups	cooked

Spring Time Couscous

What on earth could this recipe pair well with you might ask? If you are having a spiced sausage dish, this is your side. If you are enjoying some grilled chicken, this is your side. Any type of bold, meaty, spicy-flavored protein would be enhanced by these flavors.

1¼ cup fat-free
    vegetable broth
1 cup water
2 tablespoons sugar
1 cup dried fruit of your
    choice, chopped
¾ cup couscous
2 tablespoons butter or
    margarine, optional

Add all ingredients to a medium saucepan, except butter, and bring to a boil over medium-high heat. Stir to keep sugar from burning on bottom and to blend all ingredients well.

Cover with tight-fitting lid and remove from heat. Let sit 6–8 minutes, or until the couscous has absorbed all the liquid. Remove lid and toss with the butter until melted and combined well. Serve hot.

Harvest Lasagna

Should I mention this is meat free? Perfectly cheesy, perfectly spiced and perfectly comforting. If desired, go ahead and add some cooked sausage to this dish, but you won't need it.

Nonstick cooking spray
1 onion, peeled and minced
1 (10-ounce) bag fresh
    spinach leaves
6 ounces sliced, low-fat
    provolone cheese
Salt and black pepper to taste
3 cups squash or
    pumpkin, mashed
1 cup low-fat cottage or
    ricotta cheese
3 egg whites, lightly beaten
1 (15-ounce) can tomato sauce
1 teaspoon each sugar and
    Italian seasoning
12 lasagna noodles, cooked
    and drained
1 cup parmesan cheese
1 cup shredded, low-fat
    mozzarella cheese

Preheat oven to 350° F F.

Liberally grease a large skillet with nonstick cooking spray and place over medium-high heat. When hot, add onion and cook until softened, about 3–4 minutes. Add spinach leaves, toss with oil and onions, and cook until just starting to wilt, about 2 minutes. Transfer to a large bowl to cool enough to handle.

In another large bowl, whisk together squash, cottage cheese and egg whites until blended well; set aside.

In another bowl, blend tomato sauce, sugar, and Italian seasoning; set aside.

In a 13- by 9-inch baking pan or casserole dish, coat the bottom with 2–3 tablespoons tomato sauce evenly. Lay 4 cooked noodles on bottom. Spread a third of the pumpkin mixture evenly over noodles. Spread out a third of the spinach over this. Sprinkle spinach with a third of the parmesan and provolone cheese evenly. Repeat two more times, ending with the cup of mozzarella cheese over the top.

Cover loosely with foil and bake 30 minutes with a larger pan underneath to catch any sauce that may bubble over. Remove foil and bake an additional 30 minutes. Remove from oven to cool slightly before digging in.

MAKES 6–8 SERVINGS

Warm Shrimp Orzo

Although the word *orzo* is Italian for barley, it is actually very small pasta. It lends itself well to so many salads, both hot and cold, and this recipe is no different.

1 garlic clove, peeled
    and crushed
2 tablespoons pure olive oil
¾ cup fresh mushrooms of your
    choice, sliced
½ pound small Louisiana or
    salad shrimp
2 cups fat-free vegetable broth
1 cup couscous
1 cup fresh spinach, packed
1 cup cooked carrots, sliced
½ teaspoon lemon pepper
2 tablespoons malt vinegar
Salt and black pepper

In a large saucepan, over medium heat, add oil and garlic. Cook, stirring frequently, for 3 minutes. Add mushrooms and shrimp. Continue cooking and stirring until the mushrooms and shrimp are just done, about 4–5 minutes. Remove mushrooms and shrimp with a slotted spoon to a bowl; set aside.

Add broth, couscous, spinach, and carrots to saucepan. Bring to a boil, stir, and cover. Reduce heat to low and simmer 6 minutes, or until all liquid has been absorbed. Remove from heat, add the mushroom/shrimp mixture back into the pan along with vinegar and lemon pepper, and season to taste with salt and pepper. Fluff well and serve immediately.

SERVES 4

Guiltless and Simple Spaghetti Bolognese

TVP®, or texturized vegetable protein, is made from soy flour that is cooked under pressure and then extruded to make different sizes and shapes such as flakes, cutlets, tenders, chunks, and granules. The granules are used for burgers, sausage, meatballs, and sauces such as Bolognese. They absorb much better than tofu because you buy TVP in a dry state, whereas tofu is not. TVP is lower in fat than tofu and much better adapted to most recipes as a subsitute for meat. You will feel great and will not miss the meat— I didn't!

2 cups textured vegetable
    protein granules
2 vegetable bouillon cubes*
1 cup boiling water
1 tablespoon pure olive oil
½ small onion, chopped
2 garlic cloves, peeled
    and crushed
2 ounces button mushrooms,
    chopped
1 (15-ounce) can tomato sauce
    or puree
3 tablespoons tomato paste
1 tablespoon brown sugar
1 tablespoon oregano

SERVES 3–4

1 teaspoon dried basil
1 teaspoon dried
    thyme, crushed
salt and pepper to taste
1 pound spaghetti

Crumble the vegetable protein in a bowl, then add the bouillon cubes and boiling water: set aside.

In a large skillet, add oil and heat over medium flame. Once hot, add the onions and garlic, stir to combine. Cook for 3–4 minutes, or until onions have slightly softened. Add the vegetable protein mixture along with the remaining ingredients except spaghetti. Reduce heat to low and simmer for 15 minutes, or until hot and the spices have developed well.

Meanwhile, cook pasta according to package directions; strain, and set aside. Remove sauce from heat and serve this "bolognese" over pasta.

*Salt-free bouillon is great here.

Try a Little TVP

While exploring the local health food store, I was checking out some soy products. The manager noticed me and came by for a little chat. We have known each other for a while and he knew I was a meat and potatoes kind of man but didn't hesitate to introduce me to something I had never worked with before: textured vegetable protein, or TVP (a trademark of Archer Daniels Midland).

He said that if I had any hesitancy about using soy curd, or tofu, to try TVP instead. I bought an 8 ounce block of it to take home, and was shocked that it was just 99 cents a pound! And not only was it inexpensive, but when you use TVP, a half pound quickly becomes over a pound because it quickly soaks up surrounding liquid and flavors.

Textured vegetable protein has zero cholesterol and is widely accepted in breakfast and lunch programs in hundreds of public schools here in the US and many more "across the pond."

Want to compare it with other proteins, such as beef or sausage? Fair thee well animal protein, and hello vegetable. You can actually purchase sausage-flavored TVP as well as beef and ham, although flavored TVP does contain some partially hydrolyzed oil for flavor and texture. But, it is still much more healthful than animal protein. For example, sausage-flavored vegetable protein has about 16% fat with about 12% fiber.

Now for pricing comparisons. If you were to buy ground beef on sale anywhere, you would be hard pressed to find it any less expensive than 99 cents a pound. One pound of beef-flavored vegetable protein, dry, costs about $1.50. But when you rehydrate it, your cost is . . . wait for it . . . about 40 cents a pound.

Remember that one ounce of dry TVP is the equivalent of almost 3 ounces of meat in any given dish. Plus no browning or cooking is required, another bonus!

Italian-Style Soba Noodles

Compared to white-flour noodles, soba noodles contain almost half the calories. Although the calories are still mostly carbs, those are also much lower. Try them as an alternative to other pastas and noodles.

¾ cup walnuts, shelled
6 ounces soba noodles
1 tablespoon rice wine vinegar
2 garlic cloves, peeled
    and crushed
1 teaspoon hot pepper sauce
1 tablespoon chopped chives,
    dried or fresh
¼ cup soy sauce
2 cups (about ½ head)
    escarole, roughly chopped
Salt and pepper to taste
Shaved parmesan cheese

SERVES 2

In a small skillet, toast the walnuts over medium-high heat, stirring constantly until lightly browned and fragrant, about 2–3 minutes. Remove, cool slightly, and crush with either a coffee grinder, food processor, or simply with the side of a large knife; set aside.

Cook soba noodles according to package directions. Drain but don't rinse

In a large skillet over medium heat, cook the vinegar, garlic, hot pepper sauce, chives, soy sauce, and escarole until the escarole is softened, about 4–5 minutes Add the drained noodles, toss to coat evenly, then season with salt and pepper to taste.

Transfer to serving dishes, top with the nuts and shaved Parmesan cheese, and serve immediately.

Keep the Skin On

I believe I am the only one in my family, and even friends when they have visited during the holidays, that does not take the whitish, flaky skin off when I shell my walnuts. I think it may be the Yankee in me, loving my coffee so intense that my spoon stands up in it. But those of you who don't mind a very slight bitterness once in a while will be glad to know that over 80% of the phenolic acids and flavonoids (antioxidants) found in walnuts are in the flaky skin. *It's Just That Simple!*

East-West Lemon-Lobster Linguine

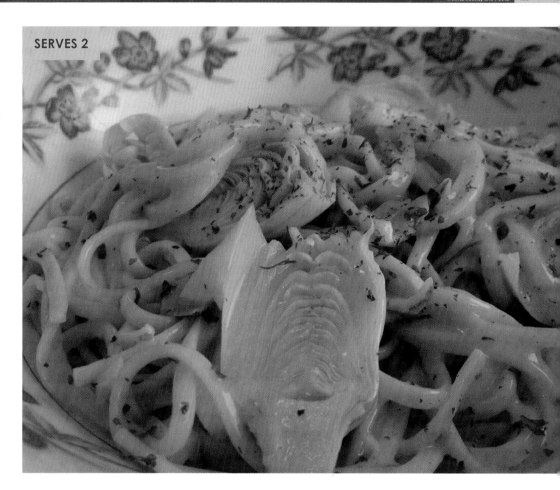

SERVES 2

A wonderful combination of lobster with just the right amount of lemon flavor to transform a once lowly addition to the supper table to a level of decadence seldom enjoyed in such a quick recipe.

½ pound linguine
2 teaspoons pure olive oil
2 green onions, thinly sliced
    (about 1 ounce)
1 cup cooked artichoke
    hearts, quartered
    .(about six ounces)
6 ounces lobster meat, cooked
    and coarsely chopped
1 cup fat-free vegetable broth
¼ cup evaporated skim milk
½ teaspoon lemon zest, grated
½ teaspoon dried
    rosemary, crushed
Salt and black pepper to taste

Cook linguine according to package directions; drain.

In a large skillet or saucepan over medium-high heat, add 2 teaspoons oil until hot. Add onions, artichokes, and lobster. Cook until the onions are softened, about 2 minutes, stirring frequently. Add broth, milk, lemon zest, and rosemary. Bring to a boil. Add drained pasta, stirring to combine well. Salt and pepper to taste and cook an additional minute. Serve hot.

Saucy Chicken Lo Mein

Enjoy this recipe using steak, seafood, or simply a variety of cooked vegetables. As for the pasta (or noodles) used, this is entirely up to you. I have often used just plain cooked spaghetti, fettuccine, angel hair, or even chow mein noodles. There is a slight difference between lo mein noodles and spaghetti, but not enough to have you run out and buy one or the other if you have one type at home already.

½ cup soy sauce
¼ cup apple juice
3 tablespoons cornstarch
3 tablespoons apple
    cider vinegar
1 teaspoon sugar
1 teaspoon sesame oil,
    optional
½ teaspoon black pepper
2 cups fat-free chicken broth
1 tablespoon pure olive oil
8 ounces chicken breast, cut
    into 1-inch cubes
½ small onion, minced
2 garlic cloves, peeled
    and crushed
2 ounces lo mein noodles or
    spaghetti, cooked
½ teaspoon dried ginger

Combine first 8 ingredients in a bowl and whisk well; set aside.

In a wok or large skillet over medium-high heat, add olive oil until hot. Add the chicken and cook 4–5 minutes or until done, stirring often. Add the onion and garlic, cooking an additional 2–3 minutes, or until onions are tender. Stir in the soy sauce mixture and boil 1 minute. Add the noodles and ginger, continuing to cook and stir a minute or two longer until everything is cooked together and heated through. Serve immediately.

SERVES 2–3

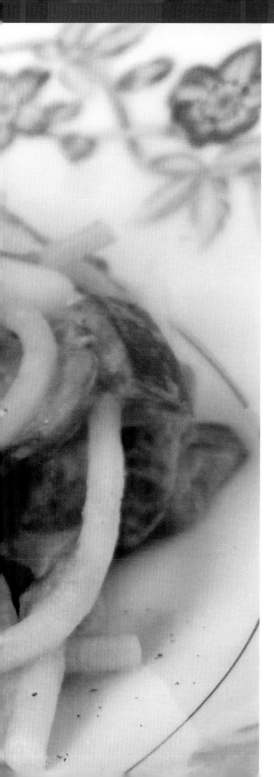

Pasta Alle Melenzana Aromatico

Whether to seed an eggplant or not is entirely up to you. It is the same as with cucumbers; the deciding factor is probably whether your body can handle seeds or not. This dish, although perhaps lacking some visual appeal, is none-the-less very satisfying and exciting in taste. This is the *only* way I can get my children to enjoy eggplant.

1 pound pasta, cooked and
    drained (such as linguine)
1 small eggplant
2 tablespoons pure olive oil
4 garlic cloves, peeled
    and crushed
½ small red onion, peeled
    and minced
¼ cup sliced mushrooms
1 small tomato, seeded
    and chopped
1 tablespoon dried basil leaves
1 cup chili sauce
1 teaspoon rosemary
Salt and cracked black pepper
    to taste
2 tablespoons yogurt or
    sour cream
4 teaspoons skim milk
Shredded parmesan cheese,
    for garnish

Cook your choice of pasta, drain and keep warm while preparing remainder of recipe. Or cook pasta while making sauce, but make sure it is well drained for it to adhere to the sauce.

Cut eggplant in half lengthwise, then slice crosswise. You can either leave the skin on or peel it off, your preference. Dice eggplant into ½- to ¾-inch cubes; set aside.

In a large skillet over medium heat, add olive oil, garlic, onion, and mushrooms. Stirring frequently, cook for 2–3 minutes, or until onions start to soften. Raise temperature to medium-high and add diced eggplant, continue cooking an additional 3–4 minutes or until eggplant is slightly tender, stirring frequently but carefully. Eggplant tends to absorb oil very rapidly so keep an eye out.

Add tomato, basil, chili sauce, rosemary, and salt and pepper to taste. Bring to scalding, stirring well.

Meanwhile, in a small bowl, whisk together yogurt and skim milk until smooth.

Remove tomato mixture from heat, stir in yogurt mixture and toss with cooked, warmed pasta. Serve with shredded parmesan over the top.

SERVES 4

Puritan Spaghetti

It must be the Yankee in me because lately I have been enjoying all sorts of dishes using pumpkin; my kids enjoy this recipe the best so far. Our ancestors, during the colonization of New England, used the "pompion" (pumpkin) in numerous ways, though many of their preparations have been lost through the years. This is a great example of yet another way to use our ingrained taste for this Yankee staple.

1 pound spaghetti, or pasta of your choice
1 tablespoon pure olive oil
2 garlic cloves, peeled and crushed
1 small onion, minced
1 small zucchini, seeded or unseeded, diced
1 small summer squash, seeded or unseeded, diced
1 (15-ounce) can pumpkin puree
2 cups skim milk*
1 cup fat-free chicken or vegetable broth
¼ cup parmesan cheese, grated
1 cup cooked white beans (I use great northern)
½ cup whole kernel corn
Salt and black pepper to taste

Cook spaghetti according to package directions. Drain and set aside.

In a large saucepan, add oil and garlic. Over medium-high heat, cook garlic for 2 minutes, stirring frequently. Add onions, zucchini, and squash. Cook, stirring frequently, until the vegetables are fork tender.

Meanwhile, in a large bowl, combine pumpkin, milk, broth, and parmesan cheese, whisking well. Add pumpkin mixture along with beans and corn. Stir together and continue cooking until heated through. Season to taste.

Add the cooked spaghetti, toss to combine and serve immediately.

* This is one of those rare times that skim milk works best in a recipe involving a cream sauce. Adding any dairy with fat here makes this recipe simply too weighty and unpleasant. Skim milk thins out the pumpkin without masking any flavor.

SERVES 4

Milk Matters

All milk sold in the United States is fortified with Vitamin D because this vitamin is needed to absorb calcium. Skim and 1% milk are often fortified with Vitamin A. According to the American Heart Association, skim milk and 1% milk contain slightly more nutrients than 2% and whole milk.

Earth's Best Great Northern Salad

This salad requires such simple preparation, yet it's packed with a tremendous amount of flavor. I recommend this side for any outdoor event as a healthier alternative to mayonnaise-based salads that can spoil.

¼ cup pure olive oil
¼ cup fresh oregano,
    chopped,
3 tablespoons lemon juice
3 tablespoons canned green
    chilies, chopped
2 tablespoons parmesan
    cheese
1 teaspoon garlic powder
½ teaspoon dried rosemary
¼ teaspoon freshly
    ground pepper
2 cups cooked and drained
    great northern beans
1 large tomato chopped
¼ cup whole kernel corn
Shredded extra-sharp, low-fat
    cheddar cheese, optional

Place the first 8 ingredients in a bowl and stir well.

In another, larger bowl, toss the beans, tomato, and corn together. Add the liquid to the bean mixture, gently blend, cover and refrigerate at least 2 hours before serving with cheese on top.

SERVES 4–6

Latin-Style Black Beans and Rice

This recipe is so uniquely delicious, you would never guess it is low in fat. With only enough butter to cook with, it may be your new favorite Yanked recipe. If desired, cook dry black beans according to package directions for this recipe, but canned beans are much easier and just as tasty.

2 tablespoons butter
    or margarine
6 ounces cooked lobster
    meat, chopped
¼ teaspoon annatto seeds
½ teaspoon paprika
Pinch of cumin
4 ounces smoked, cooked
    chicken, diced small
2 (15-ounce) cans black
    beans, well drained
2 cups Latin-style rice, cooked*
1 cup whole kernel corn

In a large skillet, melt butter over medium-high heat. Add lobster, annatto seeds, paprika, and cumin. Stir fry until heated through and beginning to sear slightly, about 5–6 minutes. Add chicken, black beans, rice, and corn. Continue cooking and stirring until everything is hot.

*Cook 1 cup rice according to package directions, but substitute pineapple juice for the water.

SERVES 3-4

Beans: To Soak, or Not to Soak?

That is the question. Whether it is easier to suffer the discomfort or to soak away the slings and arrows of gas . . . Okay, I am no Shakespeare. Some say soaking dry beans helps to keep them from causing that unfortunate side effect of eating them. It does help, but very minimally. I soak because it can shorten the cooking time in half and I end up with beans that hold their shape rather well. But if you don't have the time, don't worry about it. Just make sure you remove beans when they are just done.

Yankee Red Beans and Rice

SERVES 4

Although ham or pork would be excellent in this rendition of a Southern classic, I thought I would kick it up a notch and add some great flavor in the way of ground chicken. Add or remove spicy elements, if desired.

¼ cup apple juice or cider
2 tablespoons butter
  or margarine
1 pound ground chicken
1 green bell pepper, minced
1 small red onion, minced
1 rib celery, minced
2 garlic cloves, peeled
  and crushed
3 teaspoons Cajun seasoning
½ teaspoon cayenne pepper
1 teaspoon dried thyme
¼ teaspoon dried sage
2 (15-ounce) cans red kidney
  beans, rinsed and drained
½ cup fat-free beef broth
1 (15-ounce) can whole
  tomatoes, coarsely mashed
4 cups cooked rice, hot
Apple cider vinegar, optional

Over medium heat, add apple juice and butter to a large saucepan until butter has melted. Add the chicken, pepper, onions, celery, and garlic. Stir to break up the ground chicken and blend well. Cook, stirring frequently, until the chicken is cooked through, about 5–6 minutes. Add seasonings, beans, broth, and tomatoes, mix well, and bring back to a light boil. Reduce heat to low and simmer for 10 minutes.

Remove from heat and ladle over hot cooked rice. My family has been drizzling apple cider vinegar over our Red Beans and Rice for years, and it is delicious. Served with a side of apple sauce, you have a great, and original, Red Beans and Rice!

Go, Go, Garlic!

Garlic has been shown to actually kill cancer cells in the breasts according to the American Institute for Cancer Research (AICR).

If you have cancer, you've probably heard that eating lots of vegetables can help fight the disease and give your body the nutritional support it needs to withstand chemotherapy. One vegetable in particular—garlic—contains substances that are especially powerful weapons against cancer, says the AICR.

The Best Refried Beans

We all know that refried beans are great with burritos, dip, and quesadillas or on meatless tacos. But how about with a Mexican-style lasagna or as the base for pizza? So cheap to make, it is a wonder why more people don't make this at home anymore.

½ cup onion, minced
1 cup fat-free beef or
    vegetable broth
3 (15-ounce) cans pinto
    beans, drained
1 teaspoon garlic powder
1 teaspoon onion powder
1 teaspoon paprika, optional
1 teaspoon chili powder
1 teaspoon apple
    cider vinegar
½ teaspoon black pepper

MAKES ABOUT 4 CUPS

In a medium saucepan, bring the onion and broth to a boil over medium-high heat and cook until onions are soft, about 4–5 minutes. Add beans and continue boiling until the liquid has reduced to all but a couple tablespoons. Remove from heat and add the remainder of ingredients. Mash with a potato masher to desired consistency or transfer to a food processor to puree to desired consistency. Cover and refrigerate until needed.

You can alternately use 3 cups dried pinto beans (or beans of your choosing) and place in a slow cooker with 8 cups liquid and remainder of ingredients. Set it on high and forget about it for the next 6 hours or so. When beans are soft, remove, then let cool before transferring to a food processor or mashing by hand.

New England Couscous

Although a noted ingredient in many Middle Eastern recipes and mostly associated with Israel, couscous is, in fact, an original from Africa.

1 (15-ounce) can whole
    tomatoes in juice
2 cups clam juice
½ small onion, minced
3 tablespoons fresh basil,
    chopped and divided
1 cup whole wheat couscous
1 cup water
2 (6-ounce) cans chopped
    clams, including juice
1 teaspoon sugar
Couple dashes of hot
    pepper sauce
Salt and black pepper to taste
Fresh basil leaves, chopped
    for garnish

In the bowl of a food processor or blender, place the whole tomatoes and juice, clam juice, onion, and 2 tablespoons chopped basil. Pulse until the tomatoes are minced very fine.

Transfer to a large saucepan and add couscous, water, juice from the canned clams, sugar, and hot pepper sauce. Stir until combined and place pot over medium-high heat. When boiling, reduce heat to low, cover, and simmer 8–10 minutes, or until the couscous has plumped up and cooked. Remove from heat, stir well, adding the chopped clams and seasoning to taste. Serve with freshly chopped basil leaves on top.

SERVES 4

Polpo Ventoso

I must credit a certain Gayle Bailey (yup, another gorgeous member of my family) as the inspiration behind this recipe. My children never knew they were eating octopus until after they finished. The idea came from one of Gayle's many culinary stories from the various countries where she has traveled. In Italy, she learned to put something in her tomato sauce that she now finds indispensable: Grated lemon rind! I had to experiment, and on the first try I realized the sauce was perfectly balanced. This recipe combines that sauce with the great taste of seafood and the kick of a little chile oil: It is spot-on.

This recipe is aptly named for the lady who inspired it. Translating the title may take a little out-of-the-box thinking, but I think you will get it.

12 ounces linguine
2 tablespoons chile oil*
½ pound sliced octopus**
1 sweet bell pepper, seeded
    and diced
2 cups tomato sauce
1 cup low-fat ricotta cheese
1 teaspoon grated lemon zest
½ teaspoon chopped basil
Salt and black pepper to taste

Cook pasta according to package directions; set aside in strainer. In a small bowl, whisk together the tomato sauce, ricotta cheese, grated lemon zest, and basil. Season to taste with salt and pepper, then set aside.

Over medium heat, heat the chile oil in a large skillet until hot. Add the prepared octopus and cook for 4–5 minutes, or until just cooked through and slightly seared. Add the bell pepper and continue cooking an additional 2 minutes, stirring frequently. Add tomato sauce mixture. Stir to combine and reduce heat to low. Cover and simmer 10 minutes.

Remove lid, add the pasta, and toss (or stir) to coat well. Be careful, since the pasta is now very dry and lumped together somewhat, carefully separate strands while tossing with the sauce. Serve hot.

*Chile oil: If you don't have any chile oil on hand, add 1 cup pure olive oil to a small saucepan with 2 teaspoons red pepper flakes. Turn heat to low and let oil and pepper flakes gently warm together for 5 minutes. Remove from heat, cool to room temperature, and transfer to a container with a lid if not using immediately. This will keep very well in the refrigerator for a month.

SERVES 4–6

**You can buy fresh baby octopus at your local supermarket or use frozen (but thawed), already sliced octopus (or squid) tentacles. I removed the "suckers" for my children but feel free to leave on.

Chicken Caprese Risotto

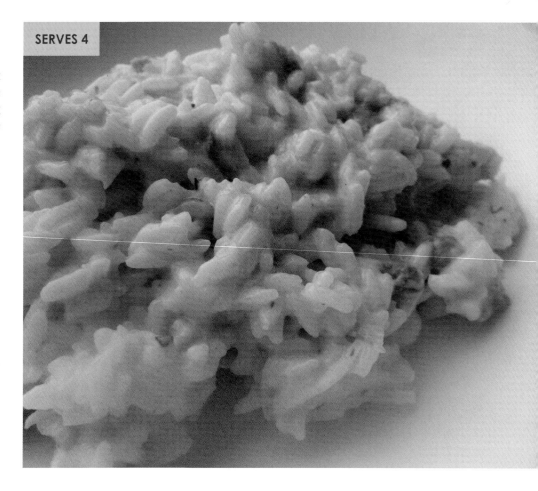

SERVES 4

I suggest prosciutto ham for this recipe but any ham, really, would make this recipe glorious. Don't be intimated by making risotto; it is fool-proof if you stand by the pan the entire time and follow directions.

3 tablespoons plain yogurt
1 tablespoon skim milk
4 cups fat-free chicken broth
2 tablespoons pure olive oil
8–10 ounces chicken breast, chopped small
2 ounces dry cured ham of your choice, chopped
1½ cups short grained rice
2 small plum tomatoes, seeded and chopped
½ cup shredded part-skim mozzarella cheese
2 teaspoons chopped, fresh basil (or 1 teaspoon dried)
Salt and black pepper to taste

In a small bowl, stir together yogurt and milk; set aside. In a saucepan, heat chicken broth until just below boiling.

In a large saucepan, heat olive oil over medium-high. When shimmering hot, add chicken and cook for 4–5 minutes, or until cooked through.

Add ham and rice to saucepan with chicken, stirring to combine well. While continuously stirring, add ½ cup hot broth and continue stirring and cooking until it is absorbed by the rice. Add another ½ cup and repeat. Continue until all the hot broth is absorbed, about 15 minutes total time. Stir in the tomatoes, cheese, yogurt mixture and basil. Remove from heat, season to taste with salt and pepper, and serve immediately.

Lobster Fried Rice, New England Style

SERVES 4

Such a treat to enjoy lobster in every conceivable manner. What is nice about this recipe, besides the taste, is the fact that it makes more than enough for two meals or four sides, without spending a fortune on lobster. What other dish lets you use only six ounces of lobster meat to feed four and still taste the sea in every bite?

3 tablespoons pure olive oil

2 garlic cloves, peeled
    and crushed

¼ cup onion, minced

¼ cup soy sauce

2 tablespoons plus 1 teaspoon
    brown sugar

½ cup frozen baby lima
    beans, thawed

3 cups rice, cooked

1 egg, beaten

6 ounces cooked lobster
    meat, chopped

¼ teaspoon black pepper

You may use egg substitute for whole eggs in all these recipes. Remember that it takes 3 whole eggs for each ½ cup measure of egg substitute. Use 3 tablespoons egg substitute for 1 egg. If you choose to use egg powder, use 2 tablespoons egg powder mixed with 2 tablespoons warm water to equal 1 egg.

In a large skillet, or wok, over medium-high heat, heat oil to shimmering. Add garlic and cook 1 minute, constantly stirring. Add onion and continue cooking until onion is soft, about 3 minutes. Add soy sauce, brown sugar, and lima beans. Stir-fry for 2 minutes. Add rice and cook, while constantly stirring to combine well, until the rice is heated through, about another 3 minutes. Make a hole in the center of the rice, add the egg and stir with a fork until it is scrambled completely. Mix it in with the rice mixture with a spoon or spatula to thoroughly combine, along with lobster and pepper. Cook until heated through. Remove from heat to serve immediately.

Pronounced *yag-a-see*, this dish is packed with protein. For those of you who are unfamiliar with preparing summer squash or zucchini, there is no need to peel either. As for the seeds, that is entirely a personal option. Some folks can't tolerate them and some have no issues. Gas and irritable bowel syndrome are the two major factors in processing these seeds.

Tempting Jagasse

Not many people know, or have even heard of, Jagasse. In the early 1800s, fishermen along the Massachusetts coast were also farmers in their non-fishing time. Of course their families had their fill of fish in meals and this dish gave them a subtle hint of the ocean while enjoying the bounty of the garden as well. They used whole fish in their Jagasse, but just the hint of the ocean is all that is needed in this delicious, original Yankee Jagasee recipe.

Nonstick cooking spray
2 ounces thinly sliced capicola
    ham, diced
1 cup fish broth or clam juice
½ small summer squash, diced
½ small zucchini, diced
1 cup whole kernel corn
½ cup red bell pepper, minced
¼ cup onion, minced
1 cup navy beans, cooked
2 cups rice, cooked
1 (15-ounce) can
    tomato sauce
1 teaspoon garlic powder
1 teaspoon onion powder
½ teaspoon red pepper flakes
Salt and black pepper to taste

Liberally grease the bottom of a large pot with nonstick cooking spray and place over medium heat. Add diced ham and cook until crisp, about 3–4 minutes. Add fish broth. Boil for 3 minutes before adding the squash, zucchini, corn, red bell pepper, and onion. Stirring occasionally, cook until the vegetables are just barely tender, about 6–8 minutes. Add beans, rice, tomato sauce, garlic and onion powders, red pepper, and salt and pepper to taste. Stir to combine and continue cooking until everything is heated through.

SERVES 4

Sticky Sweet and Smoky Rice Pilaf

I don't know if "sticky sweet" should really refer to a rice pilaf, but this side dish is truly a great combination of sweet and salty, which is what everyone and their mother is into nowadays. New England palates have been enjoying the combination of these two tastes since we first began adding salt to our apples. Heck, we have been adding salt to crab-apples for generations, yet another combination of sour and salty.

I love this recipe and I think you will enjoy my touch of sweet maple syrup saddling right up alongside the smoky flavor of bacon.

What to enjoy with this? I think some spicy grilled chicken, some poached firm-fleshed white fish or even as is, with a side of pickled vegetables.

1 tablespoon pure olive oil
½ onion, minced
2 cups rice
2 slices homemade bacon, minced (see recipe on page 140)
¼ cup maple syrup or honey
4 cups fat-free chicken broth
1 cup frozen peas
Salt and black pepper to taste

In a large saucepan, over medium heat, add the oil until hot. When ready, stir in the onion and cook until soft, about 3-4 minutes. Add the rice and homemade bacon and continue to cook an additional minute, stirring well. Add the maple syrup, stir to combine and cook an additional 2 minutes. Add broth and peas, bring to a boil, reduce heat to low and cover. Simmer for 30 minutes. Do not remove lid! At the end of 30 minutes, lift the lid to make sure all liquid has been absorbed. Fluff with a fork, season with salt and pepper to taste and serve hot.

SERVES 4

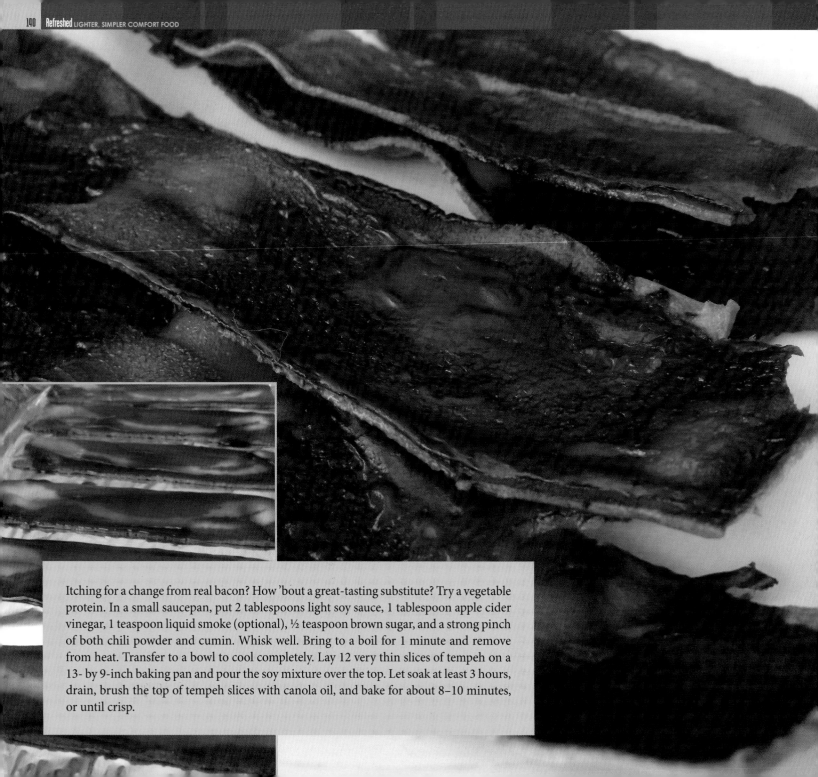

Itching for a change from real bacon? How 'bout a great-tasting substitute? Try a vegetable protein. In a small saucepan, put 2 tablespoons light soy sauce, 1 tablespoon apple cider vinegar, 1 teaspoon liquid smoke (optional), ½ teaspoon brown sugar, and a strong pinch of both chili powder and cumin. Whisk well. Bring to a boil for 1 minute and remove from heat. Transfer to a bowl to cool completely. Lay 12 very thin slices of tempeh on a 13- by 9-inch baking pan and pour the soy mixture over the top. Let soak at least 3 hours, drain, brush the top of tempeh slices with canola oil, and bake for about 8–10 minutes, or until crisp.

The Best Frying Oil?

I am constantly asked what the best oil for deep-frying is, and I think this is a topic that really has no easy answer.

First, even if you are on a low-fat diet, you don't need to skip fried foods as long as they are cooked correctly and you have a great oil. But choosing one particular type of frying oil over another is a tough decision because of the varying results from hundreds of world-wide research studies over the past 20 years alone.

In short: The three criteria that should be taken into account are a neutral taste (so flavor transfer is kept at a minimum); high smoke point (so oxidation doesn't occur rapidly, turning oil rancid); and a high oleic acid percentage.

Oleic acid, more commonly known as Omega-0, is a monounsaturated fatty acid. Oils containing monounsaturated fat are typically liquid at room temperature and begin turning solid when refrigerated. These fatty acids help reduce your bad cholesterol which, in turn, lowers your risk of heart disease and stroke. These acids also give our cells key nutrients, such as antioxidants to ward off diseases, including cancer.

The highest amounts of monounsaturated fats (oleic acids) are found in avocados, almonds, olives, hazelnuts, herring, peanut butter, olive oil, and even nonstick cooking sprays.

Believe it or not, lard (beef tallow) and goose fat (the fancy part of foix gras) are very rich in oleic acids. Closely following are palm and peanut oils.

Some oils on the market are further processed to give them a higher oleic acid percentage. For example, while sunflower oil usually has an average amount of oleic acid (50–60%), you are now able to find sunflower oils with over 75% oleic acid.

Here are my choices for the best of the best for deep-frying foods.

1. High oleic canola oil
2. High oleic sunflower oil
3. Safflower oil
4. Soybean oil
5. Peanut oil

Now why have I chosen canola oil above the rest, even though I haven't mentioned it once on this page? Because canola oil has the highest oleic fatty acid percentage, the highest stability against oxidation (which quickly breaks down oil) and the lowest saturated fat content.

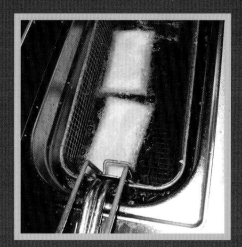

CHAPTER 5 Fish and Seafood

Although most of the literature involving fish and seafood in our diet concentrates on the benefits of Omega-3, there has also been talk for years about the negative effects of mercury consumption. After researching the benefits versus the pitfalls of each, I believe the risk is far below the value, so we should not avoid fish or seafood.

Organizations such as the International Agency for Research on Cancer (IARC) and the World Health Organization (WHO) study breast cancer incidents across different regions of the world. In regions where fish and seafood are consumed in greater amounts, there tends to be a lower rate of breast cancer. While these are not cause- and-effect studies, there does seem to me to be a link.

Take these examples from the AICR:

- Here in the US, there are 95 incidents of breast cancer out of every 100,000, while in South-Central and Eastern Asia, the incidents are below 20.
- Women in the US have about a 12% risk of getting breast cancer in their lifetime while in South Central and Eastern Asia the risk is about 3½%.

Easy As Paella

I could go on and on about different types of paella and many of these include well over twenty ingredients, with one of them being saffron. Saffron is so expensive I often substitute either the same amount of turmeric or even simply yellow curry powder. Granted the flavor may be a little different than saffron-infused recipes, but it is great tasting in its own right. As for the pan? Many Spanish chefs will tell you to *always* use a paella pan. These round, metal pans are about two and a half inches deep and are made to spread the heat evenly over hot coals, which is the traditional way of making paella. They also have two handles and come in generally two sizes, 9 inch and 12 inch. You have the equivalent at home in the form of a cast-iron skillet. Same thing, believe it or not. If you don't have either, simply use a skillet of your choice.

SERVES 4

3 (15-ounce) cans fat-free chicken broth

1 (8-ounce) bottle clam juice

1 teaspoon turmeric

1 teaspoon paprika

1 tablespoon oil

2 garlic cloves, peeled and crushed

1 link chicken sausage, sliced ½-inch thick

1 small onion, peeled and minced

1 small bell pepper, seeded and minced

1¾ cups rice

1 cup diced, canned tomatoes with juice

1 cup frozen peas

6 clams, scrubbed clean

6 mussels, scrubbed and debearded

8 (41–50 count or similar size) peeled shrimp

Combine broth, clam juice, turmeric, and paprika in a large pot and bring to a light boil over medium heat. Reduce heat to low and continue simmering while preparing the rest of the recipe.

Heat oil in a large skillet over medium heat. Add garlic and sausage, cook 2–3 minutes, or until sausage is just done. Add onion and pepper and cook 1–2 minutes or until vegetables are just starting to turn soft. Add rice and cook 2 minutes, stirring frequently. Add tomatoes with juice, peas, and the hot broth mixture. Reduce heat to low and simmer, covered, for 12–14 minutes or until the rice has absorbed all liquid. Do not stir.

Remove lid and add the clams, mussels, and shrimp. Replace lid and continue cooking an additional 5–7 minutes, or until the shells open, discarding any unopened shells. Remove from heat and serve immediately.

Salmon Cornbread Sandwiches

Don't, I repeat, *don't* be afraid of this ingredient list! If you take a quick peek at the items, most likely you will already have everything on hand. With that said, enjoy what I think is the perfect sandwich-meal.

4 squares cornbread, roughly
    4–5 inches square
Butter-flavored nonstick
    cooking spray
1 (7-ounce) can
    salmon, drained
¼ cup frozen peas, thawed
2 tablespoons low-fat
    mayonnaise
½ cup cracker crumbs
3 egg whites, lightly beaten
1 teaspoon lemon juice
1 teaspoon chives
1 tablespoon cracked
    black pepper

For the *Yanked* Egg Sauce:

2 teaspoons cornstarch
2 teaspoons water
1 cup 2% milk
1 teaspoon Dijon-style mustard
    (or yellow mustard)
½ teaspoon salt
¼ teaspoon black pepper
1 teaspoon minced water
    chestnuts, optional
1 hard-boiled egg, peeled and
    chopped

Split cornbread squares horizontally and liberally coat each cut side with nonstick cooking spray. Preheat a skillet over medium heat and place cornbread squares into skillet, sprayed-side down. Grill until crisp, about 3 minutes. Remove from heat and set aside, keeping skillet handy.

Remove bones and skin from salmon. In a large bowl, combine salmon with next 6 ingredients until well combined. The mixture should be quite dry. If need be, add a tablespoon of cracker crumbs at a time to make it just dry enough to hold together.

Taking a ball at a time, shape the salmon mixture to make 4 patties. Evenly sprinkle both sides of each patty with the cracked pepper.

Over medium-high heat, spray a large skillet with nonstick cooking spray and grill salmon patties until crisp, about 3–4 minutes. Flip and repeat cooking process.

Remove from skillet and place one patty on the bottom half of the grilled cornbread. Top with warm Egg Sauce and place the top half of the cornbread to close. Serve warm with coleslaw and that, my friends, is good eating.

To make the *Yanked* Egg Sauce:

In a small bowl, whisk cornstarch and water until smooth to make a slurry; set aside.

Mix milk, mustard, salt and pepper in a saucepan. Over medium heat, and whisking almost constantly, bring to scalding. Slowly whisk in slurry and continue cooking and whisking until thickened and smooth, another minute. Remove from heat and stir in water chestnuts and egg.

MAKES 4 SERVINGS

Baked Haddock, Tandoori Style

Not quite in the style of tandoori, which refers to a method of cooking in a tandoor oven, or clay pot, this is a great recipe nonetheless. Garam masala is a blend of spices that is never prepared the same: You could have tandoori food in one stall at a Malaysian food court and the very next one will be entirely different, in heat, flavor, and color.

3 tablespoons garam masala*
2 (8-ounce) haddock fillets
1 cup plain yogurt
Nonstick cooking spray
1 large onion, peeled and
    thickly sliced
1 large cucumber, peeled and
    sliced into thin ribbons with
    a vegetable peeler
½ teaspoon cracked
    black pepper
½ teaspoon cayenne pepper
    or chili powder
1 lemon, optional

Sprinkle garam masala on both sides of haddock. Place yogurt in a bowl and dip each haddock fillet into yogurt, evenly coating both sides. Place on a plate, cover with film wrap, and refrigerate 12 hours.

Preheat oven to 350° F. Coat the bottom of a baking pan with nonstick cooking spray. Layer the onion slices without overlapping. Remove haddock from yogurt mixture and lay on top of onion slices. Bake 20–25 minutes, or until haddock flakes easily.

Meanwhile, toss the cucumber with cracked black pepper and cayenne pepper. Divide cucumber ribbons onto 2 serving plates. Remove haddock from oven to finish plating. You can keep the cooked onion with the haddock or omit them when plating. Serve immediately with wedges of lemon.

SERVES 2

Make your own version of garam masala by mixing 1 teaspoon each of garlic powder, dried ginger, dried coriander, cayenne pepper, black pepper, and salt with ½ teaspoon each of cinnamon, ground cardamom, and ground cloves.

Homemade Hot Smoked Salmon

There is a tendency among chefs and home cooks alike to avoid putting fish on the grill but this preparation is different. By following a few easy steps, you will be eating like the bigwigs at formal, catered luncheons but on your picnic table with the kids running around.

For a gas grill, you will need to take 2 cups soaked wood chips and securely encase them in a large sheet or two of aluminum foil, making sure the seam is upright. Poke a few holes in the top with a pencil.

Place this pouch directly over a high flame in your outdoor grill until you see smoke coming from the pouch. Reduce heat to the lowest possible setting and only have on one row of flames.

Place a 6-ounce salmon fillet on a piece of tinfoil that has been lightly sprayed with nonstick cooking spray. Place this on top of a small wire rack that has, in turn, been placed on top of of a small, 2-inch sided pan half filled with water. Put this on the grill grate as far from the heat source as possible. Close the lid, and close all vent holes. Turn heat off and allow salmon to smoke for 30 minutes, or until it flakes easily with a fork. Remove to serve.

If you want to buy a larger, 2-pound salmon fillet, understand that you will first need to debone it with a small set of pliers or have your fishmonger do it for you.

SERVES 4

Fantastic Fatty Acids

Omega-3 fatty acids are known to lower your risk of heart disease. According to Jamie Stern, MS, Omega-3 is an essential fatty acid that our bodies need but can't make.

A quick way to know which fish have high Omega-3 levels is by looking at the color of the fish flesh: Darker flesh generally has higher amounts than the leaner, lighter colored fish, such as cod, haddock, and flounder.

Sardines have almost 2,000g per 3-ounce serving. Wild herring, farmed Atlantic salmon, wild king salmon, and wild mackerel have in excess of 1,500 mg per 3-ounce cooked servings.

Most health organizations suggest getting 300-500 mg per day of Omega-3s, while the American Heart Association recommends 1,000 mg a day for those with coronary heart disease. But you don't have to consume only fish to get your Omega-3s; significant amounts are found in everything from walnuts to basil to ham.

Hot Smoked Salmon with Tropical Salsa

Either follow the recipe for Hot Smoked Salmon (page 149) or simply purchase it from the store. Cold smoked salmon works especially great in this recipe as well.

2 plum tomatoes, seeded
    and diced
1 cup pineapple, diced
½ red onion, minced
½ cup fresh cilantro, chopped
2 tablespoons roasted bell
    pepper, chopped
2 garlic cloves, peeled
    4and crushed
1 hot pepper of your choice,
    seeded and minced
Juice and grated zest of 1 lime
4 (6-ounce) hot smoked
    salmon fillets

Mix the first 8 ingredients together in a bowl, cover, and refrigerate at least 2 hours before topping the Hot Smoked Salmon evenly.

If you are using cold smoked salmon, slice it very thin on the bias lengthwise and wrap it around the salsa, holding it all together with a toothpick. Serve very cold.

SERVES 4

Bar Harbor Smoked Pâté

Although pâté is typically smooth, I enjoy the slivers of smokiness that are ever-present in the Bar Harbor brand sardines. If you want it smooth, all you have to do is process another few seconds. Simple, huh? Enjoy it in a bowl and shared with toasted french bread or crackers.

MAKES ABOUT 1 CUP

1 (6.7-ounce) Bar Harbor®
   All-Natural Hardwood
   Smoked Atlantic Mackerel
⅓ cup ricotta cheese,
   drained well
2 tablespoons low-fat
   mayonnaise or
   salad dressing
2 tablespoons minced
   cucumber
1 teaspoon lemon juice
½ teaspoon red pepper flakes
1 tablespoon snipped chives
Large pinch of black pepper

In a bowl, stir together mackerel, ricotta cheese, mayonnaise, cucumber, lemon juice, red pepper, and chives until well combined and the mackerel has broken up.* Spoon into bowl, cover, and refrigerate until serving.

*If you would like a pâté that can be sliced, simply double the amounts in this recipe and add 2 beaten egg whites. Transfer to 2 greased muffin cups in a 6 cup muffin tin. Bake 15–20 minutes, or until firm and set. Remove from oven to cool slightly before transferring to a plate. Slice and serve on your favorite toasted bread or crackers.

Potato-Crusted Salmon Fillets

SERVES 4

I just cannot say enough about this recipe. The crisp potato crust reminds me of spicy french fries.

Nonstick cooking spray
1 large potato, cooked until tender, cooled
1 carrot, peeled and cooked until tender, cooled
Salt and black pepper to taste
2 teaspoons horseradish
1 teaspoon prepared mustard
4 (6-ounce) salmon fillets
2 tablespoons yogurt

Preheat oven to 400° F. Grease a baking pan with nonstick cooking spray.

Using the largest holes in your hand-held grater, grate both the potato and carrot into a large bowl. Add salt, pepper, horseradish, and mustard, combining well.

Very lightly coat each side of each fillet with yogurt. Press the potato/carrot mixture onto both sides of each fillet and place onto prepared baking sheet. Bake 15–17 minutes, or until the topping is crisp. If the fish is done but it still isn't as crispy as you would like it on top, turn off oven and turn on the broiler. Place the fish at least 3 inches from the heat source and broil for a couple of minutes until it is crispy. Remove to serve immediately.

Poached Haddock with Carrot Ginger Sauce

Talk about flavor and good, clean tastes. The ocean-tinged haddock shines through and is not muddled or lost in the deliciously fruity, spicy zest of the sauce.

1 tablespoon pure olive oil
1 small leek, sliced thin
1 tart apple, peeled, cored,
    and roughly chopped
4 carrots, peeled and sliced
1 teaspoon fresh ginger,
    peeled and grated
1 cup water
½ cup milk
½ cup plain yogurt
1 tablespoon lemon juice
¼ teaspoon curry powder
4 (6-ounce) haddock fillets
Chopped fresh or dried basil
    leaves, for garnish

In a medium saucepan, heat the oil over medium-high heat. When hot, add leek and apple, stirring to combine. Cook and stir until apple is tender. Add carrots and ginger, stirring to combine. Cook 2 minutes, add water, cover, and reduce heat to low. Simmer until the carrots are very tender, about 10–12 minutes or more, adding more water if needed. But don't overdo it, we want the carrot mixture to be as dry as possible when they are done. Uncover, remove from heat and carefully transfer to a food processor, or blender in batches.

Add the milk, yogurt, lemon juice, and curry powder to the carrot mixture. Puree on high until smooth; keep carrot ginger sauce warm.

Meanwhile, poach haddock by placing the fillets in a large skillet with an inch of water. Bring to a light boil over medium heat, reduce to low, cover, and simmer until fish just starts to flake, about 3 minutes, according to the thickness.

Ladle equal amounts of carrot ginger sauce into the center of 4 serving plates. Lift out haddock from poaching liquid, drain excess water, and place on top of sauce, garnishing with additional cooled carrots and basil leaves if desired. Serve immediately.

SERVES 4

Farmers Market Oyster Ceviche

This simple and perfect ceviche rivals any I've found prepared by a master chef. The only hard part may be the shucking. To avoid this, if you'd like, buy oysters in its own liquor, already shucked.

6 large fresh oysters, opened
    and shucked, liquor saved
¼ red onion, minced
1 tomato, seeded
    and chopped
1 jalapeño chili, seeded
    and minced
1 garlic clove, peeled
    and crushed
2 tablespoons fresh
    cilantro, shredded
½ cup fresh corn kernels,
    uncooked (from 1 ear)
5 limes, juiced
½ tablespoon pure olive oil
1 teaspoon hot pepper sauce
    (like Tabasco brand)

Chop oysters and add to oyster liquor in a bowl. Add remaining ingredients, and toss to combine well. Cover and refrigerate 1 hour so it gets very cold. Serve immediately.

SERVES 2–3

First, place your oysters in the freezer for 30 minutes. This makes shucking tremendously easier. Then, hold an oyster in your hand with a glove or towel to prevent slipping, with the rounded side facing down and the hinge facing toward you. Insert a blunt, sturdy, short-bladed knife into the hinge. Twist the knife to separate both sides of the shell. You will hear the suction let go when doing so. Now run the blade of the knife along the entire perimeter of the oyster, ending at the opposite side from where you started. You may need to continue twisting the knife.

Remember *not* to apply too much pressure because of injury. Just keep twisting your knife until it opens. Try to keep from breaking the shell into pieces that may enter the oyster meat, making for an uncomfortable dining experience. Keep the oyster flat at all times to retain its liquor. Once opened, run the knife along the bottom of the oyster meat to separate it from the shell entirely.

t are the differences between green onions, scallions and chives? Green onions and
ons are of the same genus and species and they stay small without forming a large
If harvested early enough and before the bulb is formed, the regular cooking onion
e sold as a green onion as well, also called a spring onion.

Chives are a different genus, *Allium*, which also includes garlic, shallots, and leeks.
s are confused with scallions many times when they are harvested very young. Leeks
rmer than scallions, however, and with a milder flavor.

Yankee Smoked Oysters and Fettuccine

My inspiration for this dish comes from summertime fare, healthy thinking, and the Italian favorite of carbonara. I wanted the flavor of carbonara, with a simple twist and the smell and taste of the rocky shoreline. I think you will enjoy the simple substitutions that take away some of the guilty pleasure of cream (found in carbonara). I think the subtle flavor of spinach is perfect with the sweet, briny taste of oysters. I use two-color fettuccine but feel free to substitute your own favorite pasta.

1 (8.8-ounce) package of
    2-color fettuccine
1 cup evaporated skim milk
3 egg whites, slightly beaten
½ cup parmesan
    cheese, grated
2 tablespoons chives, chopped
2 tablespoons pure olive oil
2 garlic cloves, peeled
    and crushed
¼ cup red bell pepper, roasted
    and diced
½ pound smoked oysters
Salt and black pepper to taste

In a large pot, cook the fettuccine according to package directions. Leave in colander while preparing remainder of recipe.

Meanwhile, in a large bowl, beat the milk, egg whites, cheese, and chives together well: set aside.

In a large skillet, heat the oil until shimmering over medium-high heat, about 1–2 minutes. Add garlic and red bell peppers and cook about 10 seconds, stirring constantly. Add the egg mixture and bring to scalding while constantly stirring. Gently stir in the oysters and add the fettuccine, tossing until combined. Season to taste. Remove to serving plate and serve immediately.

SERVES 2

Thai Seaside Appetizers

Thailand is known for its spices . . . and I mean spices. The hotter, the . . . well, hotter. I have toned down the heat so that the taste of Atlantic clams shines through. Mollusk shells are easily found in any craft store but if you have trouble finding them, this recipe is easily adaptable by serving it in small romaine leaves or large, crisp basil leaves.

3 tablespoons chile oil*
3 garlic cloves, peeled
    and crushed
½ teaspoon dried ginger
1 tablespoon soy sauce
Juice and grated zest
    from 1 lemon
1 cup cole slaw mix
¼ small red bell pepper,
    diced small
¼ small green bell
    pepper, minced
2 (6-ounce) cans chopped
    clams, drained
1 cup plain white or sticky rice,
    cooked and kept warm
14–16 clean clam, mussel, or
    scallop shells or romaine
    leaves or large basil leaves

In a large skillet, heat chili oil over medium heat until shimmering. Add garlic and cook 1 minute, stirring frequently. Add the ginger, soy sauce, and juice and zest from the lemon. Stir to combine, then raise the temperature to medium-high and add cole slaw mix along with both peppers. Combine and stir-fry 3–4 minutes, or until heated through and just starting to soften. Add the clams and mix well. Remove from heat.

Serve immediately with clam mixture in one half of the clam shell and rice in the other.

*To make your own chile oil, see the recipe for Polpo Ventoso, page 133.

SERVES 14–16

Iron Boost

A 3-ounce serving of cooked clams has about 25 milligrams of iron. The RDA is 18 per day for pre-menopausal women and only eight for adult men and post-menopausal women.

Clams Casino, the New England Way

Although I am proud of the Rhode Island roots of clams casino, I wanted to take a gamble. Are you ready to roll the dice? I have revamped this recipe for a much healthier version and one that you would be proud to serve at any formal or informal gathering. I use clams from Maine's Bar Harbor foods, which boasts some amazing products, many of which you won't find anywhere else (barharborfoods.com).

4 squares prepared cornbread
Butter-flavored nonstick
    cooking spray
⅓ cup onions, diced
⅓ cup red bell pepper
1 (10.5-ounce) can Bar Harbor®
    New England Style White
    Clam Sauce
¼ cup parmesan cheese,
    grated
3 ounces smoked, low-fat deli
    ham, diced small
1 (6.5-ounce) tin Bar Harbor®
    Whole Cherrystone
    Clams, drained
Salt and black pepper to taste

Put a square of cornbread on each of 4 serving plates.

Coat the bottom of a large skillet with nonstick cooking spray and place over medium heat. Add onions and bell pepper, cooking until they are tender but still crisp, stirring occasionally. Add the clam sauce, parmesan cheese, and ham. Bring to boil, reduce heat to low, and simmer 8 minutes, stirring once or twice. Add clams and season to taste. Cook an additional minute or until the clams are heated through,

Heat the cornbread in the microwave until hot. Evenly divide clam mixture over each cornbread slice and serve immediately.

SERVES 4

Have some jicama left over? Simply snack on these no-fat, vitamin C-rich tubers throughout the day. Just know that the larger the jicama is, the more it tends to become woody to the taste, converting sugars to starches as it grows.

Spiced Shrimp with Grande Salsa

Although this recipe looks lengthy and time consuming, it is super simple. Mexico is renowned for fiery flavors but many don't realize that vanilla is just as much part of Mexican heritage as corn and jalapeños. This recipe is great when you want heat tempered by the natural flavors of vanilla and the subtle tinge of cilantro.

For the Mexican Poached Peaches:

1 cup orange juice
¼ cup honey
1 tablespoon pure
   vanilla extract
2 peaches, peeled, pitted
   and wedged

For the Marinated Shrimp:

1 pound jumbo shrimp, peeled
   and deveined
2 tablespoons soy sauce
2 tablespoons lime juice
½ teaspoon red pepper flakes

For the Grande Salsa:

1 small jicama, peeled and
   diced small (about 3 cups)
3 tablespoons fresh
   cilantro, minced
1 cup whole kernel corn
½ cup onion, minced
2 tablespoons red peppers in
   adobo sauce, chopped
1 tomato, seeded
   and chopped
2 tablespoons lime juice
½ teaspoon red pepper flakes

1 tablespoon pure olive oil

Prepare poached peaches: In a small saucepan, mix all poached peach ingredients over medium-high heat. Cook until peaches are softened but not mushy. Remove from stove and transfer to a bowl, cover, and refrigerate at least 3 hours, or until cold.

Prepare shrimp: When peeling shrimp, leave tail intact. Mix in large bowl along with soy sauce, lime juice and only ½ teaspoon red pepper flakes. Cover and refrigerate at least 1 hour.

Prepare salsa: Make the salsa by mixing all ingredients together well. Cover and refrigerate at least 1 hour.

To assemble: Place oil in a large skillet over medium-high heat until shimmering. Remove shrimp from marinade, blot dry, and cook about a minute per side, or until just done. Mound salsa evenly among 4 serving plates, top with peaches, and then equal amounts of salsa. Serve immediately.

SERVES 4

Surf and Turf Shooter

SERVES 4

This is a non-alcoholic appetizer that blends the fresh taste of the surf (lobster) with the garden freshness of cucumber (turf). If you would like to make this an alcoholic appetizer, pour this recipe into shot glasses, leaving enough room to splash an ounce or so of lemon-flavored vodka on top. How to enjoy? Shoot it! But don't forget to chew.

1 large cucumber, peeled, sliced in half lengthwise and then chopped roughly
1 teaspoon lemon juice
¼ teaspoon prepared horseradish, optional
Cold cooked lobster pieces, about 2–3 ounces
4 shakes red pepper sauce
Coarse or sea salt, to taste

Prepare cucumber juice: Put prepared cucumber into blender or food processor and pulse until as liquidy as possible, about 1–1½ minutes. Remove and strain through a coffee filter or cheesecloth that has been placed in a wire strainer. If you want a more pulpy juice, omit filtering. Gently press pulp to extract as much juice as possible. Whisk lemon juice and horseradish into juice until well blended. Freeze 10 minutes to get cold.

Meanwhile, divide lobster pieces among 4 shot glasses. Add cucumber juice to barely cover lobster (you will have juice left over). Sprinkle red pepper sauce into each glass along with a small sprinkle of coarse salt on top.

Creamy Clams Torta Rustica

Don't be fooled by the name: Torta usually means a type of bread or pastry, be it cornmeal, wheat, rye, or other grains. I have omitted this kind of crust and have replaced the usual ricotta cheese with a creamy French cheese. This delicious meal creates its own crispy brown crust.

4 cups cooked spaghetti,
　　or other pasta
½ cup evaporated skim milk
5 egg whites
½ teaspoon black pepper
6 ounces chopped
　　clams, drained
4 ounces chevre
　　cheese, grated*
3 tablespoons pure olive oil

SERVES 4

Chevre cheese is great in this dish, lending a mild, tangy flavor. Mix it up a bit and purchase flavored chevre. Or, substitute other goat milk cheeses, such as parmesan and romano or even havarti.

Drain spaghetti as well as you can, then let sit for 15 minutes to dry out.

In a large bowl, whisk milk, egg whites, and pepper together well. Fold in the spaghetti, clams, and lastly, the grated cheese.

Bring oil to shimmering hot over medium heat in a large 10- to 12-inch skillet. Give the spaghetti mixture one more stir to blend the cheese evenly throughout. Pour into hot skillet, reduce heat to low, cover, and simmer. You should see a slight bubbling all around the outside of the skillet in about 8–10 minutes. If not, raise heat to medium-low. Remove from heat once the center is set and the edges have attained a brown, crispy crust. Transfer to a serving plate and slice like a pizza. Serve hot.

*Place your cheese in the freezer for about 15 minutes, remove, and grate. This works with all soft cheeses you want to shred or grate.

Singapore Sweet Lobster

This uncommon, yet unbeatable fusion of lobster and Asian-inspired ingredients tastes great. And one peek at the directions, and you will see why my motto is *It's Just That Simple!*

¼ cup fish sauce
¼ cup pineapple juice
1 teaspoon sesame oil
½ teaspoon coriander
1 hot chili, seeded and minced
¼ teaspoon each black
      pepper and garlic powder
6 ounces cooked lobster meat,
      roughly chopped
½ cup frozen California-style
      vegetables, thawed
¼ cup cooked lima beans
¼ cup cooked, french-style
      green beans

In a small bowl, whisk the first 6 ingredients well. Add remainder of ingredients, tossing gently. Cover and refrigerate at least one hour before serving cold.

SERVES 2

Want to know more about lobsters? See my article, "FYI on Lobsters, Maine Lobster!" at theyankeechef.com.

What is this recent Greek yogurt craze about? Many people simply like the texture of G[...] yogurt over regular because the liquid whey, found in many regular yogurts, has been stra[...] out. This gets rid of the extra salts and sugars that have been dissolved in it, with the [...] a thicker, creamier, and denser yogurt. This also heightens the protein levels.

Smoky Picnic Lobster Sliders

For those of you seeking that perfect summertime slider, you have found it! Combining the heat of Chinese barbecue with the ever-loved tang of its American counterpart, these sliders also feature the flavor of New England. The cooling effect of this original tzatziki sauce will have you reaching for another, then another . . . If you are unable to find this lobster juice, add extra soy, chili sauce, and Worcestershire sauce to equal ¼-cup.

For the sauce:
1 red bell pepper, roasted
3 tablespoons Greek yogurt or
   sour cream
1 teaspoon lemon juice

For the patties:
12 ounces cooked
   lobster meat
2 tablespoons imitation
   bacon bits
1 cup cracker meal, divided
2 egg whites, beaten
¼ cup lobster stock
2 tablespoons soy sauce
3 tablespoons hot chili sauce
1 teaspoon lemon juice
1 teaspoon Worcestershire
   sauce
Pinch of red pepper flakes
Pinch of cracked black pepper

Nonstick cooking spray
8 yeast rolls

Prepare the tzatziki sauce: Mash 3 tablespoons roasted red bell pepper, well drained. Stir in 3 tablespoons Greek yogurt or sour cream and 1 teaspoon lemon juice. Refrigerate until needed.

Prepare the patties: In a large bowl, break apart the lobster meat. Add bacon bits, ⅔ cup cracker crumbs, egg whites, lobster stock, soy sauce, hot chili sauce, lemon juice, Worcestershire sauce and red and black pepper. Gently toss, form into 8 patties and refrigerate at least 30 minutes, covered.

When ready to cook, remove patties from refrigerator and dip in remainder of cracker crumbs, lightly coating each side to prevent sticking. Grease a large skillet liberally with nonstick cooking spray and place over medium heat. When hot, add patties and cook until crisp and lightly browned on both sides, 3–4 minutes per side. Add additional spray as needed. Serve on split yeast rolls and top with tzatziki sauce.

MAKES 8 SLIDERS

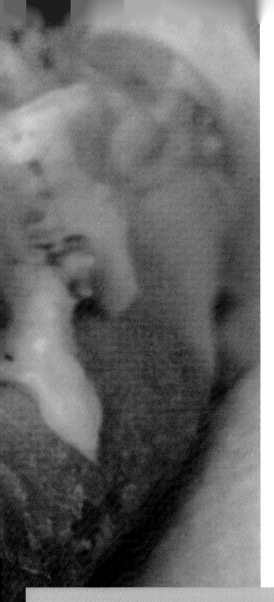

Warm Lobster Thermidor Rolls

A fantastic and different take on the fusion of two classics. *It's Just That Simple!*

Butter-flavored nonstick
    cooking spray
1 pound cooked lobster
    meat, chopped
1 teaspoon dried tarragon
½ teaspoon dried,
    snipped chives
¼ cup skim milk
1 teaspoon Dijon-style mustard
¼ cup parmesan cheese
Salt and black pepper to taste
1 cup plain yogurt
Juice and grated rind
    of 1 lemon
Hot dog rolls, toasted well
Shredded lettuce, optional

Liberally coat a large skillet with nonstick cooking spray and, over medium heat, add lobster, tarragon, and chives. Stir and cook until lobster is heated through. Blend in the milk and mustard. Continue cooking and stirring until most of the milk has been absorbed, about 3–5 minutes. Add the parmesan cheese and season to taste with salt and pepper.

In a bowl, whisk together the yogurt, lemon juice, and grated rind of the lemon.

To serve, layer some shredded lettuce in the bottom of each roll and equally divide the cooked lobster mixture. Drizzle lemon-flavored yogurt dressing over the top of each and serve immediately.

MAKES 2–4 ROLLS

What's the difference between hot dog rolls and hot dog buns? Almost as controversial and argumentative as the great New England vs. Manhattan Clam chowder debate, we here in New England are passionate about New England hot dog rolls. Unlike hot dog buns, they are crustless on the sides and stand up on their own because of the flat bottom and top slice. Frankfurter or hot dog buns have crust all around. Go ahead and fill each style with the Warm Lobster Thermador recipe and see which stands up without toppling over and spilling.

Shrimp Scampi Cakes with Sweet Tomato-Curry Sauce

With the possible powerful effects of garlic on certain types of cancer and the explosion of antioxidants such as lycopene, vitamins A and C found in tomatoes, I would not pass up the opportunity to introduce both into my diet as often as possible. This recipe is delicious as well.

3 egg whites, beaten lightly
1 cup crushed saltine crackers
½ cup fat-free vegetable broth
1 tablespoon dried, chopped basil (or 2 tablespoons freshly chopped basil)
1 tablespoon pure olive oil
3 garlic cloves, peeled and crushed
½ cup small onion, grated
1 pound small shrimp, such as Maine or Louisiana
Nonstick cooking spray

For the Sweet Tomato-Curry Sauce:
1½ cups plain yogurt
2 teaspoons cornstarch
1 garlic clove, peeled and crushed
1 medium tomato, seeded and chopped
½ teaspoon dried ginger
1 teaspoon curry powder
Salt and black pepper to taste

In a large bowl, combine egg whites, crushed saltines, broth and basil: set aside.

Add oil to a large skillet and place over medium-high heat. When hot, add garlic, cooking for 2 minutes, stirring frequently. Add onion and well drained shrimp. Continue cooking until onions are just tender and the shrimp is completely cooked through, about 4 minutes.

Add additional olive oil to prevent shrimp from sticking, or as needed. Remove from heat, drain any fat and add to crumb mixture, lightly mixing well. Cover and refrigerate at least 30 minutes.

Make Sweet Tomato-Curry Sauce: In a small bowl, whisk together the yogurt and cornstarch until well blended. Set aside. In a small saucepan, cook the garlic over medium heat, constantly stirring, until fragrant and softened, about 3–4 minutes. Add chopped tomato and continue cooking, and stirring occasionally, until tomatoes have broken down and are softened, about 3–4 minutes. Add ginger and curry, cooking and stirring for 15 seconds. Reduce heat to medium-low and add the yogurt mixture, blending well. Simmer and stir constantly until sauce is well blended and heated through, about 2 minutes. Remove from heat and season to taste with salt and pepper. Set aside.

When ready to cook, scoop out shrimp cakes in desired amounts. Use 2–3 tablespoons for mini cakes for luncheons or ½ cups for entrée-size cakes.

MAKES 12–14 MINI CAKES OR 6 ENTREE-SIZED CAKES

Liberally coat a large skillet with nonstick cooking spray and place over medium-high heat. Drop cake mounds in hot skillet and flatten with the underside of a spatula. Grill cakes over medium-high heat until well browned on both sides, about 4 minutes per side. Continue until all shrimp mixture is cooked, coating the skillet as needed with nonstick cooking spray. Serve hot or at room temperature with Sweet Tomato-Curry Sauce.

Spicy Shrimp Tostadas with Roasted Carrot Smash

There truly isn't anything more inviting than tasting fresh, sweet Maine shrimp.

2 pounds carrots, peeled
    and halved
6 (6-inch) tortillas, flour or corn
2 tablespoons honey
2 tablespoons lime juice
3 tablespoons pure olive oil
1 poblano chili pepper,
    seeded and minced
8 ounces small shrimp*
2 tablespoons chili powder
½ teaspoon salt
½ teaspoon black pepper
Low-fat sour cream, optional
Grated lime zest for garnish

SERVES 6

Preheat oven to 350° F. Place the carrots on a baking sheet and bake for 40-45 minutes, or until tender. When there is about 7–8 minutes remaining, add the tortillas directly on a middle rack and cook until crisp, about 6–7 minutes. The tortillas should be crisp yet a little pliable. When carrots are done, place in a large bowl with the honey and lime juice. Mash well, cover with film wrap, and set aside.

In a large skillet, heat oil over medium-high. Add the poblano pepper and cook 1 minute. Add the shrimp, chili powder, salt, and pepper. Saute, stirring constantly, until shrimp is cooked through, about 1 minute.

To assemble: Place crisp tortilla shells on 6 serving plates and mound an equal amount of smashed carrots on each. Top with equal amount of shrimp and top each with sour cream and grated lime zest.

* Larger, shelled and deveined shrimp are fine as well. Just dice small and follow recipe.

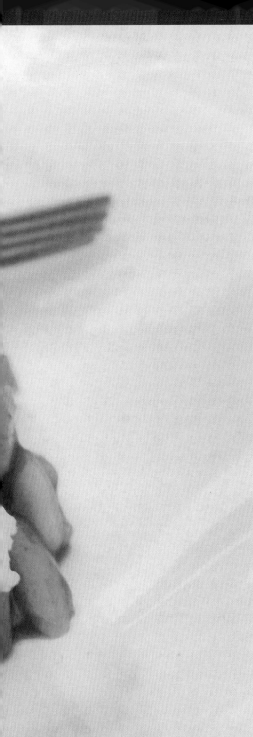

Mexican Orzo and Clams

Dried chilies give a uniquely piquant flavor to any recipe, but when you briefly toast them, their flavor really explodes. If you cook them too long, however, they become noticeably bitter. Try this fragrant hot tomato-chili sauce tossed with any pasta for an imaginative trip to the Southern Hemisphere.

2 dried chili peppers of
    your choice
½ cup hot, fat-free
    vegetable broth
1 garlic clove, peeled
    and crushed
½ teaspoon salt
½ (15-ounce) can diced
    tomatoes in juice
½ (15-ounce) can
    tomato sauce
1 (6-ounce) can tomato paste
1 teaspoon dried oregano
3 cups cooked orzo,
    kept warm
2 (6.5-ounce) cans chopped
    clams, drained well

Place a large skillet over medium-high heat. When hot, add the whole, dried chilies and toast for 15 seconds, then roll them over and toast for same amount of time, completely toasting the outside. Immediately remove from pan and let cool until you can handle them. Split each in half, lengthwise, removing the stem, seeds, and pith (the white membrane) and discard. If you want more heat, retain the seeds. Roughly chop and place in a bowl with the hot broth, garlic, and salt, mixing to combine. Let hydrate for 30 minutes.

Place the liquid and chilies in the bowl of a food processor or blender and pulse, on high, until size desired. Transfer to a large saucepan with diced tomatoes and juice, tomato sauce, tomato paste, and oregano. Blend well and bring to scalding over medium heat. When hot, remove, then add cooked orzo, 1 can chopped clams; stirring well. Divide among 3 serving plates, topped with additional hot, chopped clams and serve immediately.

SERVES 3

Seared Scallop Salpicon

I use sea scallops here but by all means, substitute bay if you want a sweeter, less expensive, taste. I have made this recipe time and time again on request and when you start digging in, you will be making it more often than not as well.

12 sea scallops, dry packed
1 mango, pitted, peeled,
    and diced
1 cup tomato, seeded and
    chopped
¼ cup onion, minced
¼ cup fresh cilantro, chopped
2 jalapeño peppers, seeded
    and thinly sliced
⅓ cup apple cider vinegar
1 tablespoon lime juice
1 teaspoon salt
½ teaspoon black pepper
1 small sweet potato, peeled,
    diced, and cooked
1 cup cream-style corn
Milk, as needed
Salt and black pepper to taste
2 tablespoons butter or
    margarine
1 strip turkey bacon, cooked
    and finely chopped

Wipe scallops with paper towels and set aside on a paper towel–lined plate in refrigerator until needed.

In a large bowl, toss together next 9 ingredients. Cover and refrigerate until needed.

Put potato and corn in a blender or bowl of a food processor. smooth as possible, about 1 minute on high. If you need to, add milk, a tablespoon at a time, until you have a puree. Season with salt and pepper to taste; cover with film wrap and set aside.

Add butter to a large skillet. Over medium-high heat, carefully place the scallops in hot butter and cook 2–3 minutes per side, or until well seared, browned, and just done.

To serve, place a quarter of the corn puree in the middle of each plate. Top with 3 seared scallops and equal amounts of the Salpicon mixture. Top with chopped bacon and serve.

SERVES 4

Why choose diver scallops? Scallops are harvested in different ways, according to many different factors. First let me explain that sea scallops are much larger, and less sweet, than bay scallops, although both are tremendously delicious.

Bay scallops can be caught either by dragging nets along the ocean floor or by using suspended nets. If you care about the environment and the future of fishing, please ask your fishmonger (or check the package if buying frozen scallops) to check on the harvesting technique and go with scallops caught with suspended nets. Nets that are dragged damage the habitat by scooping up *all* life forms from the sea floor.

As for sea scallops, these large bivalves are taken by either trawling or diving. I don't need to tell you that diver scallops will be more expensive but this is because they are hand selected for market.

One more note for scallop buyers: "Dry" simply means that they have never been frozen, making them probably the only type of scallop suitable for that perfect sear when grilling. Try using a "wet" (frozen then thawed) scallop for your searing. No matter how much you hand-dry them, it truly isn't the same.

Savory Spiced Scallops with Asparagus

Easy, quick, and delicious, this has the elements of a great entree. This recipe is also great with smaller, sweeter bay scallops—just watch the cooking time.

1 pound sea scallops
½ cup oatmeal powder*
2 tablespoons butter
    or margarine
2 garlic cloves, peeled
    and crushed
½ pound asparagus, cut into
    2-inch segments
½ cup fat-free vegetable broth
1 tablespoon lemon juice
1 tablespoon soy sauce
1 tablespoon chili sauce
½ cup carrots, cooked
    and sliced
1 tablespoon dried basil leaves
½ teaspoon dried ginger
½ teaspoon lemon rind, grated
2 cups rice, cooked and hot

Drain scallops well and toss with oatmeal powder; set aside.

Heat oil over medium heat in a large skillet. When butter has melted, carefully add the scallops and cook 3–4 minutes, turning over when one side is lightly browned. Remove with a slotted spoon onto a plate; set aside.

Cook garlic in skillet, stirring, for 1 one minute. Add asparagus, vegetable broth, lemon juice, soy sauce, and chili sauce. Mix well and bring to a boil. Add scallops back into the skillet, along with carrots, and continue cooking 1 additional minute. Remove from heat to blend in the basil, ginger, and lemon rind. Serve over hot rice.

*Take ¾ cup rolled oats and blend them in a food processor or blender until they form a powder.

SERVES 3

Summertime Outdoor Mussels

For an alternative, try these smoked by following the cooking instructions for Hot Smoked Salmon (page 149), but using this recipe instead, closing all dampers, and smoking for 30 minutes.

1 pound mussels, scrubbed and debearded

6 garlic cloves, peeled and crushed

3 ounces cooked, smoked ham of your choice, minced

1 teaspoon dried chives

½ teaspoon chili powder

1 cup dried bread crumbs, unseasoned

¼ cup parmesan cheese, grated

2 tablespoons apple jelly, slightly heated and whisked smooth

SERVES 2

Mussels are a type of shellfish related to scallops, oysters and clams, and because the method for farming them is environmentally sound, Monterey Bay Aquarium awards them a "best choice" in its Seafood Watch. And did you know that mussels can be found in many rivers as well? With species popularly called pigtoe, monkeyface, and maple leaf, they are almost indistinguishable from each other.

Preheat outdoor grill to medium heat.

Meanwhile, bring 1 cup water and garlic to boil over medium-high heat in a large saucepan. Add mussels, cover, and boil for 2 minutes, or until shells open completely. Carefully strain and allow mussels to cool enough to handle. Remove mussel meat from the shells, discarding any remaining beard found; set aside. Wash the shells clean and set aside. Chop mussel meat and add to a bowl with remainder of ingredients, mixing well. Equally divide the mussel mixture into as many halved mussel shells as able.

Carefully place filled shells onto grill grate over indirect heat. Close lid and cook 6-8 minutes, or until heated through and the top is starting to crisp. Remove and serve with lemon wedges if desired.

Spicy "Pickled" Mussels

I adore mussels no matter how they are prepared. Having a cold appetizer of tangy mussels mixed with beans and mushrooms is both super satisfying and a great preface to a seafood entree.

12 ounces shiitake mushrooms, cleaned and sliced
½ cup apple cider vinegar
1 teaspoon lemon juice
1 (15-ounce) can pinto beans, drained
12 ounces mussels, cooked and smoked*
¼ cup pure olive oil
2 tablespoons prepared mustard
1 teaspoon garlic powder
½ teaspoon dried oregano
¼ teaspoon allspice
¼ teaspoon red pepper flakes
Salt and black pepper to taste

MAKES ABOUT 3 CUPS

Put the mushrooms in a saucepan with vinegar and lemon juice. Bring to scalding over medium-high heat, stirring once. Immediately remove from heat, covering with tight-fitting lid, letting mushrooms steep until softened, about 5 minutes. Remove lid to cool 15 minutes before adding remainder of ingredients. Toss to combine, transfer to a bowl, cover, and refrigerate at least 2 hours. Serve cold.

*You can buy frozen, cooked, smoked mussels in 6-ounce containers at most supermarkets. They are also available in cans, but they are too soft to use here. You can also buy mussels in a shell for this recipe. Just scrub, debeard, cook, and shell before use.

CHAPTER 6 Meat and Poultry

Studies are still being done about the relationship between the consumption of meat and breast cancer. This truly is an argument with no answer . . . yet!

Some tremendously innovative and quite substantial research was conducted by Maryam Farvid (PhD, department of nutrition at the Harvard School of Public Health, Boston) and administered by the Nurses' Health Study II. It followed the dietary lives of nearly 90,000 women, aged 26–45, for a span of twenty years. The women were meticulously questioned about their eating habits, and it was found that those who ate above one and a half servings of red meat a day increased their breast cancer risk by nearly 25% compared to those who ate just one 3-ounce serving a week. It was also noticed that the culprit may be Heterocyclic Amines (HCAs), chemicals that form when meat is cooked fast and on high heat, such as hamburgers and steaks.

At the same time, the study seems to show that eating poultry may actually decrease the risk of breast cancer. Substituting one serving of poultry for one serving of red meat a day decreased the risk by 17% in premenopausal women and as much as 24% by postmenopausal women.

However, this study has its critics. Betsy Booren, vice president of scientific affairs at the American Meat Institute Foundation noted that the findings were "extremely weak" because the results were based on self-reporting and, therefore the study "doesn't add much to our current knowledge on this complex condition." And Dr. Stephanie Bernick, chief of surgical oncology at Lenox Hill Hospital at NYC has said that the results of the study are open to interpretation: "The women who ate less red meat may have a healthier lifestyle, and that reduces their risk of cancer. The increased risk tied to red meat might only stand in for other unhealthy behaviors. A healthy lifestyle can lower your risk of cancer in general."

While the potential link between breast cancer risk and the consumption of red meat has not been conclusively shown to exist, the American Institute for Cancer Research recommends eating no more than 18 ounces of red meat per week, including beef, pork, and lamb.

As Jamie Stern, MS, notes, "Humans are omnivores. This means we are well-suited to eat meat. Early man used to hunt and gather. Meat was a celebration or would help man survive long winters when there was little vegetation available for consumption. Meat, especially red meat, *is* high in saturated fat and protein but both are macro nutrients, essential for life."

Sunshine Sausage Barigoule

SERVES 3

Barigoule is a French Provençal stew-like dish traditionally prepared with wine and incorporating onions and carrots. I have replaced the wine with broth and added in a nutrient-rich yellow bell pepper. The consistency is also heartier than a stew, and I've used chicken sausage, a healthier choice.

1 tablespoon pure olive oil
3 garlic cloves, crushed
2 (99% fat-free) chicken
    sausage links, sliced
1 small carrot, peeled and
    slivered with peeler
1 sweet bell pepper, seeded
    and julienned
1 teaspoon dried basil leaves
¼ teaspoon celery or
    fennel seeds
¼ teaspoon crushed rosemary
½ cup fat-free beef or
    vegetable broth
8 ounces frozen artichoke
    hearts, thawed
Salt and black pepper to taste

In a large skillet over medium heat, add the olive oil and garlic. Cook, stirring frequently, for 2–3 minutes, or until garlic is softened and aromatic. Add the sausages, carrot, and bell pepper, cover and cook for 7–10 minutes or until the sausages are done and no longer pink in the middle. Remove cover and remove sausages.

Add basil, celery seeds, and rosemary to skillet and cook for 1–2 minutes. Add the broth and bring to a boil. Reduce heat to medium low and simmer until reduced and thickened, about 4–7 minutes, uncovered. Add the artichokes and sausage, tossing to combine with salt and pepper. Serve hot.

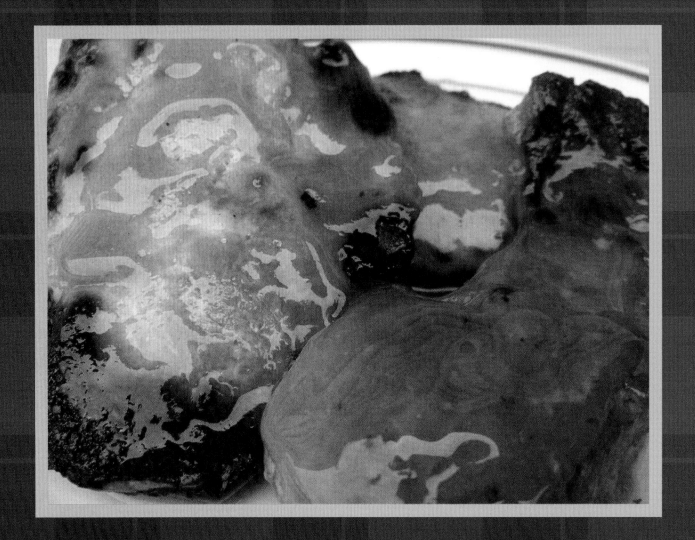

New England Quick Ribs

If you are unable to find the citrusy, orange blossom honey, clover honey will work perfectly. The difference? One comes from clover blossoms and is slightly less sweet than the other, which derives from the blossoms of orange trees.

1½ pounds pork
    tenderloin, trimmed
2 cups apple jelly
¼ cup orange blossom honey
3 tablespoons apple
    cider vinegar
2 tablespoons brown sugar
1 teaspoon black pepper
2 teaspoons prepared mustard
1 teaspoon garlic powder
½ teaspoon red pepper flakes
½ teaspoon chili powder

Throw the pork in the freezer for about 30 minutes, or until just partially frozen, which will help you slice it evenly. Remove and lay on a cutting surface. Slice pork into pieces about the size of half a playing card lengthwise and ¾-inch thick. Meanwhile, preheat grill to medium-high heat.

Make the glaze: In a bowl, combine remainder of ingredients and whisk until well combined.

Lay the pork on the grate of your grill and cook 1–2 minutes over indirect heat with the cover closed. Flip over and continue cooking an additional 1–2 minutes. Start basting with your glaze and continue cooking until meat is done, about another 4–5 minutes per side. Continue liberally basting on both sides. (Never mind what television chefs tell you about only flipping meat over only once; this is complete foolishness with meat this thin.) Remove from grill and enjoy with any remaining glaze drizzled over, heated of course.

SERVES 4

Vitamin B1's Boost

Vitamin B1 (a.k.a. thiamine and part of the B complex set of vitamins) is widely referred to as the "morale vitamin'" because it helps to control stress and nervousness and benefits mental attitude. The three important chemicals of your brain—serotonin, dopamine, and epinephrine—are reliant on Vitamin B1.

According to Shannon Clark, personal trainer, health and fitness guru and a contributing wellness and fitness writer for this book, of the top 10 vitamins everyone should have in their diet, Vitamin B1 is number one not only because of its tremendous ability to keep us "level-headed" but because it helps transform carb intake into usable energy.

Great sources of B1 include fish (trout and salmon are good choices), lean pork, seeds (such as sunflower and sesame), nuts, and wheat bread.

Spicy Beef with Corn Salad

Flank steak is considered lean because it comes from the section of the animal that is regularly exercised. I would still trim any excess connective tissue and fat from it, however. And as with all lean meat, flank steak should be cut on the bias, which is a fancy word for "at a slant."

¼ cup soy sauce
3 tablespoons maple syrup
3 tablespoons ketchup
1 (1-pound) flank
    steak, trimmed
½ red onion, sliced thinly
⅓ cup fresh cilantro, chopped
2 tablespoons lime juice
½ teaspoon green chili
    pepper, minced
1 tomato, chopped
1 cup baby corn, halved
    if large

In a large, shallow bowl, whisk together the soy sauce, maple syrup, and ketchup. Add the steak and let marinate for at least 4 hours, turning every hour. Remove steak and discard marinade. Either grill your steak on an outdoor grill to your desired temperature or cook in a skillet, over medium heat with butter until desired doneness.

While steak is cooking, combine remainder of ingredients in a large bowl and toss well. Divide among 3 serving plates. When steak is done, slice on the bias and top each plated salad with equal amounts.

SERVES 3

Here are a couple quick rules of thumb when it comes to beef. Anything that is labeled loin or round is generally considered lean.

The leanest cuts of beef are round tip, eye round, top round, bottom round, top loin, tenderloin and top sirloin.

Trim all meats of fat.

Choose ground round or sirloin when preparing anything that requires hamburger.

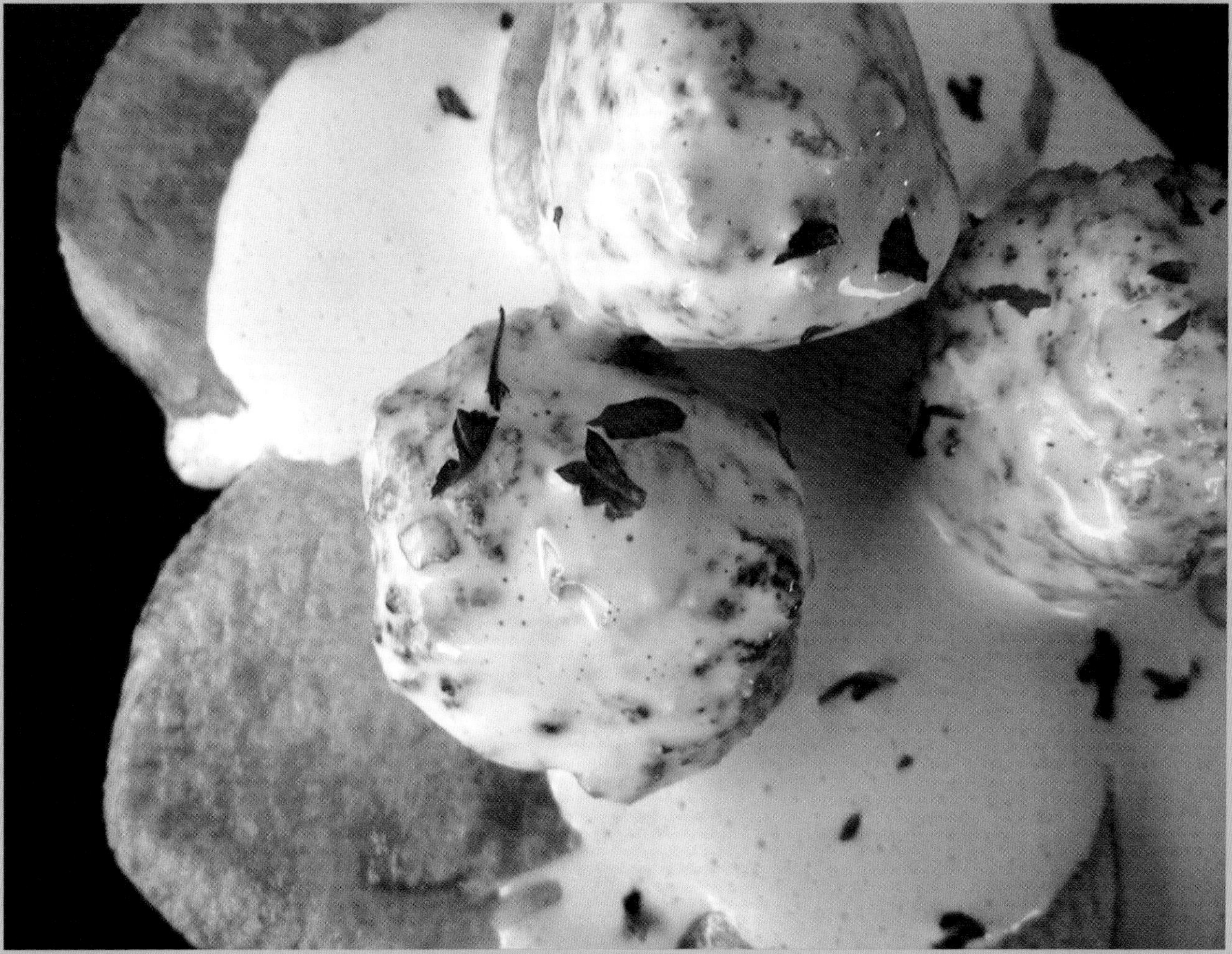

Southern "Fried Chicken" Meatballs

What a great alternative to fried chicken. Supremely southern, with a twist.

1 pound ground chicken
    or turkey
4 egg whites, beaten well
½ cup dried breadcrumbs
½ teaspoon each black
    pepper, oregano,
    celery salt, garlic, and
    onion powder
¼ teaspoon salt
2 strips turkey bacon, cooked
    and crumbled

For the gravy:
2 cups 2% milk
1 tablespoon Worcestershire
    sauce
½ teaspoon black pepper
¼ teaspoon salt
3 tablespoons cornstarch
    mixed with ¼ cup water

2 tablespoons pure olive oil,
    or as needed
1 pound potatoes, peeled and
    sliced ¼-inch thick
1 cup fat-free chicken broth

Preheat oven to 350° F.

In a large bowl, combine chicken, egg whites, breadcrumbs, spices, salt, and turkey bacon and mix well. Form into 1½-inch meatballs. Place meatballs on a baking sheet with at least an inch-high side. Bake 15–20 minutes, or until cooked throughout.

Prepare gravy: In a large saucepan, mix milk, Worcestershire sauce, black pepper, and salt. Whisk well and bring to scalding over medium heat. Do not let it boil. When milk is scalding, reduce heat to low and whisk in cornstarch slurry until smooth. Remove from heat; set aside.

Remove meatballs from the oven and transfer to saucepan with gravy using a slotted spoon, gently coating each meatball. Keep warm while preparing potatoes.

In a large skillet, heat olive oil over medium-high heat until shimmering hot. Add potato slices in a single layer. Set aside any potatoes that don't fit. Cook potatoes until lightly browned on one side. If you have more potatoes to add, simply lift out cooked potatoes onto a plate while browning remainder. When all potatoes are browned, after about 2–3 minutes, return any potatoes you removed to pan and add chicken stock. Reduce heat to medium, cover, and cook until crisp tender. Remove cover and continue cooking potatoes, without mixing, another 3 minutes, or until most of the liquid has evaporated and the potatoes are very tender.

To assemble, evenly divide potatoes, decoratively, in the center of each plate. Top with equal amounts of meatballs and sauce and serve hot.

SERVES 4

Spicy Curried Beef and Eggplant

Whole grain rice has triple the dietary fiber of white rice. It is one of the best sources of Vitamin E and folacin as well. And the cost? Just a tad more than white, but the benefit your body receives far outweighs the cost. And besides, this dish is fantastic.

1 (14-ounce) can evaporated
    skim milk
½ cup almond or soy milk
½ pound sirloin steak, trimmed
    and cubed
2 tablespoons curry powder
2 tablespoons pure olive oil
Grated rind and juice
    from 1 lime
½ small eggplant, diced
1 red bell pepper, seeded
    and diced
½ small onion, minced
½ cup freshly chopped basil
2 cups whole wheat rice,
    cooked and kept warm

Whisk together evaporated milk and almond milk well; set aside.

Toss the sirloin with curry powder, coating evenly. In a large skillet, over medium-high heat, add oil. When oil is hot, add steak and cook until desired doneness. Remove beef with a slotted spoon and set aside.

With pan still over medium-high heat, add milk mixture and lime juice and zest, stirring to lift up the fonds at the bottom of the skillet. When scalding, reduce heat to medium and add eggplant, bell pepper, onion, and basil. Cook, stirring frequently, until the eggplant is tender, about 5–7 minutes. Add back the steak, toss to combine. Evenly divide the warm rice among serving dishes and immediately serve curried beef on top.

SERVES 3

Chinese Red Cooked "Ribs"

This healthier version of the classic Chinese ribs tastes just as good as the original. By using the leanest cut of pork possible, the content of fat and cholesterol drops significantly. Because there are literally hundreds of that "perfect" Chinese barbecue sauce recipes, I offer two of my all-time favorites. They both are true Chinese red barbecue sauces but the second recipe has ketchup added, for those of you who think tomato should be the base of *all* barbecue sauces.

2–3 pounds pork tenderloin, trimmed and cut into 3- by 2-inch chunks

For Red Marinade #1:

1 cup soy sauce
½ cup brown sugar, packed
1 cup apple juice or cider
½ cup apple cider vinegar
2 teaspoons red pepper flakes or cayenne pepper, or to taste
2 teaspoons Chinese 5-spice powder
1 teaspoon dried ginger (or 1 tablespoon minced fresh)
1 teaspoon garlic powder
5 drops red food coloring

For Red Marinade #2:

1 (12-ounce) bottle ketchup
⅓ cup hoisin sauce
⅓ cup soy sauce
¼ cup pomegranate juice
1 tablespoon Worcestershire sauce
2 teaspoons garlic powder
¼ cup molasses
3 drops red food coloring
1 teaspoon Chinese 5-spice powder
1 teaspoon grated orange rind
Juice from 1 orange

At least 4 hours before cooking, whisk together all ingredients for whichever marinade recipe you choose.

Place your pork in a single layer in a large pan with at least 2-inch sides. Pour marinade over the top, turn the pork a few times, and refrigerate at least 4 hours, or until you are ready to cook.

When ready, heat your grill to about medium hot. Take the pork directly from the marinade onto the cooking racks, shaking excess liquid from "ribs." Make sure the heat source is at least 3 inches from meat. Close the grill and start cooking, basting every 5 minutes with marinade, turning over every time you baste. After 15–20 minutes, start checking for doneness. They should be crispy and perfect at about 20–25 minutes.

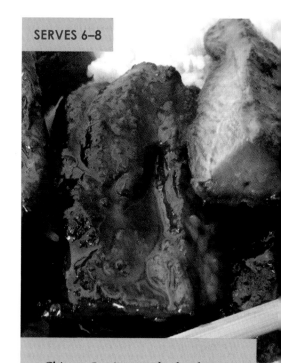

SERVES 6–8

Chinese 5-spice powder has been a staple in Asian cooking for centuries. So called, not for its spices but, because it stands for the five elements that are present all around us. Wood, earth, metal, water, and fire are the elements that are needed to keep yourself in check, according to ancient Chinese medicine, or you will suffer from a wide variety of illnesses and ailments.

Yanked Pork and Beans

SERVES 4

I developed this recipe with one of my ancestors in mind. He wrote back in 1793 that he had shared his meager supper, consisting of a "small piece of pork and a parcel of beans," with a Scotsman. I took that and ran with it, so to speak. I think you will find this modern approach to pork and beans delightfully tasty. I serve these beans with grilled pork chops, but add whatever protein you desire or simply enjoy them topped with some fried or poached eggs. Use frozen lima beans that have been thawed or canned beans that have been drained.

1 tablespoon oil
¼ small onion, minced
2 garlic cloves, peeled
    and crushed
1 (15-ounce) can diced
    tomatoes
8 ounces lima beans, cooked
1 cup whole kernel corn
2 tablespoons tomato paste
1 teaspoon Dijon-style mustard
½ teaspoon each salt,
    oregano, basil, sugar, and
    black pepper
Salt and black pepper to taste
Cooked pork of your choice*

In a large skillet, heat oil over medium heat. Add onion and garlic. Cook, while stirring frequently, until onions have softened, about 4–5 minutes.

Add remainder of ingredients, except pork, stirring to combine well. Reduce heat to low and simmer 10 minutes to give the sauce a chance to thicken. Remove from heat and season to taste with salt. Serve hot with pork.

*I suggest a simple, trimmed boneless loin chop sprinkled with black pepper and garlic powder. Grilled or pan fried in olive oil until thoroughly cooked, it is both lean and very flavorful.

Smoked Ham Slices with New England Red-Eye Gravy

The South has nothing on my version of a classic red-eye gravy, which adds my own little touch. The flavor of apple is a "no-brainah" when it comes to ham, or any pork product actually. May I suggest using cranberry juice as well, or even a combination of each?

Nonstick cooking spray
½-1 pound smoked boneless ham, about ½-inch thick
1 cup brewed coffee*
1 cup apple cider or juice
¼ cup molasses
2 tablespoons evaporated skim milk
¼ teaspoon ground cloves
Salt and pepper, to taste

Liberally coat a large skillet with nonstick cooking spray (I use cast iron for this recipe). Place over medium heat and add ham steak, cooking 5–7 minutes per side, or until nicely browned. Remove to plate, cover with tin foil to keep warm, and set aside.

Add coffee and cider to same skillet. Bring to a boil, scraping the bottom of the skillet to lift the fonds. Continue boiling an additional 3 minutes. Add molasses, milk, and cloves, whisking well. Continue cooking and stirring until smooth

SERVES 2

It is easy to make ham less salty. For ham steaks, simply put the steak in a shallow bowl and pour lemon-lime soda over the top to cover. Place in your refrigerator for at least 3 hours, changing the soda every hour. When ready to cook, remove ham, rinse in cold water, pat dry, and continue with recipe. I allow my ham slice to soak for at least 8 hours. I counteract the lack of saltiness with my Red-Eye Gravy.

and thick, about 1 minute. Remove from heat, season to taste with salt and pepper, and serve with ham steak.

* Your coffee should be very strong. I suggest you take 2 cups brewed coffee and boil it down to 1 cup.

Jack's Sweet Pork, Southern-Style

Kentucky bourbon is the "Jack" in this recipe and the "Southern" is Georgia-inspired peaches. The addition of blueberries? Well, let's just say that we here in New England love our blueberries. The cornbread mentioned in the recipe can be made from a box, or use my recipe on page 10.

4 tablespoons Kentucky
    bourbon
4 tablespoons orange juice
2 tablespoons pure olive oil
1 teaspoon dried
    rosemary, crushed
1 teaspoon garlic powder
1 pork tenderloin
    (about 1 pound)*
Butter-flavored nonstick
    cooking spray
½ cup blueberry preserves
1 pan (13- by 9-inch)
    prepared cornbread

For the Simmered Peaches:
1 cup orange juice
3 tablespoons honey
1 tablespoon brown sugar
3 peaches, halved, pitted,
    wedged, and each wedge
    cut in half cross-wise
Simmered Peaches,
    recipe below

SERVES 4 SERVINGS

Mix bourbon, orange juice, oil, rosemary, and garlic powder in a small bowl. Place pork in large resealable plastic bag or glass dish. Add marinade; turn to coat well. Refrigerate at least 4 hours.

Preheat oven to 375° F. In a high-sided baking pan, add the pork and marinade. Roast 45–60 minutes or until cooked thoroughly, turning occasionally and basting with marinade while cooking. Remove from oven and discard marinade. Let rest, covered with foil, while preparing the remainder of the recipe.

Cut each cornbread into roughly 4- by 4-inch squares and spray with nonstick cooking spray. Place cornbread in large skillet, over medium-high heat, and grill 1 to 2 minutes on each side or until starting to brown, turning once with a spatula. (Do not use tongs as cornbread is fragile and tends to crumble.)

In another large skillet, over medium-high, heat and stir orange juice, honey, and brown sugar. Add peaches when mixture is hot. Reduce heat to medium-low and simmer, uncovered, for about 6–8 minutes, or until peaches are crisp tender. Keep stirring and flipping peaches over to evenly cook.

Meanwhile, cut pork tenderloins into ¼-inch thick slices. To serve, warm the blueberry preserves and spread evenly on cornbread squares. Place 1 slice pork tenderloin on top, followed by peaches.

*If you have trouble finding a 1 pound pork loin, cut a larger loin down to size and save the rest for another dinner.

Yanked Cincinnati Chili

Cincinnati chili is markedly different than most other chilis in that it most often contains either chocolate and/or a pasta. Although I adore chili, I just can't bring myself to mix it with pasta, so here is my take on this Cincinnati classic.

1 small onion, peeled
    and minced
1 small bell pepper, seeded
    and minced
4 garlic cloves, peeled and
    crushed
½ pound ground round
    or sirloin
½ pound ground chicken
    or turkey
2 tablespoons brown sugar
2 tablespoons chili powder
1 tablespoon unsweetened
    cocoa
2 teaspoons ground cumin
1 teaspoon salt
½ teaspoon black pepper
1 (20-ounce) can fat free
    beef broth
1 (15-ounce) can red kidney
    beans, drained
1 (15-ounce) can diced
    tomatoes, undrained
3 ounces 70% or higher cacao
    chocolate, chopped
4 cups rice, cooked and
    kept warm

SERVES 4

In a large pot or saucepan, combine the onion, bell pepper, garlic, ground round, and ground chicken, breaking the meat apart. Place over medium-high heat, uncovered, and cook until thoroughly done, about 6–8 minutes. Continue breaking apart as you are cooking.

While the meat is cooking, in a small bowl mix together brown sugar, chili powder, cocoa, cumin, salt, and black pepper. Add to meat mixture and stir well. Reduce heat to low and add the remainder of ingredients except rice. Stir to combine and cook an additional 30 minutes, or until heated through and thickened slightly, making sure the chocolate has thoroughly melted.

Divide rice into serving dishes and ladle chili on top.

So many people are being led astray that I must add something about "dark chocolate": Buyer beware. The United States Food and Drug Administration asserts that there is no such thing as "dark chocolate." However, I will state that whenever you see me write about "dark chocolate," I mean at least 70% cacao chocolate. This raw form of chocolate is loaded with antioxidants. Although you may find the taste slightly bitter, when mixed with a sweetener (as you will see in many recipes here) you will love the flavor.

I use 85% cacao, or raw chocolate, in most recipes; to get the full effect of the great benefits of cacao, use 70% or higher. The lower the percentage, the less bitter it will be.

And before you ask, certainly you can replace all cacao listed in my recipes with your favorite chocolate, whether it's milk or the so-called "dark."

Family-Style Classic Pastitsio

There are many ways of preparing this Greek dish, and some of them are complicated, requiring the preparation of either a mornay or béchamel sauce, along with many other herbs and/or seasonings. Here is a simplified version with the same great flavor.

If I were to choose one vegetable that goes perfectly with lamb, it would be green beans. Both the first and second Yankee Chefs, my grandfather and father, agreed and always, when able, prepared lamb with green beans.

8 ounces elbow macaroni
½ cup egg substitute
¼ teaspoon nutmeg
Nonstick cooking spray
1 cup green beans,
    cooked and cut into
    1-inch segments
1 pound lean, ground lamb
½ small onion, minced
2 garlic cloves, peeled
    and crushed
1 (8-ounce) can tomato puree
1 teaspoon oregano
¾ teaspoon black pepper
½ teaspoon cinnamon
    or allspice
1 ½ cups evaporated skim milk
½ cup plain yogurt
½ cup grated
    Parmesan cheese

SERVES 4

Cook pasta according to package instructions. Drain well and transfer to a large bowl. Stir the egg and nutmeg into the pasta well; set aside.

Spray nonstick cooking spray on the bottom and half-way up the side of a 2 quart casserole dish or 9-inch square baking pan. Lay the prepared pasta in the bottom of the dish followed by the green beans evenly over the top; set aside.

Preheat oven to 350° F. In a large skillet, cook lamb, onion, and garlic over medium heat until done, breaking up meat as you cook. Drain fat from skillet and stir in tomato puree, oregano, pepper, and cinnamon. Reduce to low heat and simmer 5 minutes. Spread this mixture over the pasta.

In a bowl, whisk together milk and yogurt well. Pour over the meat mixture and sprinkle with Parmesan cheese. Bake 30–35 minutes or until set and the top is bubbling.

The Best Italian Meatballs

I adore meatballs and could eat spaghetti and meatballs every single day of the week. After years of experimenting, and although I never made a meatball I didn't like, I believe sincerely these meatballs are the best of the best.

4 garlic cloves, peeled
    and crushed
1 tablespoon pure olive oil
1 small onion, minced
¾ cup California-style
    vegetables
¼ cup fat-free vegetable or
    beef broth
¾ cup cooked farina*
1 pound ground round or sirloin
1 pound ground chicken
2 cups black or white beans,
    cooked, drained
    and mashed
4 egg whites, beaten
1½ cups dried bread crumbs,
    plus more if needed
½ cup parmesan cheese
1 tablespoon Italian seasoning
2 teaspoons celery or
    fennel seeds
1 teaspoon each of salt and
    black pepper

Preheat oven to 350° F.

In a large skillet, over medium heat, cook garlic in oil Cook for 2 minutes, stirring often. Add the onion and cook until softened, about 3-4 minutes; set aside.

In the bowl of a blender or food processor, pulse vegetables and broth until the veggies are pureed very small. Transfer to a large bowl along with farina and remainder of ingredients. Mix well, adding more bread crumbs as needed to hold together. Form into desired sized meatballs and place onto an ungreased baking pan. Make sure your pan has sides that are at least an inch high. Bake until done and firm to the touch, about 30 minutes.

*Measure 6 tablespoons farina and mix in a small saucepan with ¾ cup water. Bring to a boil, reduce heat to low and cover. Simmer for about 6 minutes, or until farina has absorbed all the liquid. Fluff up. If desired, you may opt out of farina and simply double the amount of California-style vegetables.

MAKES ABOUT 30 MEATBALLS

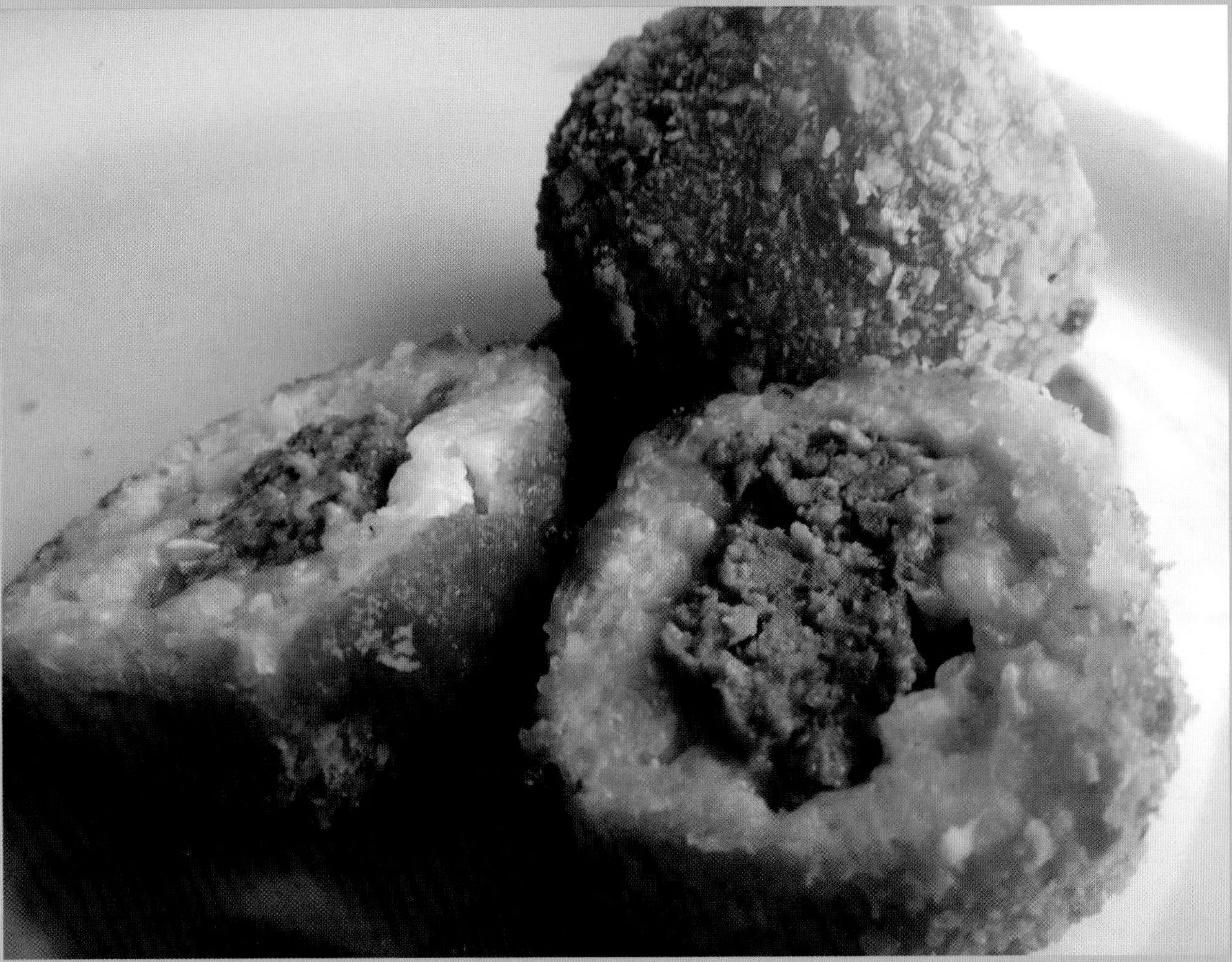

Simple Italian Meatball Arancini

This recipe is a favorite at my home. My kids have fun with these little crunchy critters, but not too much fun. After all, being Yankees, we take a lumberman's approach to dinner: Be happy, but eat!!! The cheese-infused rice is such a great way to accent the tasty meatball inside, and with marinara sauce for dipping, your kids will certainly have no problem eating this Italian street food favorite.

You can also bake these by lining an oven pan with waxed or parchment paper, then spraying each arancini with nonstick cooking spray and baking for about 20 minutes, or until crisp and hot.

1½ cups fat-free beef or
   chicken broth
¾ cup uncooked rice
10 prepared meatballs,
   room temperature
½ cup egg substitute
½ cup shredded cheese
   of your choice
2 tablespoons flour
½ teaspoon each salt and
   black pepper
1 teaspoon hot sauce,
   if desired
1 quart canola oil for frying
1½ cups crushed crackers
Nonstick cooking spray
1¼ cups hot marinara sauce

MAKES 10 MEATBALLS

Over high heat in a medium saucepan, bring broth to a boil. Add rice, stir, reduce heat to low, cover, and cook 15–17 minutes, or until rice has absorbed all of the liquid. Remove from heat and set aside for a few minutes before transferring to a bowl. Cover and refrigerate to cool completely. This will take at least 3 hours.

When ready, remove rice from refrigerator and stir in egg substitute, cheese, flour, salt, pepper and hot sauce. Mix well. It should be sticky and hold together well. If not, add a tablespoon flour at a time until it holds together.

Heat oil to 350° F over medium heat in a heavy pot, or use deep fryer according to manufacturer's instructions. Wet palms of both hands with water and grab a couple tablespoon measures of rice mixture. Flatten out rice in one palm and take a meatball, placing it in the middle of the rice. Now wrap the rice around it, rolling the mixture between the palms of your hands to completely hide the meatball. Repeat with remainder of meatballs. Then roll each meatball in crushed crackers, pressing firmly to coat.

Fry 4 rice balls at a time for 4–5 minutes, or until nicely browned. Transfer to a paper towel-lined platter to drain. Give yourself a minute or two to let oil come back up to temperature before continuing with remaining arancinis. Serve with hot marinara sauce.

Yankee Meatball Bites

Actually more than a bite, these Yankee "cornbread-plated" meatballs are perfect for elegant dining as well as finger food for that great game. Use your favorite cheese in lieu of cheddar if desired. A heavily smoked low-moisture cheddar or swiss would be great as well. But then again, we New Englanders are quite partial to any form of cheddar.

Nonstick cooking spray
¾ cup cornmeal
¾ cup flour
1 tablespoon sugar
2 teaspoons baking powder
½ teaspoon cayenne or red pepper flakes
½ teaspoon salt
2 tablespoons melted butter or margarine
3 egg whites, beaten
¼ cup skim milk
10 prepared meatballs, cold
1 cup marinara sauce
Dried oregano
5 slices low fat, smoked cheese slices, cut in half, optional

Preheat oven to 350° F. Spray a cookie sheet or baking pan with nonstick cooking spray: set aside.

In a large mixing bowl, combine cornmeal, flour, sugar, baking powder, cayenne, and salt. Stir in melted butter, egg whites, and milk until well incorporated. It will be thick.

Scoop 2-tablespoon measures of cornbread mixture onto prepared pan, leaving 2 inches between mounds. Place one meatball in the center of each mound and bake 10–12 minutes, or when cornbread is firm to the touch. Carefully pull out oven rack, ladle a tablespoon and a half of the marinara sauce over each meatball, a sprinkling of oregano, and a half slice of cheese. Return to the oven for 2 minutes for cheese to melt. Remove and serve hot.

Smothered Beef and Onions

Well worth your patience and time, the preparation of true smothered beef and onions results in fall-apart beef and the great taste of seasoned onions with beef gravy blanketing the entire dish. I shortened the preparation time and spiced the dish up a bit.

1 teaspoon cracked pepper

4 teaspoons lemon
    juice, divided

4 tablespoons pure olive
    oil, divided

8 ounces cubed lean beef

3 tablespoons fat-free
    beef broth

1 tablespoon tomato paste

1 tablespoon cornstarch

2 garlic cloves, peeled
    and crushed

½ small yellow onion, julienned

½ small red onion, julienned

8 green onions, cut into
    2-inch segments

SERVES 3

Mix together cracked pepper, 2 teaspoons lemon juice, and 2 tablespoons olive oil in a large bowl, then add the beef. Stir, cover, and refrigerate at least 1 hour.

Whisk together beef broth, remainder of lemon juice, and tomato paste; set aside.

When beef is marinated, heat remainder of oil in a large skillet over high heat. Remove meat from marinade, blot dry with a paper towel, and add to skillet with the garlic. Discard marinade. Stir-fry beef and garlic until beef is no longer pink in the middle, about 2–3 minutes, depending on how large the beef cubes are. Add all onions and cook 2 minutes longer, stirring constantly. Add the tomato paste mixture and cook one additional minute, stirring constantly, until thickened. Remove and serve hot.

Tender Marinated Flank Steak with Caramelized Onion

I just can't say enough good about caramelized onions. You could put these bad boys on an old sandal and they'd probably still taste good. Here, they are combined with one of the best marinades around.

¼ cup brown sugar
1 tablespoon curry powder
1 tablespoon coarse-grained salt
2 teaspoons garlic powder
½ teaspoon ground ginger
½ teaspoon cardamom powder
½ teaspoon cracked black pepper
1½ pounds flank steak, trimmed

For the Onions:
1 tablespoon pure olive oil
1 onion, peeled, sliced, or julienned
Large pinch of salt and black pepper
1 teaspoon sugar, optional
¼ cup balsamic vinegar, optional

Make the spice rub by combining first 7 ingredients in a small bowl.

SERVES 2–3

Fire up your grill to medium-high heat and while that is heating, rub the steaks thoroughly with the spices on both sides and let sit for 10 minutes. Grill the steak for about 4–5 minutes per side, with the lid open, for medium rare, adding a minute or so longer per side for medium. Remove steak and serve piled with caramelized onion.

To Make the Onions:
Heat the oil in a large skillet over high heat until shimmering. Add the onion and stir fry to break apart for 2–3 minutes, or until starting to soften. Stir almost constantly. Reduce heat to low, salt and pepper, and cover. Let cook for 30 minutes, stirring often, or until as dark as you would like them. During the last 5 minutes, remove lid if you would like the onions less moist.

If you would like to use the vinegar, after 15 minutes, remove lid and add the vinegar and continue cooking without the lid.

Simple, Unadorned Cashew Turkey

David Leong, a Chinese chef in Springfield, Missouri, began making his version of cashew chicken back in the '30s at his restaurant, the Grove Supper Club. It is a simple dish that is still being prepared the same way by his son at another family-owned restaurant. David's recipe inspired my rendition of the Grove Supper Club's famous dish, but I use turkey instead.

Nonstick cooking spray
1 pound boneless turkey
     breast, cut into 1-inch cubes
1 cup water
1 tablespoon plus 2
     teaspoons cornstarch
2 tablespoons soy sauce
2 tablespoons oyster or
     hoisin sauce
1 tablespoon canola oil
¼ small onion, minced
1 cup unsalted cashews,
     divided
2 garlic cloves, peeled
     and crushed
½ teaspoon dried ginger
4 cups rice, cooked and
     kept warm

SERVES 4

Coat a large skillet with nonstick cooking spray and place over high heat. When hot, stir-fry half the turkey cubes until cooked through, 3-5 minutes. Remove and set aside. Add more spray to skillet and cook remaining turkey, also setting aside when done.

In a bowl, whisk together water, cornstarch, soy, and oyster sauce until the cornstarch is mixed thoroughly.

Heat canola oil in same skillet over high heat and add onions, ¾ cup of the cashews, and garlic. Cook 1 minute.

Add cornstarch mixture along with the ginger and continue stir-frying until liquid boils and thickens, about another minute.

Divide rice among four serving plates and evenly dish out the turkey, sauce, and remainder of cashews over the rice.

Heartland Chicken

Want a dish that will get your kids to start eating more veggies? This is the one! Substitute their favorite vegetables here if desired. *It's Just That Simple!*

3 tablespoons tomato paste
½ teaspoon each salt and
    black pepper
½ teaspoon garlic powder
½ teaspoon oregano
1 (10.5-ounce) can fat-free
    chicken broth
½ cup evaporated skim milk
2 egg whites
¾ cup cracker crumbs
1 tablespoon pure olive oil
2 (6-ounce) chicken breast
    halves, cut in half
    lengthwise
¼ cup minced onion
1 cup diced summer squash
1 cup diced zucchini
1 cup cooked, diced carrots
1 firm apple, peeled, cored,
    and diced*
4 cups rice, cooked and
    kept warm

In a large bowl, whisk tomato paste, salt, black pepper, garlic powder, oregano, and chicken broth; set aside. In a shallow bowl, whisk together milk and egg white; set aside. Place the cracker crumbs in a shallow bowl; set aside.

Heat oil in a large skillet over medium heat. Dredge chicken in egg wash, then evenly coat with cracker crumbs. When oil is hot, add the chicken, partially cover and cook until well done throughout, about 4–5 minutes per side. Transfer chicken to a plate and set aside.

Add onions to same skillet, cooking for 3 minutes. Add both squashes, carrots, and apple. Increase heat to medium-high and stir-fry for about 4 minutes, or until vegetables are crisp tender. Reduce heat to low and add chicken broth mixture and chicken back into the skillet. Cover and simmer 10 minutes.

Divide the rice among 4 serving plates, top with equal amounts of chicken and vegetable tomato sauce. Serve hot.

SERVES 4

*Granny Smith, Cortland, Jonagold and Winesaps are good choices.

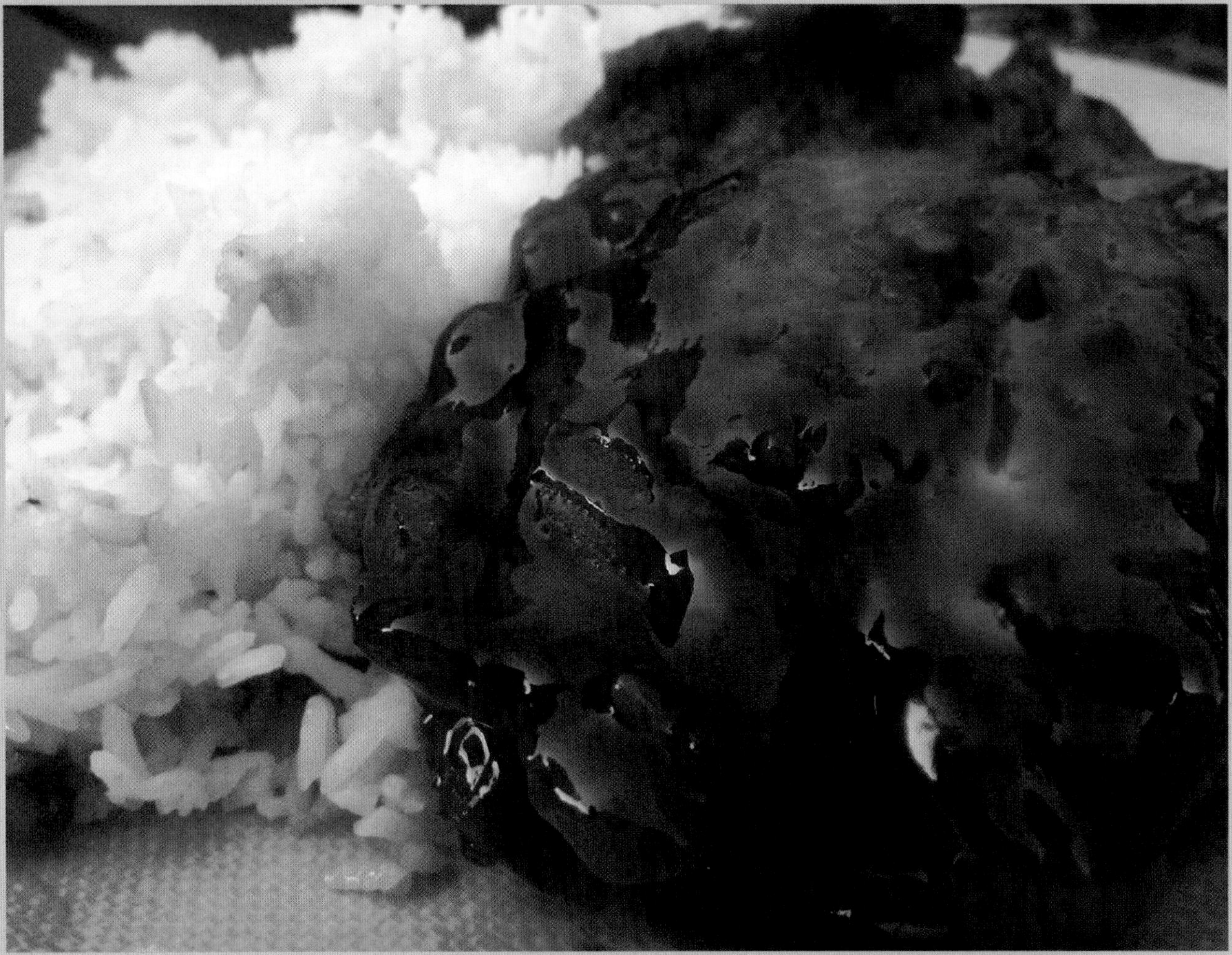

General Tsao Chicken for the Grill

Think you need to be a whiz when cooking Chinese food? Think again. Not only is this dish spot-on when it comes to true Tsao flavor, but when you cook anything outside on the grill, doesn't it always taste better? I didn't make this overly hot, but if you want more heat, simply mince a hot pepper or two and add it to the sauce.

½ cup apple juice
½ cup fat-free chicken broth
    or stock
¼ cup tomato paste
2 tablespoons brown sugar
3 tablespoons soy sauce
¼ cup rice vinegar
½ teaspoon garlic
    powder, optional
½ teaspoon cayenne pepper
1 teaspoon sesame oil
2 tablespoons cornstarch
2 tablespoons water
3 chicken breast halves
3 cups white rice, cooked and
    kept warm

Preheat outdoor grill on medium heat.

Prepare the sauce: In a small bowl, combine first 9 ingredients and whisk well. In another small bowl, whisk together the cornstarch and water until smooth, then mix into the apple juice mixture; set aside.

Cook chicken over indirect heat on grill until the chicken is cooked completely through, about 4–6 minutes per side. Remove from grill and add to sauce. Add this sauce back onto your grill, over low heat, and let the chicken simmer for at least 15 minutes, stirring frequently to prevent scorching on bottom; the sauce will thicken as it simmers.

Evenly divide the rice onto 3 serving plates and put one half breast on each. Spoon extra sauce over each chicken breast.

SERVES 3

Gà Kẹo Caramel

Want something completely different, but that still has a familiar, great taste? Here it is! A spicy (yet not too spicy) simmered chicken dish that has an American/Asian flair. This is a great protein with a side of satay noodles.

2 tablespoons pure olive oil
2 pounds bone-in chicken
   (I prefer thighs)
½ cup granulated sugar
1 garlic clove, peeled
   and crushed
1 hot chili, seeded and minced
1 cup chili sauce
¼ cup pomegranate juice
2 tablespoons apple
   cider vinegar
½ teaspoon dried ginger
1 tablespoon molasses

SERVES 3

Heat oil in a large skillet over medium-high heat until shimmering. Add the chicken and let cook for 6–7 minutes without moving the pieces. Gently loosen the chicken with a spatula and turn over to brown an additional 4–5 minutes, or until browned on bottom.

Remove the chicken, leaving the fond in the pan, and add the sugar, garlic, and minced chili. Let sugar melt and stir for 1 minute while cooking.

Meanwhile, in a small bowl, mix well the remainder of ingredients

Add the chicken back into the skillet and glaze both sides of the chicken with the melted brown sugar mixture. Reduce heat to low, add the bowl of chili sauce mixture, cover and simmer 20–22 minutes, or until chicken is done throughout.

Turn over the chicken half-way through simmering. When done, remove from skillet and serve immediately.

Sweeter with Molasses

Molasses! This original Yankee sweetener is abundant with calcium, with over 200 mg in just 3½ ounces. Other important benefits of molasses are that it contains over 60% of your RDA of magnesium and over 40% of your RDA of potassium. According to the *Journal of the American Dietetic Association* (January 2009), substituting molasses for other sugars could increase your antioxidant intake to the level of berries, such as blueberries. All this in just 3½ ounces!

Savory Chinese Garlic Chicken

While at first glance this may look complicated, you probably already have most of the ingredients on hand. This is also a quick dish. It will be ready before the twenty minutes you need to cook the rice!

You also don't have to stick with the vegetables listed. Add some sliced water chestnuts, bamboo shoots, cauliflower, green beans, or anything your heart desires.

For the sauce:
2 tablespoons apple
　　cider vinegar
1 tablespoon brown sugar
2 tablespoons fat-free
　　chicken broth
1 tablespoon soy sauce
2 teaspoons tomato paste
½ teaspoon cayenne pepper
1 teaspoon cornstarch

For the chicken:
1 teaspoon cornstarch
2 egg whites, beaten
2 tablespoons fat-free
　　chicken broth
½ teaspoon dried ginger
4 chicken breast halves, diced
　　into ¼-inch pieces
3 tablespoons pure olive oil
1 small onion, diced

SERVES 4

1 small green bell pepper,
　　seeded and chopped
3 cups broccoli florets
½ carrot, sliced very thinly with
　　vegetable peeler
4 garlic cloves, peeled
　　and crushed

Mix all the sauce ingredients together and set aside.

Beat 1 teaspoon of cornstarch with egg whites, chicken broth, and dried ginger. Add the chicken pieces and mix well so all chicken is coated. Place in refrigerator for 15 minutes.

Remove chicken from marinade and dry well; reserve marinade. Heat oil in a large skillet or wok over medium-high heat until the oil is shimmering and very hot. Add the chicken pieces and stir-fry until nicely browned and cooked through, about 3–4 minutes.

Add the onion, pepper, broccoli, carrots, and garlic, cooking until vegetables are crisp tender, about 3–4 minutes. Add reserved marinade, bring to a boil and cook 1 minute.

Add the sauce, bring to a boil and continue to stir and cook until sauce has thickened, about 1–2 minutes. Remove from heat and serve as is or over warm rice.

Tender and Simple Chicken Chow Mein

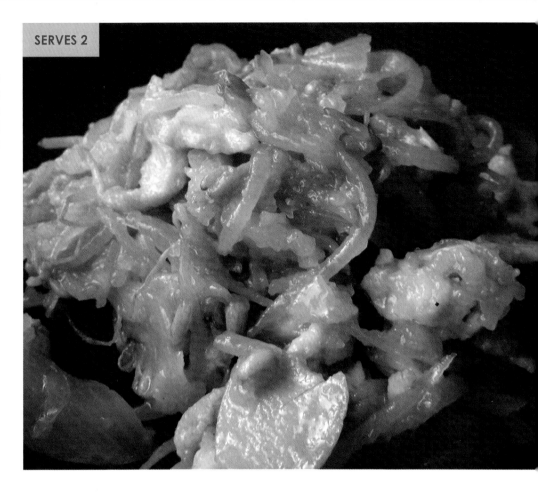

SERVES 2

Although not one of the prettiest dishes you'll see, this is one of the famous comfort foods of the "other East"—Asia. Although many chow mein recipes include a myriad of other ingredients, I find bean sprouts satisfying, in taste, bulk, and nutrition.

¼ cup soy sauce

2 tablespoons cornstarch

1 tablespoon pure olive oil

1 small onion, thinly sliced
    or julienned

2 ribs celery, thinly sliced

2 garlic cloves, peeled
    and crushed

1 (6-ounce) chicken
    breast, chopped

1 (7-ounce) package (4 cups)
    fresh bean sprouts

1 cup fat-free chicken broth

1 tablespoon brown sugar

In a small bowl, whisk together soy sauce and cornstarch until smooth, set aside.

In a large skillet over medium heat, combine oil, onion, celery, and garlic and stir. Cook, stirring frequently, about 6–8 minutes. Add the chicken and continue to cook and stir an additional 4–8 minutes (depending on the size of the cut chicken) or until chicken is done throughout. Raise the heat to medium-high and add bean sprouts. Stir-fry until the sprouts are softened, about 3–5 minutes. Add soy sauce mixture, broth, and brown sugar. Continue cooking and stirring until thickened and hot throughout, about 2–3 minutes. Serve immediately.

Yankee Grilled Skewers

You want a true New England equivalent of teriyaki chicken on a stick? This is it! Taste the New England flavors of maple and apples "caramelizing" on thin strips of chicken over a smoky fire.

¾ cup maple syrup
¼ cup apple cider vinegar
½ cup jalapeño, peach,
    or apple jelly
¼ teaspoon ground ginger
Salt and black pepper to taste
3 boneless chicken
    breast halves
6 skewers
1 tablespoon cornstarch
1 tablespoon water

MAKES 6 SKEWERS.

In a bowl, whisk together maple syrup, vinegar, jelly, ginger, and salt and pepper to taste. Put chicken between 2 sheets of film wrap and gently pound them with the bottom of a skillet until they are ½ inch thick. Place the chicken breasts into the marinade and let sit for at least 1 hour, covered, in the refrigerator.

Heat grill on low and remove chicken from marinade, shaking excess liquid off, and reserving liquid. Cut chicken into long, 1 ½-inch wide strips and pierce onto skewers. I place these skewers on the top rack of my grill, where the flame does not touch the rack. Close lid and cook 3–4 minutes before turning to cook on

the other side until done. Depending on your rack placement, you may need to cook chicken longer until it is cooked through.

While chicken is cooking, heat the marinade in a saucepan over high heat until boiling. Whisk cornstarch with a tablespoon of water and stir into boiling marinade until thickened. Remove from heat and dip your cooked chicken skewers into the sauce.

Grilled Chicken Dumplings with Asian Blueberry Dipping Sauce

This is a two-step process, but don't be dismayed! They are well worth the time it takes to prepare from beginning to end. The dipping sauce is the perfect accompaniment to these gently spiced dumplings.

1 cup minced, cooked, low-fat
   deli chicken
½ cup mashed potatoes
2 tablespoons plain yogurt
   or sour cream
2 tablespoons parmesan
   cheese
2 tablespoons onion, minced
2 egg whites, beaten
1 teaspoon garlic powder
Salt and black pepper to taste
Nonstick cooking spray

For the Asian Blueberry Dipping Sauce:

1 cup blueberry preserves
   or jelly
1 tablespoon soy sauce
½ teaspoon garlic powder
½ teaspoon dried ginger

In a large bowl, combine first 8 ingredients, mixing very well.

Bring a medium saucepan half-full of water to a gentle simmer over medium-low heat. Make quenelles* of the chicken mixture with 2 teaspoons or simply shape the chicken mixture as best as you can into oblong forms. Carefully drop them into the simmering water and cook 2–3 minutes, or until they float and feel firm. Remove with a slotted spoon into a colander. Refrigerate for at least 30 minutes.

Coat a large skillet with nonstick cooking spray and place over medium heat. When hot, add dumplings and cook until browned on both sides, tossing as needed. This will take about 10–12 minutes.

In the meantime mix dipping sauce ingredients in a microwave-safe bowl, cover with film wrap, and heat for 30 seconds in microwave, or until hot and bubbling. Carefully remove film wrap and whisk again. Serve hot grilled dumplings with your heated blueberry sauce.

*Here is a quick and easy lesson in making quenelles. Simply scoop a teaspoon or tablespoon of your mixture with one spoon and scoop it out with another, following the contour of the original spoon. Keep scooping 3 or more times until the perfect (or as best as you can muster) oval-shaped quenelle is formed. It only takes a couple minutes to master this technique.

SERVES 6–8

Here is another great dip that can be used for so many other recipes as well, including as a spread on bagels or toast. Puree 3 tablespoons milk or plain yogurt with 1½ tablespoons lemon juice and 1 cup cottage cheese in a blender or food processor until very smooth, at least 1 full minute on high. Transfer to a bowl, cover, and refrigerate. It will thicken upon cooling.

CHAPTER 7 Cookies, Cakes, and Bars

Yup! With all the hype about sugar and obesity, I had to go and put this chapter in the book. Just remember, as in most things in life, moderation! I also use as many fruits as possible in these recipes, taking away some of the guilt and adding some great benefits in the way of antioxidants. Let me give you just a quick glimpse at sugar.

Fructose is a simple sugar found in fruits, vegetables, and nature's syrups such as maple and honey, but it is also made in a lab as high-fructose corn syrup. Fructose has become the most prevalent sweetener in our diets because it is sweeter than sucrose and used in many processed foodstuffs, including sodas and fruit-flavored drinks. Because high-fructose corn syrup (HFCS) makes a beeline almost straight to your liver, where it more readily converts to fat more often than other sugars, HFCS increases the risk for diabetes and weight gain.

Glucose, also known as blood sugar and the "lesser of three evils," is your body's preferred source of energy. Glucose is formed when your body breaks down starches. The primary responses of insulin is the elevated blood levels of glucose. Your glucose levels are easier to regulate by your body's insulin than with either sucrose or fructose. This helps maintain weight and keep your energy level on a more even keel.

Sucrose is the equal mixture of glucose and fructose, and is commonly known as table sugar. It is obtained from sugar cane or sugar beets. Fruits and vegetables also naturally contain sucrose.

The American Heart Association suggests limiting added sugars to 25 g (6 teaspoons) per day for women and 37 g (9 teaspoons) per day for men. Staying within these guidelines is quite easily achieved with these desserts because I have significantly reduced added sugars by substituting fruits and berries for that extra sweet kick.

Orange-Maple Cinnamon Roll Cookies

These cookies are soft like cinnamon rolls, but with the addition of maple syrup, half the normal amount of sugars than other sugar cookie recipes, and a hint of orange, they are simply delicious. If you would like crispier cookies, slice them half as thick, but cook 2 minutes less.

¾ stick butter or margarine,
    cold and diced
½ cup apple sauce
¼ cup brown sugar plus 2
    tablespoons, firmly packed
4 egg whites, well beaten
Rind from 1 orange, grated
3 cups flour
2 tablespoons plus
    1 teaspoon cinnamon
2 teaspoons baking soda
Nonstick cooking spray
½ cup real maple syrup

For the Glaze:
¾ cup powdered sugar
Juice from one orange
    (about 3 tablespoons)

MAKES 10-12 COOKIES

In a large bowl, beat butter, apple sauce, all but 2 tablespoons brown sugar, egg whites, and grated orange rind on high with an electric mixer until well combined. Reduce speed to low and slowly add, while beating, the flour, 2 tablespoons cinnamon, and baking soda until thoroughly mixed.

Spray one side of a large sheet of waxed paper with nonstick cooking spray. Spread the cookie dough out until it is about 12 inches long by 10 inches wide. You may want to wet your hands so dough doesn't stick to them. Evenly spread the maple syrup over the top, leaving an inch all around without syrup. Evenly sprinkle 2 tablespoons brown sugar and cinnamon on top of syrup. As you would a cake roll, start rolling the dough up as tightly as possible from the long side. Remove waxed paper and tightly wrap in film wrap. Place in the freezer for 30 minutes.

Preheat oven to 350° F. In a small bowl, whisk together powdered sugar and orange juice until smooth; set aside. Coat 2 cookie sheets with nonstick cooking spray; set aside.

Remove dough from freezer and unwrap. Place on cutting surface and slice into ½-inch thick slices using a sharp, non-serrated knife, dipping it into water. Place slices on prepared cookie sheets, 3 inches apart. Bake 9–11 minutes, or until the bottoms are medium brown in color and the top is soft, but cooked. Remove from oven to cool for a couple of minutes before transferring to platter or rack to cool completely. Drizzle orange glaze over the top and enjoy.

Reminder: Always make sure your work surfaces, utensils, pans, and tools are free of gluten. Always read product labels. Manufacturers can change product formulations without notice. When in doubt, do not buy or use a product before contacting the manufacturer for verification that the product is free of gluten.

Gluten-Free Hamantaschen Cookies

Hamantaschen cookies are three-cornered cookies that resemble Haman's hat and traditionally eaten for Purim, the Jewish holiday. But, of course, I love these cookies year-round. The kids will love them because they can pick out their favorite jam, jelly, preserves, or even chocolate as filling, though traditionally, they are filled with poppy seed, prune, or raisin filling.

Nonstick cooking spray
¾ cup brown rice flour
1 tablespoon tapioca flour
    or cornstarch
½ cup sugar
½ teaspoon baking powder
¼ teaspoon baking soda
Pinch of guar or xanthan gum
¼ cup butter or margarine
½ teaspoon vanilla extract
2 egg whites
1 tablespoon skim or
    dairy-free milk
About 1 cup jam or preserves*

Preheat oven to 350° F. Line a large baking sheet with parchment paper or lightly grease with nonstick cooking spray; set aside.

In a medium bowl mix all dry ingredients. Cut butter into small cubes and add to the dry ingredients. Use an electric mixer (hand-held or stand mixer) and mix just until crumbly. Add vanilla, egg whites, and milk, beating until smooth. Refrigerate 15 minutes.

Remove from refrigerator and roll dough out on a floured surface using a third of the dough at a time; roll it just under ¼-inch thick. Cut into 3-inch circles, adding a tablespoon of preserves to the center of each. Fold the sides upward to create a triangular window of fruit in the center. Seal corners well by squeezing firmly.

Although the 3 sides of dough should be folded over and under each other, it is far easier to simply pinch the sides together once you bring them up, something like folding the top of a box together, but with three flaps instead of four.

Place on prepared baking pan and refrigerate another 15 minutes. Meanwhile, preheat oven to 375° F. Bake the chilled cookies 8–12 minutes, until edges are light golden brown. Remove them from the oven at the first sight of this golden color, otherwise the filling will bubble up and over the sides. Let cool slightly before transferring to a plate or rack to cool completely.

*Or use your favorite jelly, jam, preserves, or mashed fresh fruit.

MAKES ABOUT 1 DOZEN COOKIES.

Yanked Ma' Jouls

Shortbread-like Ma' Joul cookies are an Easter staple from the Gulf state and are usually filled with chopped dates and nuts. I am Yanking this recipe using blueberries. I also added a marshmallow cream dip.

For the filling:

1 pint fresh or frozen blueberries
1 teaspoon cornstarch
Juice from one orange
2 tablespoons sugar
Pinch of cinnamon

For the pastry:

¼ cup butter, room
    temperature
¼ cup apple sauce
2 tablespoons powdered sugar
2 tablespoons evaporated
    skim milk
1 tablespoon lemon juice
1 cup flour

For the marshmallow dip:

1 cup marshmallow creme
1 cup plain yogurt
1 teaspoon lemon juice
1 teaspoon grated lemon zest

MAKES ABOUT 15

Make the filling: In a bowl, coat the blueberries with cornstarch evenly and then place in a medium saucepan with next 3 ingredients. Cook over high heat until boiling, stirring often. Reduce heat to low and simmer for 4–5 minutes, stirring constantly, or until very thick, breaking up the blueberries.

Remove from heat, transfer to a bowl and cool in refrigerator, uncovered, until completely cold, about 30 minutes.

Meanwhile, make the pastry. Preheat oven to 300° F. With a mixer, beat butter and apple sauce with sugar until creamy. Beat in the milk and lemon juice well. Reduce speed to low and mix in flour, a little at a time, until well incorporated.

With your hands, knead dough until it comes together and holds its shape. Pinch off a walnut-sized piece of dough and roll into a ball. With your thumb, make a well in the center and fill with a tablespoon of chilled blueberry filling. Close and seal this hole back up and roll to form a circle with your hands.

Place on an ungreased cookie sheet, flattening the bottom slightly to stand sturdy. Repeat until all dough is used, leaving an inch between each ball.

Bake 16–20 minutes or until firm and set. Cool on pan for 5 minutes before transferring to plate or rack.

While cooling, make marshmallow dip: In a bowl, combine 1 cup marshmallow creme, 1 cup plain yogurt, 1 teaspoon lemon juice, and 1 teaspoon grated lemon zest.

Not Just Pumpkin Cookies

Gooey with amazing dark chocolate, scented with molasses, and sweet with cranberries, how could you say no to these cookies? Note: Cacao is widely available in supermarkets.

Nonstick cooking spray
2 cups flour
1½ cups rolled oats
1 teaspoon baking soda
2 teaspoons cinnamon
1 teaspoon nutmeg
½ teaspoon dried ginger
1 cup mashed, ripe banana
¼ cup (½ stick) butter or
    margarine, softened
1¾ cups sugar
½ cup molasses
1¼ cups canned pumpkin
½ cup egg substitute, or 3 egg
    whites, beaten
1 cup chopped 70%, or higher,
    cacao chocolate, or dark
    chocolate chips
1 cup dried cranberries

MAKES ABOUT 36 COOKIES.

Preheat oven to 350° F. Spray a cookie sheet with nonstick cooking spray. In a large bowl, combine well the flour, rolled oats, baking soda, cinnamon, nutmeg, and ginger.

In another bowl, beat mashed banana, butter, sugar, and molasses, on high, until light and creamy. Add the pumpkin, egg substitute, cacao, and cranberries and continue beating another 10 seconds, or until well incorporated.

Reducing the mixer to low, beat in the dry with the wet until mixed well. Drop dough onto prepared baking sheet using a heaping tablespoon measure. Leave an inch in between cookies. Bake 14–15 minutes, or until the bottoms are lightly browned. Remove; let cool a few moments before transferring to a platter or rack to cool slightly before eating these gooey treasures.

While canned pumpkin is convenient, every once in a while, I still like to make my own puree for that fresh, earthy taste. Here's how to do it.

First, and foremost, make sure you buy a pie pumpkin, not the kind used to make jack-o'-lanterns. Pie pumpkins have a deeper orange color on the outside. Cut off the stem end and then halve the pumpkin top to bottom. With a large tablespoon, scoop out the seeds as well as a half inch of the stringy pulp that clings to the seeds.

Slice it, peel it, and cut into 2-inch chunks. Steam them by placing the cut pieces in a steamer above simmering water until tender, about 15–20 minutes. Remove to cool slightly before pureeing them in a food processor until smooth. That's it!

Pink Memories

Ever since I can remember, my mother made Divinity. She called it Divinity Fudge, while others in the family called it Divinity Candy or just Divinity. It was strictly white with little flavor other than that of sweetened meringue. This is one of two *Yanked* recipes for Divinity that I've made in honor of Mom and those who have struggled with breast cancer. This one is aimed more at children, and includes some crunchy candy.

3 egg whites
Pinch of salt
4 tablespoons raspberry or
   strawberry gelatin
¾ cup sugar
½ teaspoon apple
   cider vinegar
2 peppermint candies or
   canes, crushed

MAKES 25

Preheat oven to 225° F. Beat, on high, the egg whites with salt until soft peaks form. Add gelatin, sugar, and vinegar and continue beating until stiff peaks form. By hand, gently mix in the crushed peppermints. Spoon or pipe into small circular mounds on a cookie sheet covered in parchment paper. (To pipe, I use a small plastic bag with the corner cut out.) Bake 60 minutes, turn oven off, and allow to sit for an additional 45 minutes. Remove from oven and allow cookies to cool completely.

Cranberry Memories

Here's my second *Yanked* recipe for Divinity, this one for more grown-up tastes.

3 egg whites
½ teaspoon apple
    cider vinegar
Pinch of salt
¾ cup sugar
Red food coloring
1 cup dried cranberries,
    chopped

Preheat the oven to 225° F. Line cookie sheets with aluminum foil or parchment paper.

In a large glass or metal bowl, beat egg whites, vinegar, and salt to soft peaks. Gradually add sugar while continuing to beat until stiff peaks form, about 5 minutes. Add 3 or 4 drops red food coloring and beat a few seconds longer, or until it is all pink. Fold in the chopped cranberries. Drop by heaping teaspoons, or use a piping bag or a small plastic bag with the corner cut out, onto the prepared cookie sheets, 1 inch apart. Bake for 60 minutes in oven, turn off heat and let sit in oven 45 additional minutes. Cool on baking sheets.

MAKES 25

Just a Spoonful of Vinegar

For some unknown reason, researchers have paid little attention to vinegar's effects on everyday health as well as certain types of cancer. And that is a shame because vinegar leads the way (along with garlic) in all its potential healing properties. For example, it has been shown that sipping on our beloved Yankee apple cider vinegar before a meal may help lower your blood sugar, according to the *Journal of Functional Foods*. Just a tablespoon mixed with 8 ounces of water does the trick. And we here in New England have known about this tonic for centuries. Our Haymaker Switchel, a mixture of water, vinegar, and molasses, was enjoyed by our forefathers when they were using a scythe in the fields right up until the late 1800s.

Hearthside Apple-Sugar Cookie Tart

SERVES 6–8

Nibble on these sweetly crisp treats with a cup of hot cocoa.

For Sugar Cookie Crust:

2 tablespoons butter
    or margarine,
      room temperature
2 tablespoons apple sauce
⅔ cup sugar
2 egg whites, beaten
1 teaspoon rum extract
    or vanilla
1 cup flour
Powdered sugar for rolling out

For Caramelized Apple
    Topping:

2 tablespoons butter
    or margarine
2 tablespoons brown sugar
2 tablespoons
    granulated sugar
1 large or 2 small apples,
    peeled, cored, and cut into
    ¾-inch wedges
Cinnamon
Nonstick cooking spray

Make sugar cookie crust by combining the butter, apple sauce, and sugar in a large bowl. With a stout spoon, mix well together. It doesn't have to be smooth and fluffy, just well combined. Add the egg whites and rum extract, continuing to mix together. Add the flour and mix until well incorporated.

Sprinkle some powdered sugar on a work surface, transfer cookie dough and knead for 30 seconds. Roll out to about a ½-inch thick and a size that will fit inside a 8- or 9-inch nonstick, oven-safe skillet. If you don't have nonstick, a cast-iron pan will work just fine.

Place rolled cookie dough on a sugar-dusted plate and put in refrigerator until needed.

In the meantime, preheat oven to 375° F. Heat 2 tablespoons butter in your oven-safe skillet over medium-high heat. When melted, sprinkle both sugars over the butter evenly. Now let cook until it becomes a light brown, or amber-colored. Keep an eye on this because once it starts to brown, it can burn in a matter of seconds.

Remove from heat and lay your apple wedges in a circular pattern or however you choose. Reduce heat to medium and cook apples for 5 minutes. Carefully, with a fork, flip each apple wedge over to cook on the other side, keeping your pattern. Dust with desired amount of cinnamon and let cook an additional 5 minutes. Place your sugar cookie dough carefully over the apples, pricking the top of the dough to form vent holes. Immediately put the skillet into the oven and bake 12–14 minutes, or until the cookie is starting to brown. Immediately remove from oven to rest for 1 minute, but *no longer*. Grab a plate the same size or larger, and carefully invert your creation onto the plate.

Spray a pizza cutter with nonstick cooking spray, or use a sharp, non-serrated knife that has been sprayed, and cut into wedges. Enjoy while warm or let it cool to form an amazingly crispy, sugary, caramelized crust all around.

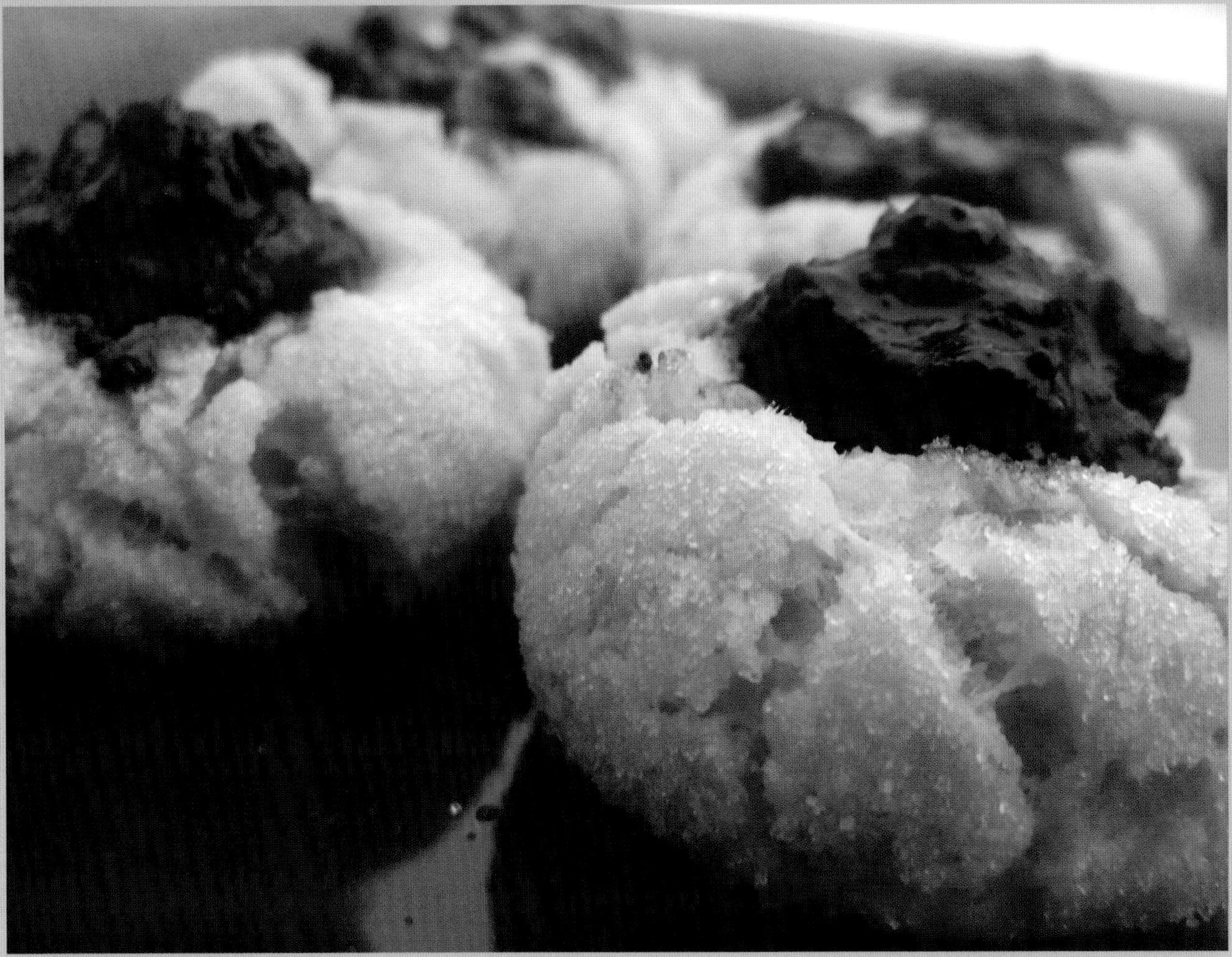

Savory Blueberry Thumbprints

Combining New England favorites such as cheddar cheese and blueberry chutney is sensational. I think Worcester's Blueberries makes the best blueberry chutney; it's made with wild blueberries and perfectly spiced with raisins, orange, ginger, and a touch of vinegar.

Nonstick cooking spray
½ cup flour
½ cup cornmeal
1 teaspoon garlic powder
1 teaspoon baking powder
1 cup shredded low-fat
    cheddar cheese
6 tablespoons fat-free cream
    cheese, softened
4 egg whites
Sugar
½ cup prepared
    blueberry chutney

Preheat oven to 350° F. Spray a cookie sheet with nonstick cooking spray; set aside.

In a large bowl, mix together flour, cornmeal, garlic, and baking powder. In a separate bowl, with an electric mixer, beat both cheeses and egg whites until creamy, on high. Reduce speed to low and beat wet ingredients in with the dry. The mixture will be very thick so you may have to stir with a wooden spoon after a few seconds. Pinch off a 2-tablespoon amount of dough and roll it into a ball with the palms of your hands. If it is too wet and sticky, add a little flour or cornmeal at a time to make it manageable. Roll each ball in sugar, pressing it in firmly. Place balls on prepared cookie sheet an inch apart. Bake 10–11 minutes, or until firm to the touch. Remove from oven and immediately make an indent in the middle of each ball with a teaspoon. While still hot, place a teaspoon of chutney in these wells and let cool completely before eating.

MAKES ABOUT 15 COOKIES

Long Live the Blueberry King!

You may know that blueberries have the highest antioxidant levels of any berry or fruit, but did you know that wild blueberries are the king of antioxidants? Because of the 5 different anthocyanins (the strongest antioxidant flavanoid) that are concentrated in the skin, blueberries are protected from the sun and other environmental stresses. A great key to remember when picking blueberries is that the darker the skin, the more antioxidants they contain. How's this for a boost? Just one ⅔ cup serving of wild blueberries gives you as much antioxidant power as 5 servings of apples, squash, and carrots and gives you the same antioxidant power as 1,730IU of Vitamin E and more protection than 1,200 mg of Vitamin C.

Gingerbread Tiramisu Cookies

Taking tiramisu to a level where children would enjoy it was simple. I *Yanked* this adult dessert into sticky cookies that can be dipped in a classically prepared whipped, tiramisu cream.

Nonstick cooking spray
1 cup flour
½ teaspoon baking powder
¼ teaspoon baking soda
½ teaspoon each cinnamon
    and dried, ground ginger
½ cup molasses
½ cup butter or margarine
½ cup sugar
2 teaspoons instant
    coffee granules or
    powdered espresso
2 teaspoons vanilla

For the dip:
4 ounces softened
    mascarpone cheese
1 cup marshmallow creme
½ cup powdered sugar
½ cup skim milk
¼ cup maple syrup

Preheat oven to 350 ° F. Spray 2 large cookie sheets with nonstick cooking spray; set aside.

MAKES 15 COOKIES WITH DIP

In a medium bowl, blend flour, baking powder, baking soda and spices; set aside. In a medium saucepan, mix molasses, butter, sugar and coffee and bring to a boil over medium heat. Once boiling and butter has completely melted, turn heat off but leave on burner, stirring to combine. Sift the flour mixture into the molasses mixture along with vanilla, whisking until smooth.

Drop by the tablespoon onto prepared pans, leaving 3 inches between mounds. Bake 8–10 minutes, or until the edges are darker than the center, and the center springs back when touched. Immediately remove from oven to cool 3 minutes before transferring to rack to completely cool. I wouldn't suggest a paper towel-lined plate because these are very sticky.

Meanwhile, make dip by using an electric mixer to beat ingredients until light and fluffy. Keep refrigerated when not using.

New England Blueberry Buckle Cake

You don't need fancy streusel topping for this ultra moist cake. This simple topping is perfectly crunchy and accents the flavor of the blueberries. And the secret to moist cake? For one, use room temperature real butter! It has more fat than margarine, which retards the production of gluten. Also, I add a bit more sugar than usual as well. Another great tip? Once your cake has cooled, always wrap tightly with film wrap and keep at room temperature. Refrigerating cake dries it exponentially.

2 cups frozen blueberries,
    divided
¾ cup granulated
    sugar, divided
½ teaspoon grated lemon zest
Juice from 1 lemon
3 tablespoons butter or
    margarine, softened
2 tablespoons apple sauce
3 cups flour
1 tablespoon baking powder
½ cup skim milk
½ cup plain yogurt
2 eggs, lightly beaten*
1 cup brown sugar,
    lightly packed
1 teaspoon cinnamon

In a small saucepan, mix 1 cup frozen blueberries, ¼ cup granulated sugar, lemon zest, and juice. Boil over medium heat, stirring and crushing blueberries, until thickened, about 10–12 minutes. Remove from heat to cool slightly.

Preheat oven to 350° F. Beat butter, applesauce, and remainder of sugar until creamy. Add flour and baking powder, incorporating until just blended either by hand or on a low-speed mixer. Add milk, yogurt, and eggs. Blend until it is just incorporated. Fold in remainder of blueberries. The batter will be lumpy.

Lightly grease a 9-inch square baking pan. Pour half the batter evenly into prepared pan. Drizzle thickened blueberry mixture over the top. Cover with remainder of the batter.

In a small bowl, stir together brown sugar and cinnamon well. Sprinkle over the top of cake and bake 25–30 minutes, or until it springs back when touched in the middle.

*Many chefs swear by using only egg yolks in cake mix for the maximum moistness. Use 4 egg yolks instead of 2 whole eggs if desired.

SERVES 6

SERVES 6

Sweet Apple Baden Cake

Don't let the list of ingredients fool you. This recipe is simple, inexpensive, and, by far, the most extraordinary apple cake you will ever have. I purposely made the cake slightly less sweet than ordinary coffee cake–like desserts, because I wanted the apple to shine through, and it certainly won't let you down. Use your favorite sweet, hard apple here.

Nonstick cooking spray
2 cups apple cider
1½ cups flour
¾ cup brown sugar
1 teaspoon baking powder
1 teaspoon cinnamon
½ stick butter, melted
2 egg whites, beaten
1 large or two small Liberty apples, peeled, cored and diced

For the topping:
1 cup flour
¾ cup brown sugar
2 tablespoons apple jelly, heated and whisked smooth
1 teaspoon cinnamon
½ teaspoon ground nutmeg

For the glaze:
1 cup powdered sugar
2 teaspoons vanilla
2–3 tablespoons milk

Preheat oven to 350° F. Spray nonstick cooking spray into a 9-inch pie pan or a 9-inch square pan.

Reduce the apple cider. Boil 2 cups apple cider until it reduces to make 1 cup. (Or substitute 1 cup frozen apple juice concentrate, thawed or 1 cup maple syrup.)

In a large bowl, combine flour, brown sugar, baking powder, and cinnamon, mixing well. Stir in the apple cider reduction, melted butter, and egg whites until just blended; lumps are fine. Transfer to the prepared pie pan. Evenly spread the diced apples over the top.

In a small bowl, combine all topping ingredients. Every bit of the topping must be damp so if you need more apple jelly, add a tablespoon at a time. Evenly sprinkle it over the apples.

Bake 30–35 minutes, or until firm in the center when touched. Remove to rack to cool for just a little bit, as you'll want to serve this beauty warm. While waiting, make your glaze by combining all ingredients and mixing until smooth. Start out with 2 tablespoons milk and add more if needed to drizzle.

SERVES 6–8 PEOPLE

Self-Glazing Chestnut Cake

This cake is the epitome of what should be served in the winter holidays, with the taste of roasted chestnuts evident in every bite. What is nice about this cake is that you can substitute any peanut in place of the chestnuts and replace the apple jelly with a jelly of your choice as well.

For those of you who are on a gluten-free diet, replace the flour with corn, buckwheat, or quinoa flours because the jelly will keep the cake moist, regardless of what type of flour you use.

1¾ cups apple jelly
2 teaspoons vanilla
2 teaspoons lemon juice
½ teaspoon ground cloves
Nonstick cooking spray
¾ cup brown sugar
2 teaspoons cornstarch
½ teaspoon cinnamon
1¼ cups flour
¾ cup granulated sugar
2 teaspoons baking powder
1 teaspoon nutmeg
¾ cup almond milk
¾ cup chopped, cooked
  (roasted) chestnuts
2 tablespoons melted butter
  or margarine

Combine apple jelly, vanilla, lemon juice, and cloves in a small microwavable bowl, cover loosely, and heat for 45 seconds. Remove to stir. If the jelly hasn't melted completely, continue heating another 15 seconds; set aside.

Preheat oven to 350° F. Spray an 8- by 8-inch pan with nonstick cooking spray; set aside.

In a small bowl, mix together brown sugar, cornstarch, and cinnamon until well combined; set aside.

In another bowl, blend flour, granulated sugar, baking powder, and nutmeg. Add the milk, chestnuts and melted butter to flour mixture, stirring just enough to combine. Pour into prepared pan. Sprinkle brown sugar mixture over the top. Pour melted apple jelly evenly over the top but do not stir in. Bake 30 minutes, or until the top springs back when touched. The jelly will have pooled in the center of the cake, so test the cake along the side.

Remove from oven, let cool for a few minutes and scoop out cake to serve as is, or with ice cream or whipped topping if desired.

SERVES 6

Rum-Raisin Depression Cake

SERVES 6–8

This kind of cake was a popular treat during the Depression era in the US; the cake is made without eggs, butter, or milk because these were rationed and expensive during that time. On the same hand, apples were abundant, cheap, and used excessively. Yankees have been using apples in every aspect of home life since the Puritan era, so it was only natural we incorporate this taste, along with New England maple syrup, into this delicious cake.

The use of boiled raisins as a topping goes back to days before the Civil War. You will notice, as well, that there is no leavening agent other than a pinch of baking soda: You won't believe the reaction of soda and vinegar in this recipe. This cake is higher than if you used baking powder or eggs. And the texture and taste are out of this world.

½ cup raisins
3 cups apple juice or cider
¼ teaspoon ground cloves
2 teaspoons lemon juice
Nonstick cooking spray
1⅓ cups flour
½ cup crushed
   graham crackers
½ cup sugar
1 teaspoon baking soda
1 teaspoon cinnamon
1⅓ cups apple sauce
¾ cup maple syrup
¼ cup pure olive oil

2 teaspoons rum extract
   (or vanilla or almond)
2 teaspoons apple
   cider vinegar

Make spiced raisin sauce: Boil raisins, apple juice, and cloves in a medium saucepan over medium heat for 15 minutes, adding more juice if needed to keep liquid just above raisins. Remove, stir in lemon juice, and transfer to a bowl. Cover and refrigerate until cold.

Preheat oven to 350° F. Spray a 9-inch cake pan with nonstick cooking spray; set aside.

In a large bowl, combine flour, graham crackers, sugar, baking soda, and cinnamon; mix well. Add apple sauce, maple syrup, oil, rum extract, and vinegar, stirring into the flour mixture until just combined. Pour into prepared pan and bake 36–38 minutes, or until nicely browned on top and the cake springs back when touched in the middle. Remove from oven to cool slightly before transferring to a plate or serving platter.

Remove sauce from refrigerator, stir to combine, and serve over cake. Add whipped topping if desired. (Sauce can also be warmed before serving.)

Blueberry Crunch Cake

Remember when your grandmother made the best blueberry cake around? I still think there is no cake around that can rival the taste of blueberries. *It's Just That Simple!*

Nonstick cooking spray
½ cup yellow cornmeal
¼ cup plus 2 tablespoons flour, divided
¼ cup plus 2 tablespoons sugar, divided
1 teaspoon baking powder
½ cup buttermilk or evaporated skim milk
½ cup egg substitute
1 tablespoon plus 1 teaspoon pure olive oil
2 teaspoons vanilla
1½ cups fresh blueberries
Pinch of cinnamon
1 teaspoon powdered sugar

Preheat oven to 425° F. Spray an 8-inch round baking pan or spring-form pan with nonstick cooking spray.

In medium bowl, combine cornmeal, ¼ cup flour, ¼ cup of the sugar, and baking powder. Add milk, egg substitute, oil, and vanilla; stir just to combine. Pour into prepared pan; top with berries.

In a small bowl, combine the remaining sugar, cinnamon; sprinkle evenly over berries. Bake until golden, 25–30 minutes. Cool 10 minutes; sprinkle evenly with powdered sugar, and serve warm.

SERVES 6–8

Blackberry Cream Ricotta Cake

SERVES 6–8

This deliciously moist cake is a cross between a pound cake and cheesecake. It has moistness and body that few other cakes can stand up to. Nonstick cooking spray

1½ cups flour
½ cup sugar
1 cup low-fat ricotta cheese,
    beaten smooth
¼ cup pure olive oil
5 egg whites
Juice and grated rind
    from 1 lemon
1 cup fresh blackberries,
    raspberries or blueberries

Preheat oven to 350° F. Liberally spray a round cake pan with the cooking spray; set aside.

In a large bowl, mix the flour and sugar until combined. Add the cheese, oil, egg whites, and juice and rind from the lemon, and beat well. It doesn't have to be completely lump free. Fold in the berries and pour into prepared pan. Bake 30–35 minutes, or until nicely browned on top and when toothpick inserted in center comes out clean. Remove from oven to cool for a few minutes before removing to a serving platter. Serve warm or chilled with whipped cream and extra berries.

Cranberry Swirl Cake

Nicely balanced in taste, yet bold enough to complement your holiday dinner, this cake is a favorite among true foodies. You can use other berries that will be just as delicious, such as blueberries, raspberries, or any fruit compote.

Nonstick cooking spray
¼ cup whole berry or jellied
    cranberry sauce
1 cup flour
¾ cup sugar
½ cup cornmeal
1 teaspoon baking powder
Grated zest and juice
    from 1 lemon
½ cup cinnamon, golden or
    any flavored fat-free
    eggnog of your choice
4 tablespoons butter or
    margarine, melted
3 tablespoons apple sauce
4 egg whites

For the cranberry cream:
1 cup jellied or whole berry
    cranberry sauce
½ cup evaporated skim milk
2 tablespoons honey

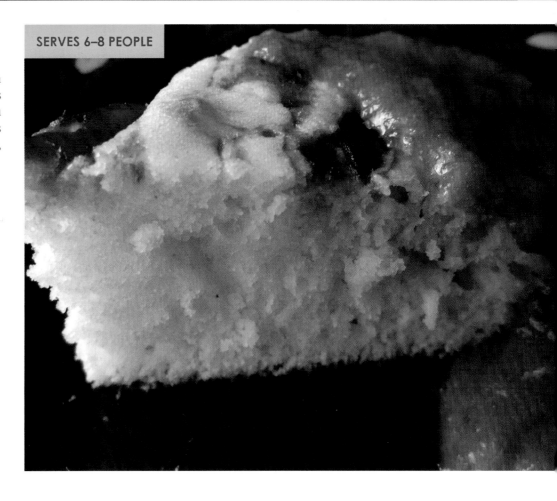

SERVES 6–8 PEOPLE

Preheat oven to 350° F. Spray a 9-inch pie tin with nonstick cooking spray. In a blender or food processor, puree cranberry sauce until it is liquidy; no need to get the lumps out. You can also do this with a wire whisk, by hand if needed. Set aside.

In a large bowl, mix together flour, sugar, cornmeal, baking powder, and lemon zest. In a separate bowl, combine eggnog, lemon juice, melted butter, applesauce, and egg whites. Combine the wet with the dry until well incorporated; no need for the batter to be lump-free. Pour into prepared pie tin and drizzle prepared cranberry sauce over the top in a spiral. Bake 30 minutes, or until the cake springs back when touched.

Make Cranberry Cream by placing ingredients in the bowl of a food processor or blender and pulsing until as smooth as possible, about 15 seconds. Remove and keep cold until needed.

When the cake is done, allow to cool and top with cranberry cream.

NOT Grandma's Date Bars

This recipe is easily adaptable to the classic look of date bars by using an 8- by 8-inch baking pan. These updated bars are super crunchy all around with a delicious tart sweetness.

Nonstick cooking spray
1¼ cups flour
1¼ cups rolled oats
½ cup brown sugar
½ cup grape, strawberry,
   or apple jelly, heated
   and whisked
¼ stick butter or
   margarine, melted

For the filling:
1 cup whole berry
   cranberry sauce
¾ cup dried cranberries
   or cherries
½ cup raisins
½ cup orange or apple juice
1 teaspoon cornstarch

MAKES 6

Preheat oven to 350° F. Spray a 6-cup muffin tin with nonstick cooking spray, or use cupcake papers, sprayed liberally. In a small bowl, blend the flour, oats, and brown sugar well. Stir in jelly and butter until the mixture is moist throughout.

To make the filling, add all the ingredients to the bowl of a blender or food processor and puree, on high, until all the raisins are minced. Remove and transfer to a bowl. Add 1½ tablespoons flour mixture into the bottom of each muffin cup, tamping down slightly, making sure the pan isn't showing through the mixture. Add a tablespoon of the raisin mixture, spreading out to make it level. Add 2 tablespoons flour

mixture on top, again, tamping down gently. Bake 15–18 minutes, or until lightly browned and crisp on top. Remove to cool for at least 15 minutes before running knife around edges to loosen. Cool completely at room temperature before lifting out.

CHAPTER 8 More Desserts

This is a chapter I'm excited about: You will notice a general theme, and it is fruits, fruits, and more fruits (and berries). To take this idea a step further, it is quite acceptable to substitute much of the fat contained in many baked goods and desserts with a healthier alternative: Yup, you guessed it! More fruit. According to Jamie Stern, MS, "Fruit purees, including applesauce and pumpkin, work especially well when used in 50% of the total fat of a recipe—cakes, cookies, and gingerbread being just a few that result in a moist and desirable flavor and texture. Pureed pears and prunes are fantastic in brownies, spice cakes, scones and muffins. Fat-free dairy products have equally satisfying 'ends to the means' as well. Buttermilk and yogurt can be used at a 50-50 ratio when using solid fats and up to 75% of the total liquid fat amount in desserts, without creating a negative texture or taste." Enjoy!

Yankee Sticky Quince

If quince is not your thing, fresh apples can be easily substituted. The sweet sap of fruit and scent of cloves are comforting.

4 quinces
¼ cup fresh cranberries
¼ cup apple cider or juice
1 cup prepared mincemeat
¼ cup brown sugar
½ teaspoon ginger
¼ teaspoon ground cloves
2 tablespoons maple syrup

Preheat oven to 375° F. Slice off a quarter of the entire quince from the top; discard.

In a small saucepan, combine the cranberries and apple juice. Put over medium-high heat with a lid ajar to let steam out but keep the mixture from splattering while cooking. Boil 2½–3 minutes, or until cranberries have become soft and are popping. Remove from heat, stir and let sit for 3 minutes. Remove the cranberries from the liquid into a bowl. Add the mincemeat, and stir to combine. Set aside the cooking liquid from the cranberries.

In another bowl, combine and mix the brown sugar, ginger, and cloves; set aside.

With a paring knife peel, core, and empty most of quince flesh, leaving half an inch wall all around. I cut my quince so it has straight sides, purely for decorative purposes. Spray the outside with cooking spray and roll in brown sugar mixture.

Spray 4 cups of a muffin tin with nonstick cooking spray. Place the sugar coated quinces in each and fill the inside of each empty quince with the mincemeat/cranberry mixture.

Sprinkle any remaining brown sugar mixture over the top and bake for 40–50 minutes until quince is nicely browned but still firm to the touch.

Remove to serving plate, and pour some of the cranberry liquid and maple syrup over the top of each.

SERVES 4

Irish Apple Bread Pudding "Pie"

This bread pudding is anything but typical. It is beautifully sweetened, less dense and "gummy" than many other equivalent puddings, and the sweet, caramelized crust that forms makes you want to pick it off first then eat the rest later. Use whatever muffin you desire; I just happen to adore cinnamon. Whichever muffin you choose, be sure that once you cut them up, you have 5 cups' worth. *Taitneamh a bhaint as!* (Enjoy!)

4 large cinnamon muffins
Butter-flavored nonstick
    cooking spray
3 large apples, peeled, cored,
    and diced, divided
1 cup apple juice or water
¼ cup maple syrup
¾ cup skim milk
½ cup egg substitute
⅓ cup brown sugar
1 teaspoon cinnamon
1 teaspoon vanilla or
    almond extract
Juice and grated rind
    of 1 lemon
½ teaspoon dried ginger

For Irish Butterscotch Cream:

1 cup evaporated skim milk
2 tablespoons brown sugar
2 tablespoons Bailey's
    Irish Cream
1 tablespoon apple jelly
1 teaspoon vanilla

Slice muffins horizontally about 1-inch thick and spray cut sides with nonstick cooking spray. Grill over medium heat until well browned, about 2 minutes per side. Place on a plate and let cool in refrigerator for an hour, preferably overnight to dry out.

Meanwhile, add ⅔ of the diced apple to a saucepan along with apple juice or water and maple syrup. Bring to a boil over medium heat, stir, reduce to low, and simmer 6–8 minutes, or until it has thickened and apples are done, but still firm. Remove from heat and set aside.

Spray a 9- or 10-inch cake pan with nonstick cooking spray liberally; set aside. Preheat oven to 350° F.

Cut grilled muffins into cubes and place in a bowl along with remainder of diced apple.

In another bowl, whisk together milk, egg substitute, brown sugar, cinnamon, vanilla, juice and grated lemon rind and ginger. Pour over muffin cubes and gently toss to evenly coat. Transfer to prepared cake pan, smoothing out the top. Spoon cooked apple mixture over the top evenly and bake 40–45 minutes, or until it is firm when touched in the center with a spoon or fork. Remove pudding to cool slightly before running a dull knife around the edge to loosen.

Make Irish Butterscotch Cream while pudding is baking: Put milk in a saucepan with brown sugar and Bailey's Irish Cream and apple jelly. Over low heat, bring to a simmer while stirring frequently to prevent scorching. After 3–4 minutes, it will be thicker. Stir in 1 teaspoon vanilla and remove from heat.

Cut pudding into wedges and serve drizzled with Irish Butterscotch Cream.

SERVES 6–8

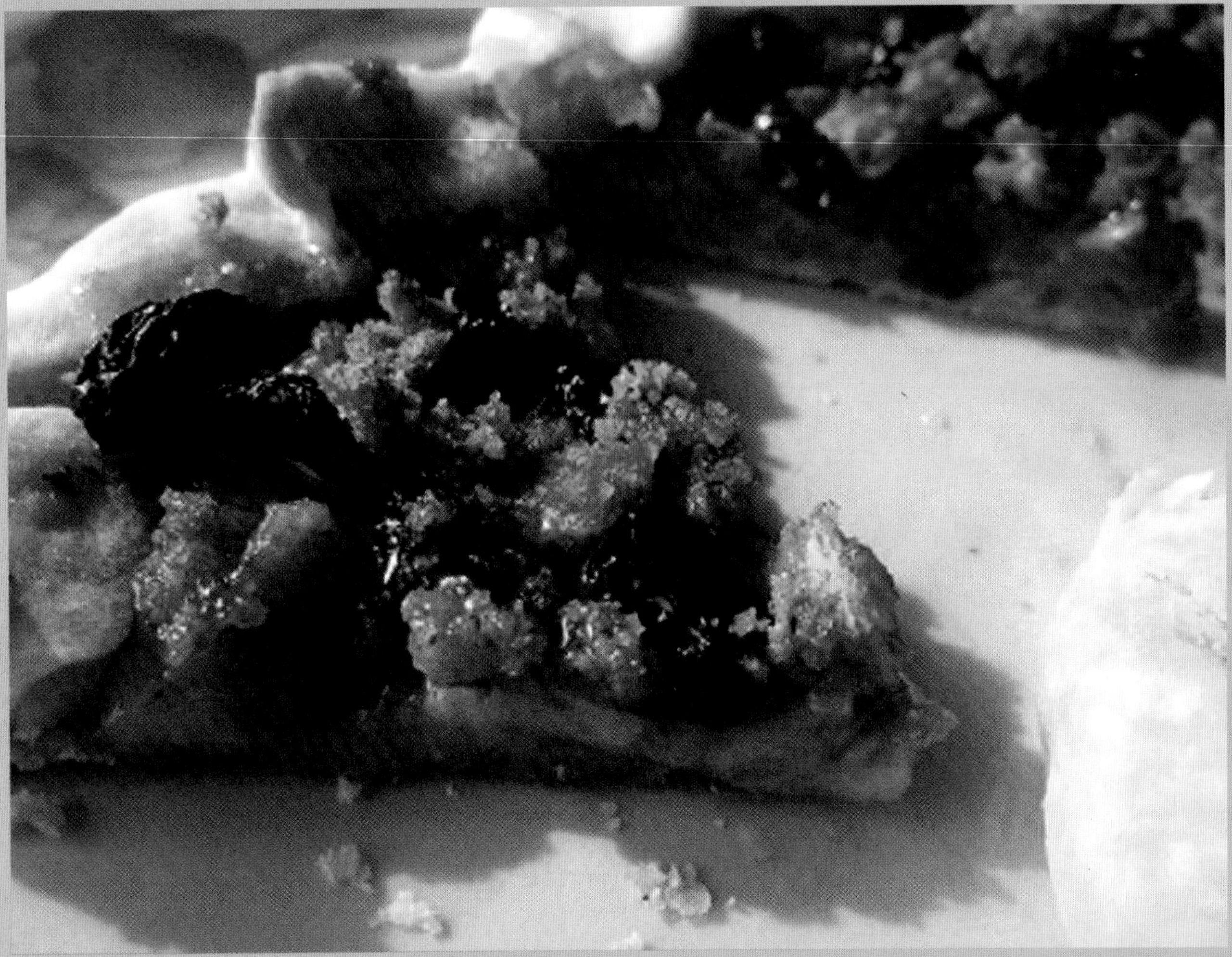

Yanked Caramel Banana Galette

For those of you who have never had a galette, you are in for a treat. For those of you who don't care for alcohol, substitute ½ teaspoon rum extract for the dark rum.

⅓ cup raisins
2 tablespoons dark rum
¼ cup apple juice
    or cider, boiling
½ (15-ounce) package
    refrigerated pie crust dough
3 cups ripe bananas
    (diagonally sliced,
    ¼-inch thick)
½ cup loosely packed
    brown sugar
½ apple, peeled and grated
2 teaspoons lemon juice
½ cup sugar
2 tablespoons water

Combine raisins, rum, and apple juice; set aside.

Preheat oven to 400° F. Roll pie dough into a 10-inch circle and place on an ungreased baking sheet. Arrange banana slices in one long spiral on dough, starting from an inch from the edge and spiraling toward the center. Fold the edge of the pie dough an inch over bananas, partially covering the outside ring of sliced bananas.

Drain the raisins, then sprinkle them evenly over the top of the galette.

In a small bowl, combine brown sugar with grated apple and lemon juice. Sprinkle this evenly over the bananas and raisins.

Bake 30 minutes, or until crust is golden brown.

Meanwhile, combine sugar and water in a saucepan. Over medium heat, cook until medium brown in color without stirring, about 7 minutes. Remove from heat and pour over the cooked galette. Cut into wedges.

SERVES 6–8.

Slow-Cooker Figgy Pudding

Traditional Figgy Pudding is a steamed dessert that resembles a very firm mousse more than anything. The *only* modern method of preparation that closely resembles the original intent of this English pudding uses a slow cooker. It comes out to an almost cake-like consistency while still having that pudding-like texture. Light, fluffy, and packed with flavor, this almost melt-in-your-mouth version is superior to that of any other figgy pudding I knowf.

Originally, this classic included figs, breadcrumbs, pepper, almonds or walnuts, dates, raisins, and a hard sauce. Dark rum was often added, as well, and you can add it here if you like: Simply add ½ cup dark rum or 2 teaspoons rum extract.

1 cup skim milk
1 cup molasses
1 cup dried figs, dates or plums (prunes), pitted and minced
½ cup dried cranberries, craisins, or raisins
3 tablespoons butter or margarine, melted
1¼ cups flour
1 cup fresh rye, white, or wheat breadcrumbs
¾ cup brown sugar
¾ cup cocoa
2 teaspoons baking powder
¼ teaspoon cinnamon
¼ teaspoon nutmeg
1 teaspoon grated lemon zest
1 apple, peeled, cored, chopped fine

For Red Currant Hard Sauce:

½ cup apple or pumpkin butter
2 tablespoons butter or margarine, softened
1–1½ cups powdered sugar
2 tablespoons orange juice
½ cup red currant jam, jelly, or preserves

In a medium saucepan, stir the milk, molasses, figs, cranberries, and butter. Place over medium heat. When it starts to simmer, reduce heat to low and allow figs and cranberries to cook for 10–12 minutes, or until they are softened, mixing occasionally. Remove from heat to cool 15 minutes.

Meanwhile, in a large bowl, combine the remainder of ingredients (except for the sauce ingredients!) until thoroughly mixed. Add the milk/fig mixture and stir to combine. If there are lumps, that is perfectly fine.

Preheat slow cooker on medium heat. Transfer the pudding to slow cooker, cover, and reduce heat to low. Cook for 1½–2 hours, or until cake bounces back when touched on top.

Make hard sauce: With a hand mixer or tabletop mixer, beat apple butter and butter on high for 1 minute, or until it is very creamy and fluffy. Reduce speed to low and beat in a half cup of powdered sugar. Keep adding powdered sugar until it resembles peanut butter. Beat in the orange juice to thin out to the consistency of whipped cream. Fold in the red currant jam by hand so that it is streaked throughout. Substitute your favorite jam or preserves here if you'd like, or substitute real dark rum or rum extract to stay with tradition.

Pour sauce over warm pudding; sauce will thin out and "melt."

SERVES 4–6

Warmly Scented Apple-Jam Danish with Maple Cream

The Yankee Apple Jam you'll make for this recipe contains a substantial amount of very, *very* strong coffee.

4 Granny Smith apples,
    peeled, cored, and
    cut into large chunks
2 cups very strong coffee
3 tablespoons brown sugar
½ cup raisins
1 teaspoon lemon juice
¾ cup maple syrup
3 tablespoons plain yogurt
1 tablespoon lemon juice
2 sheets puff pastry, thawed

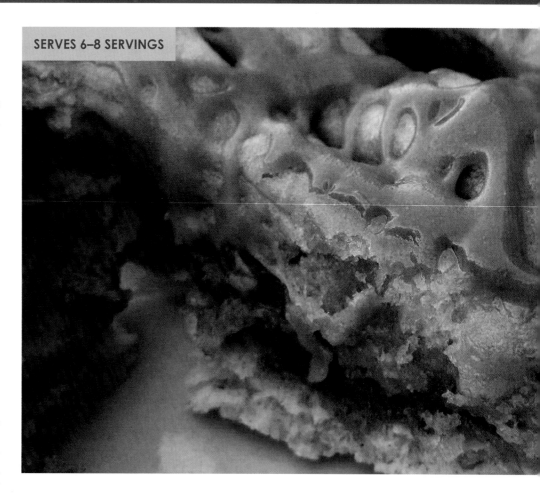

SERVES 6–8 SERVINGS

Make Yankee Apple Jam: Add first 5 ingredients to a medium saucepan and cook over medium-high for 13–15 minutes, or until most of the liquid has evaporated. Remove from heat and mash well or puree in a food processor or blender just until mashed, but not smooth. Transfer to a bowl, cover and refrigerate until needed. Makes about 2 cups.

Make Maple Cream: In a small saucepan, heat the maple syrup over medium heat until just starting to bubble. Remove from heat and whisk in yogurt and lemon juice. Remove to bowl to cool while making remainder of recipe.

Preheat oven to 350° F. Cover the bottom of a baking sheet with waxed or parchment paper.

Lightly flour a work surface and lay out a layer of puff pastry onto the flour, coating both sides. Gently roll out each sheet to remove the creases and enlarge just slightly. Equally cut each sheet into 3 squares.

Place equal amounts of Yankee Apple Jam mixture in the center of each pastry square, spreading slightly to conform to the shape of the pastry square if needed. Bring all sides to the center of the square, overlapping a little.

Place on prepared baking sheet, seam-side down and flatten to move the apple jam evenly throughout the danish. With a sharp knife, make 3-5 slits on top of each danish. Bake for about 22–25 minutes, or until lightly browned on top. The slits will open as the danish cooks. Remove from oven and let cool slightly before topping with the Maple Cream.

Blackberry-Orange Crunch Pie

Just that little hint of orange juice enlivens this pie enough so that you can get two different citrus tastes in one. The tartness of the lemon rind in the streusel topping is just . . . well, icing on the pie!

Pie pastry for a single 9-inch pie
6 cups (1¾ pounds)
    blackberries
½ cup sugar
3 tablespoons cornstarch
1 tablespoon frozen orange
    juice concentrate, thawed
4 tablespoons honey

For the streusel topping:
1 cup flour
¼ teaspoon dried ginger
¼ cup granulated sugar
¼ cup brown sugar
3 tablespoons apple jelly,
    melted and whisked smooth
1 teaspoon grated lemon zest

SERVES 6–8

Preheat oven to 350° F. Spread the pastry onto a 9-inch pie plate, and crimp, if desired, around the edges. In a large bowl, combine blackberries, sugar, cornstarch, and orange juice so that all blackberries are coated. Remove to prepared pie pan and drizzle with honey.

Make streusel topping by combining all ingredients in a bowl and mixing well.

Top the pie evenly with Streusel Topping, place onto a baking sheet, and bake 50–55 minutes or until filling is bubbly and topping is crispy brown. If the topping is browning too fast, tent a piece of tin foil over the pie. Remove from oven and let cool thoroughly before serving.

Baked Chocolate Jam Ganache "Cake"

A salty-sweet and crispy crust. A thick, soft layer of chocolate, pudding-like cake. And a thin layer of sweet jam topped with a thin layer of soft, ganache-like gooey chocolate. Simply delicious!!!

2 cups mini pretzels
2 tablespoons cocoa powder
1 tablespoon sugar
2 tablespoons grape jelly,
    melted and whisked smooth
Nonstick cooking spray
12 ounces 70% or higher cacao
    chocolate bar, chopped
    and divided
1½ cups evaporated skim milk
4 egg whites, beaten
1 teaspoon vanilla
½ cup strawberry jelly,
    preserves or all fruit
3 tablespoons 2% milk
1 teaspoon honey

Crush pretzels: place about 2 cups mini pretzels, cocoa powder and sugar in the bowl of a food processor and pulse until fine crumbs are formed. With your fingers, mix in the grape jelly to evenly moisten all crumbs.

Spray a 9-inch pie tin with nonstick cooking spray and press crumb mixture against the bottom and up the sides; set aside.

In a saucepan, melt 6 ounces (1 cup) chocolate in milk over medium heat, stirring almost constantly. The chocolate will thicken before thinning. Remove from heat the moment chocolate has melted. Slowly stir in egg whites and vanilla and pour into prepared pie crust. Bake 20–22 minutes, or until puffed up. Remove to refrigerator to cool completely, about 2 hours uncovered.

Meanwhile, melt jelly in microwave for about 15 seconds, or until it is smooth when stirring. Pour over cooled pie, spreading evenly over the top. Place back in refrigerator for 10 minutes, or until jelly has gelled again.

Heat skim milk, remainder of chocolate and honey together in a saucepan, or microwave, until chocolate has completely melted. Remove from heat and let cool for 5 minutes. Evenly pour over pie and for the last time, place back into refrigerator until the chocolate top has completely cooled, about another hour, uncovered.

SERVES 6–8

Mango Confit Gratins

This is a great take on two popular desserts from the past and present. Does anyone remember grapefruit gratins? A fancy title for slicing your breakfast grapefruit in half, sprinkling it with sugar and broiling it until it browned. Confits are simply anything slowly stewed, even savory dishes. By combining the two desserts and *Yanking* the preparation of both, you end up with a beautifully tasty fruit treat where the mango flavor explodes.

3 medium mangoes
1 cup white grape juice
½ cup apple jelly
2 tablespoons mint
    leaves, shredded
½ cup crushed
    macadamia nuts*
1 tablespoon brown sugar
1 teaspoon pure olive oil
Berries of your choice

Peel mangoes and cut as close to the flat pit as possible, creating large slices that you can then slice into wedges, enough to fill 4 (1-cup) ramekins.

Put the wedged mangoes in a large bowl. Transfer the peelings and any leftover mango pieces to a saucepan with the juice, jelly, and the mint leaves. Bring the peelings to a boil over high heat, reduce to low, and simmer 10 minutes.

Remove peeling mixture from stove and strain the juice into the bowl of sliced mangoes, stirring to coat well. Evenly divide among 4 ramekins. Preheat broiler.

Meanwhile, in a small bowl, toss macadamia pieces with brown sugar and olive oil. Sprinkle over mango ramekins and broil 4–6 minutes, at least 3 inches from heat source. When nut mixture is starting to brown, remove from under broiler and let cool slightly before topping with berries and serving.

*To easily crush macadamia nuts, put them in a plastic bag, fold it over and hit them with the bottom of a small skillet. Or use a rolling pin.

SERVES 4

Coconut-Apple Caramel Flan

This super creamy flan is an all-time favorite not only because of the flavor but because of its ease of preparation and the super short ingredient list. If you have never made your own caramel before, it is much easier than you think. But a word to the wise. You truly need to keep a close eye on it because once it starts to turn color, it does so *very* quickly.

1 cup evaporated skim milk
1 cup apple juice
4 egg whites
1⅔ cups shredded
    coconut, divided
1 cup sugar
3 tablespoons water

In the bowl of a blender or food processor, combine milk, apple juice, egg whites, and 1½ cups coconut. Blend for 10 seconds on high, leaving it in the container while preparing caramel. This will be your flan batter.

Preheat oven to 350° F. In a saucepan, stir the sugar and water over medium-low heat, allowing sugar to melt completely, about 4–5 minutes. Once melted, raise the heat to medium and cook until it is medium brown in color. If you want lighter flavored caramel, cook the sugar to a lighter brown color. The darker the color, the more intense the flavor. Be careful not to scorch or burn the sugar, for it happens very quick and will be bitter tasting. Quickly pour into a 9-inch cake pan.

Give the flan batter one more whirl to combine and immediately pour over the caramel. Bake 40–45 minutes, or until it has puffed up and started to change color on top. Remove from oven to cool slightly before carefully inverting it onto a plate or platter that is larger than the cake pan. Sprinkle the top with remainder of coconut and let cool before serving.

Yanked Apple Charlotte

I created this fantastic recipe for a wonderful Maine company, Bar Harbor Foods. Their lineup is second to none if you want the original flavors of New England any time of year.

1 (15-ounce) can prepared Indian pudding (I use Bar Harbor brand)
2 cups dried, unseasoned breadcrumbs
1 cup brown sugar
Butter-flavored nonstick cooking spray
2 tablespoons butter or margarine
3 large Granny Smith apples, peeled and cored
1 cup apple cider or juice
1 cup apple jelly
1 teaspoon Chinese 5-spice powder
⅓ cup whole berry cranberry sauce

SERVES 6

Slice Indian pudding into 6 equally sized rounds; set aside.

In a shallow bowl, combine breadcrumbs and brown sugar well; set aside.

Place the Indian pudding rounds, one at a time, into the bread crumb mixture and gently press the crumbs into both sides, then placing the round in a dish.

Liberally spray a large skillet with nonstick cooking spray. Place skillet over medium-high heat and add the coated Indian Pudding slices into the skillet. Cook until browned on bottom, about 6–7 minutes. Flip and brown the other side. Reduce heat to low, cover, and cook 4 minutes per side, or until softened and hot.

Meanwhile, slice apples into 8 wedges each.

Heat butter in another large skillet over medium heat until melted. Add apples and cider, and toss and cook until just crisp tender, about 4–5 minutes. Add apple jelly, Chinese 5-spice powder, and cranberry sauce. Stir to combine well and continue cooking until the apples are tender.

Serve pudding rounds immediately, topped with the glazed apples.

Blackberry-Lemonade Cobbler Pie

SERVES 6–8

Wild blackberries are difficult to pick. Their thorns make rose bushes seem like a walk in the park. But I would stray time and time again through those brambles to pick overripe berries for this pie. I say overripe because there simply isn't enough juice in under-ripe or even ripe berries to make a greatly flavorful blackberry pie. Look in the supermarket for jumbo, overripe blackberries to make this pie.

6 cups (1¾ pounds)
    overripe blackberries
Pie pastry for a single 9-inch pie
½ cup sugar
3 tablespoons cornstarch
2 teaspoons lemon juice
4 tablespoons honey

For lemonade cobbler dough:
1½ cups flour
½ cup sugar
2 teaspoons baking powder
½ teaspoon salt
¼ cup butter, margarine,
    or shortening
¼–½ cup skim milk
4 tablespoons frozen
    lemonade concentrate,
    thawed (or frozen orange
    juice concentrate)
½ cup plain yogurt or
    sour cream

Leave the blackberries out at room temperature for at least 4 hours before making this pie. It gives them time to soften a bit, thereby emitting more juice.

When ready, preheat oven to 350° F. Spread the pastry onto a 9-inch pie plate, and crimp, if desired, around the edges.

Make the lemonade cobbler dough: In large bowl, combine flour, sugar, baking powder, and salt. With your fingers or a fork or two, work the butter into the flour mixture until it resembles peas. Add the milk, lemonade concentrate, and yogurt. Combine until a soft, almost pourable dough is formed, starting with ¼ cup milk and adding more if needed.

In a large bowl, combine blackberries, sugar, cornstarch, and lemon juice; mix well so that all blackberries are coated. Pour into prepared pie crust, spreading out evenly. Drizzle honey over the top and dot with lemonade cobbler dough, covering as much of the top as possible, but leaving small holes here and there. Place on a baking pan and bake 45–50 minutes, or until dough is nicely browned. Remove from oven to cool completely before serving.

Snow White Haupia

Similar to the French blancmange seen in high-end restaurants of old, haupia is a creamy, almost pure white and decadent, dessert found at luaus. Expensive, store-brand coconut milk is replaced by making an excellent substitution here. The touch of lemon is so perfect. These literally melt in your mouth.

1¾ cups flaked
    coconut, divided
Nonstick cooking spray
1¼ cups buttermilk
Grated zest of ½ lemon
5 tablespoons cornstarch
½ cup sugar
1 teaspoon lemon juice

MAKES ABOUT 10 SQUARES

Preheat oven to 350° F. Spread 1 cup coconut onto a pie pan and bake 7–8 minutes, or until well browned, Immediately remove from oven and transfer to a plate.

Spray a loaf pan with nonstick cooking spray and evenly sprinkle half the cooked coconut on the bottom; set aside.

In a saucepan, combine buttermilk, lemon zest, and remainder of coconut. Bring to scalding (but don't let boil) over medium heat, stirring almost constantly. Remove from heat and let cool 10 minutes before transferring to the bowl of a food processor or blender. Puree for 30 seconds, or until coconut is finely ground. Strain through a fine metal sieve into a medium saucepan. Add cornstarch and sugar, whisking until smooth. Bring to scalding over medium heat, continuing to whisk constantly. Do not let this boil! After 2 minutes, it will thicken to the consistency of a roux. Stir in the lemon juice and immediately remove from heat. Carefully pour into prepared pan.

Sprinkle remaining cooked coconut evenly over the top, pressing the coconut down slightly to even out. Cover with film wrap. Refrigerate until firm, about 2 hours. Remove to cut in desired sizes and serve cold.

Deliciously Sweet and Natural Watermelon-Mint Gel

I remember the first time I made these for the kids, they didn't know what to think. "What? No seeds to spit?" This will be your new "go-to" summertime treat. Any adult who wants to make a watermelon mint julep just needs to add a splash of bourbon.

5 cups cubed, seedless
    watermelon
1 cup honey, sugar,
    or corn syrup
1 tablespoon lemon juice
2 (0.25-ounce) envelopes
    unflavored gelatin
½ cup cold water
1 teaspoon peppermint or
    spearmint extract

Puree the watermelon in a blender or food processor on high until as smooth as possible. This will only take a minute, and do in batches if necessary. Transfer to a large saucepan, and whisk in the honey and lemon juice. Bring to a boil over medium-high heat, stirring often. Keep cooking if you are using sugar until the sugar has dissolved.

Meanwhile, sprinkle gelatin over the top of the cold water in a bowl and let sit for a couple of minutes to soften. Remove watermelon mixture from heat and whisk in the softened gelatin and water until it is mixed in very well. Stir in the extract and immediately pour into one large bowl or 4 individual dishes. Cover and refrigerate until chilled and set.

If you would like to unmold it, simply set the dish in hot water for a few minutes, run a knife around the edge and invert.

SERVES 4

Cheers to Plum Pudding

Using a little Yankee ingenuity, I've given this traditional dessert a burst of flavor.

Nonstick cooking spray
2 cups skim milk
1 cup sugar
1 cup pitted dried
    plums (prunes)
1 (10-ounce) jar cherries
    without stems, in syrup
½ cup dark or flavored rum, or
    2 teaspoons rum, almond,
    or vanilla extract
1 tablespoon lemon juice
2 teaspoons cinnamon
1 teaspoon nutmeg
1¼ cups egg substitute
3 tablespoons butter or
    margarine, melted
1½ cups flour
Whipped topping or frozen
    yogurt if desired

Preheat oven to 350° F. Spray a 9-inch cake pan with nonstick cooking spray; set aside.

In a blender or food processor, pulse milk, sugar, dried plums, cherries (with the syrup), rum, lemon juice, cinnamon, and nutmeg until well blended and the plums have been reduced to very small bits.

Transfer to a bowl, and stir in egg substitute and melted butter. Stir in the flour until well incorporated and almost lump free.

Pour in prepared pan and bake 35–37 minutes, or until the the middle is set and the edges spring back when touched. Remove from oven to cool slightly before serving with whipped topping. This is great completely cooled as well.

Chew on Cherries

Cherries are just now being studied for their effectiveness in fighting breast cancer. So far what is known is that they are filled with powerful flavonoids. And when I say powerful, I mean so powerful they are special flavanoids called anthocyanins, which are not even found in blueberries! Tart cherries are tops. Although sweet cherries are good, they don't hold a candle to tart.

New England Tipperary "Apple" Pudding

Many of you may wonder, "Why barley in a dessert?" Many centuries ago, in Ireland, barley was a cereal grain that was widely used in kitchens during St. Patrick's time, which is surmised as being in the fifth century. Barley was used as a thickener in porridge, breads, pastries, and, of course, through natural progression, desserts of all kinds.

5 large Asian pears,
    peeled, cored, and
    roughly chopped
5 tablespoons pearl barley
2 cups water
2 cups apple juice
3 tablespoons lemon juice
⅓ cup sugar
½ teaspoon each of
    cinnamon and nutmeg
1 cup nondairy, fat-free
    whipped topping
¼ cup dried cranberries
¾ cup cranberry juice or
    orange juice

SERVES 3–4

Note: Pearl barley has been processed, therefore it is not classified as a whole grain. But if you would like to add hulled barley(a.k.a. pot barley or barley groats) in order to obtain the fiber, simply cook twice as long, and you will need to add one extra cup of liquid because of the longer cooking time. The consistency will not be altered because of the addition of other ingredients. And don't forget to rinse it before cooking to help keep that stickiness down.

In a large saucepan, bring the pears, barley, water, and apple juice to a boil over medium-high heat. Reduce heat to medium-low, cover, and simmer for 20–25 minutes, or until barley is soft. Remove from heat and strain, reserving any liquid.

Add apple mixture to a food processor bowl, or in batches using a blender, and puree until it resembles chunky applesauce. Add reserved liquid if needed to puree or more apple juice if the liquid has been fully absorbed.

Transfer mixture to a large bowl and add lemon juice, sugar, and spices, mixing well. Cover and refrigerate until cooled or serve warm.

Meanwhile, make cranberry "sauce": In a small saucepan, combine cranberries and juice. Bring to a boil over medium-high heat. When boiling, reduce heat to low and simmer 10 minutes, or until cranberries have started to take in the juice and swell. Transfer to a blender or food processor and puree until smooth. This sauce will thicken perfectly while pureeing because of the very high, natural pectin levels in the cranberries. Pour into a bowl and refrigerate until cooled.

To serve, spoon apple pudding into serving dishes, top with whipped topping, and drizzle sauce over the top.

Epilogue

Jamie Stern, the nutrition consultant who gave me so much help with this book, offers her "recipe" for a fulfilling and pleasurable life: "I like the idea that when you spend the time cooking at home, using fresh foods and trying new recipes, a healthy body and mind will follow. When home-cooked meals are balanced with physical activity and the right amount of sleep, it is the best recipe for a long life." Jamie goes on to repeat a mantra that I have often stated over and over again: "Gather your friends and family around the table and celebrate life and the change of seasons as often as possible. This cookbook by The Yankee Chef should be a staple in every person's kitchen that shares my philosophy. Home cook, with love, and celebrate."

I do hope that many of you will sit back and truly enjoy the lives that we have been blessed with. As both my dad and mom always said, everything happens for a reason and a purpose. Mom dying when we were so young from a disease that thinks it can run rampant throughout our society has brought me to the front lines with many of you. I am never without my pink chefs coat. If anyone takes a second out of their lives to honor and think about those who have suffered with breast cancer, then my mission is accomplished. If someone who reads this book changes their eating habits for one day because it makes them feel better, then my mission is complete.

So take a look at your life close-up. Make changes simply because you want to live and love.

It's Just That Simple!

Index

Jim Bailey

Jim Bailey is a third-generation chef, food columnist, and food historian. Chef Jim is best known as the Yankee Chef, constantly devoting his time and energy for many worthy causes. He rose from the first rung of the culinary ladder at age fourteen to become a leader in simple and healthy cooking who restaurant leaders and home cooks turn to. When not traveling as a food judge, creating recipes, and enjoying time in Maine with his four children, Jim is an unending supporter of breast cancer awareness and proudly sports his signature pink chef's coat.